MACKINTOSH

Publisher and Creative Director: Nick Wells
Development and Picture Research: Melinda Révész
Project Editor: Polly Willis
Editor: Sarah Goulding
Designer: Colin Rudderham
Production: Chris Herbert & Claire Walker

Special thanks to: Geoffrey Meadon, Sara Robson and Helen Tovey

FLAME TREE PUBLISHING
Crabtree Hall, Crabtree Lane
Fulham, London, SW6 6TY
United Kingdom

www.flametreepublishing.com

First published 2005

08

7 9 10 8 6

Flame Tree is part of the Foundry Creative Media Company Limited

The CIP record for this book is available from the British Library.

ISBN 978 1 84451 258 4

Printed in China

MACKINTOSH

Author: Tamsin Pickeral   Foreword: Anne Ellis

Charles Rennie Mackintosh, *A Southern Town*

FLAME TREE PUBLISHING

Charles Rennie Mackintosh, *Rome, Arch of Titus*

Contents

How To Use This Book 8
Foreword 10
Introduction 12

Life 20

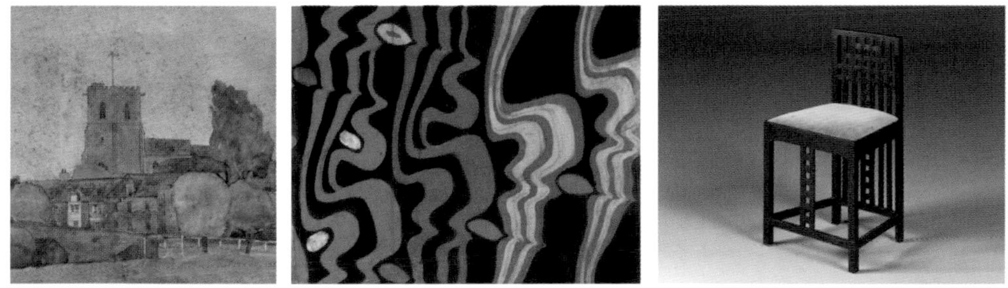

Charles Rennie Mackintosh, *Wareham, Dorset*; Textile design; Sidechair

Society 94

Charles Rennie Mackintosh, Interior of the stair tower of Scotland Street School; Sign for the Willow Tea Rooms; *La Rue du Soleil*

Places 148

Charles Rennie Mackintosh, *Study of a doorway, Naples, S. Trinita Maggiore*; Glasgow School of Art: exterior from the north-west; Glasgow School of Art: the boardroom

Influences 224

William Richard Lethaby, Design for a room; Augustus Welby Northmore Pugin, Table with carved and chamfered decoration; Herbert MacNair, *Ysighlu*, from *The Yellow Book*

Styles & Techniques 310

Charles Rennie Mackintosh, Railing from the Willow Tea Rooms; Writing desk for The Hill House; Bedroom at 78 Derngate

Biographies and Further Reading 378

Index by Work 380

General Index 382

How To Use This Book

The reader is encouraged to use this book in a variety of ways, each of which caters for a range of interests, knowledge and uses.

- The book is organized into five sections: **Life**, **Society**, **Places**, **Influences** and **Styles & Techniques**.
- **Life** provides a snapshot of how Mackintosh's work developed during the course of his career, showing the different media in which he worked.
- **Society** shows how Mackintosh's artefacts and designs reflect contemporaneous society, and how events of the time were a source of inspiration and frustration to him.
- **Places** looks at the work Mackintosh did in the different places he lived in and travelled to: Glasgow, Italy, London, Suffolk and France.
- **Influences** reveals Mackintosh's sources of inspiration, including the 'Group of Four', artistic movements including Arts and Crafts and Art Nouveau, and how much of his work anticipated Modernism.
- **Styles & Techniques** delves into the different techniques he used to produce his architectural designs as well as his furniture, textiles and paintings.

366

Design for a clock face for W. J. Bassett-Lowke, 1917

© Christie's Images Ltd

The design of Mackintosh's clocks is another example of the extraordinary attention to detail that was characteristic of him. It was this attention to detail that made him difficult to work with, but that also ensured his designs were the most impressively cohesive. An amusing indication of the artist's fastidiousness was his insistence that the trees at The Hill House be pruned to the exact shape of the trees in his original architectural drawings and, not content with just that, he apparently rebuked Mrs Blackie for her flower arrangement in the hall at The Hill House because the colours clashed with his interior scheme!

This preliminary drawing for one of the clocks at Derngate expresses the geometry of its intended surroundings and shows Mackintosh developing his colour scheme. The finished clock face was supported by ten columns and the decorative details seen in his drawing were achieved through in laid ivory and green erinoid. This clock is similar in concept, although more stunning, than one he had designed for The Hill House. Here the black-lacquered surround vividly contrasts with the ivory and erinoid creating a dramatic effect.

CREATED
London

MEDIUM
Pencil and watercolour

SERIES/PERIOD/MOVEMENT
London designs

SIMILAR WORKS
Wall clock by Margaret Gilmour

367

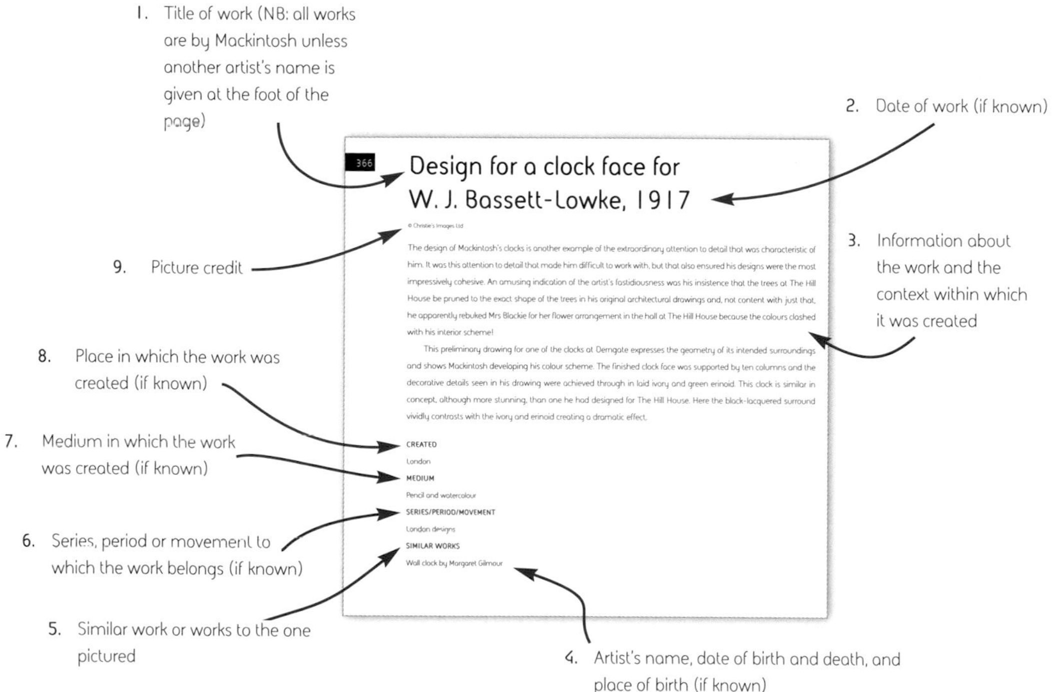
1. Title of work (NB: all works are by Mackintosh unless another artist's name is given at the foot of the page)
2. Date of work (if known)
3. Information about the work and the context within which it was created
4. Artist's name, date of birth and death, and place of birth (if known)
5. Similar work or works to the one pictured
6. Series, period or movement to which the work belongs (if known)
7. Medium in which the work was created (if known)
8. Place in which the work was created (if known)
9. Picture credit
366
Design for a clock face for W. J. Bassett-Lowke, 1917
© Christie's Images Ltd
The design of Mackintosh's clocks is another example of the extraordinary attention to detail that was characteristic of him. It was this attention to detail that made him difficult to work with, but that also ensured his designs were the most impressively cohesive. An amusing indication of the artist's fastidiousness was his insistence that the trees at The Hill House be pruned to the exact shape of the trees in his original architectural drawings and, not content with just that, he apparently rebuked Mrs Blackie for her flower arrangement in the hall at The Hill House because the colours clashed with his interior scheme!
This preliminary drawing for one of the clocks at Derngate expresses the geometry of its intended surroundings and shows Mackintosh developing his colour scheme. The finished clock face was supported by ten columns and the decorative details seen in his drawing were achieved through in laid ivory and green erinoid. This clock is similar in concept, although more stunning, than one he had designed for The Hill House. Here the black-lacquered surround vividly contrasts with the ivory and erinoid creating a dramatic effect.
CREATED
London
MEDIUM
Pencil and watercolour
SERIES/PERIOD/MOVEMENT
London designs
SIMILAR WORKS
Wall clock by Margaret Gilmour

Foreword

'There are things more precious, more beautiful, more lasting than life.'
Charles Rennie Mackintosh

Every biography ought to add to our knowledge of the subject. The problem with the straightforward chronological route, particularly when the subject is as artistically diverse as the Scottish architect Charles Rennie Mackintosh, is that generally you can explain everything except the bit that matters. The methodology of this particular approach is to examine his life, the society in which he lived, the places where he practised his profession, the sources from which his inspiration flowed and the styles and techniques he employed to express his individuality; then to scrutinize it further through examples of his work. It is far from the usual worthy but occasionally dry sequential progress. What is offered is an analytical survey that gives a rounder, truer notion of not only his artistic development, but the effects and influences of the extraordinary flourish that became known as the Glasgow Style: a biographical technique very much in line with Mackintosh's own belief that the artist '...depends very greatly for his success upon a kind of synthesis, an integration of myriads of details and circumstances'.

For every piece of work by Mackintosh, there is also illustrated either a contemporary piece or earlier work with a similar aim: points of comparison that illuminate the man and act as a benchmark for his progress. Learning, after all, is being able to see the relationship between things. The evolution of a unique artistic style is therefore traceable through distinct areas of influence, and as a consequence the aesthetic inheritance can be better assessed and therefore better appreciated.

No artist can be measured in isolation; Mackintosh rose and flourished, as did his native city of Glasgow, when the fantasy of Art Nouveau was at its height. His artistic dreams were shared by countless others both on the Continent and America – Horta, Gaudi, Hoffmann, Guimard, Klimt, Tiffany, Wright – all young men, and all, like Mackintosh, trying to escape the vulgar excesses and the drab drudgery of the Victorian Industrial Revolution. Escape was a common artistic denominator: symbolism an issue of no little importance. Design, far from being an invisible act of industry, became a visible expression of both nationalism and culture. All were seeking a new vocabulary of forms that would truly express the spirit of the age. Mackintosh set himself the 'task of clothing in grace and beauty the new forms and conditions that modern developments of life ... insist upon'. Another Art Nouveau obsession was the search for *gesamtkunstwerk*, the total work of art. It was when he was working freely, for himself or for an enlightened patron like Walter Blackie of The Hill House, that Mackintosh came nearest to achieving the concept.

Although there were personal circumstances, depression, decline and a tendency to drunkenness, Mackintosh's professional downfall was very much a shared experience. Factors affecting his practice were neither peculiar nor restricted. Many of his contemporaries were hit by a similar failure to procure architectural commissions. Some, like Mackintosh and Voysey, succumbed; others like Lutyens, Hoffman, and Frank Lloyd Wright were able to ride out the storm. Very few continued to stamp a personal mark on the ensuing era. In Mackintosh's case there was a change of style: Derngate, in Northampton, vividly represented a new and modern approach more in accord with the jazz age. Unfortunately, although it featured in *Ideal Home* magazine, Mackintosh's name was not attached, and so an important contribution to the modern era of architecture and interior design went unrecognised. In addition, by a savage quirk of fate, he was deprived of his main champions. Gleeson White, the editor of *The Studio* magazine who had heralded Mackintosh as the leader of a new style, died. Muthesius, author of *The English House*, who had introduced his work to a German and Austrian public, was on the wrong side of the First World War. And Miss Cranston, the redoubtable doyen of the Glasgow Tea Room movement, sold off her tea rooms and retired on the death of her husband.

Of course, as this book ably demonstrates, Mackintosh was more than just an architect and interior designer. His furniture, light fittings and cutlery designs are still being manufactured. The fact that they continue to have a separate existence from the very specific location for which they were designed in some way demonstrates the skill and artistry of the man. His work as a textile designer and watercolour artist, a rather neglected and therefore lesser known area of his artistic oeuvre, is also evaluated. The real impact of Mackintosh's work and life must be measured in the context of the early twentieth-century history of art, architecture and design. It is an important and still viable contribution, and his lasting popularity demonstrates how what seemed to have been a life of failure has left a lasting legacy of international significance.

Anne Ellis, *2005*

Charles Rennie Mackintosh, Master bedroom at The Hill House

Introduction

Genius, innovator, visionary, perfectionist, forerunner of Modernism and precursor to Art Deco, Charles Rennie Mackintosh has become synonymous with any number of labels. The inevitable habit of categorizing is never more poignant than when applied to Mackintosh, and yet he is by the very nature of his work indefinable. His unique expression and the language of his artistic energy set him apart from his contemporaries and those that followed, while providing a bridge spanning the chasm from Victoriana to the new century.

'Old forms in new ways' was Mackintosh's premise as he grappled with the diversity of translating the traditional into a modern context. Mackintosh's vision was for a new language of expression, a new way forward for architecture and designing and one that would be led by the Scottish. He sought to influence those around him, to redefine their artistic goals, and yet he never became the 'leader' or figurehead that he should have been in order to achieve a 'school' of design. He trod a solitary path and, so doing, was not able to see his vision for the future of architecture realized. It was a great tragedy that the fiercely nationalistic Mackintosh was never given the recognition that he deserved in his home town or country. Despite this, it was his intuitive perception of artistic endeavour that undoubtedly opened doors for those to follow. The Glasgow School of Art was visionary and inimitable in its conception; the dawn of the 'white room' and his simple, uncluttered approach to interior and exterior design was immediately at odds with the Victorian sensibilities of the time. Was it modern? Yes, within its context, although Mackintosh never sacrificed ornament or decorative detail to achieve his distinctive look. His modernity was inviolable, his expression unique, yet it was Peter Behrens who was credited with building the first 'modern' building when he designed New Ways for Mr Bassett-Lowke in 1925. Mackintosh was the ultimate master of synthesis: synthesis of form for function and of ornament with modernity. Part of Mackintosh's brilliance lay in his ability to meld the organic and the geometric seamlessly, the decorative and the functional, with neither at the aesthetic or utilitarian expense of the other.

That Mackintosh's life was beset with poor timing, bad luck and irony is a given. He died in poverty at a relatively young age, having lived the last years of his life abroad in isolation from his friends. But to view his life and works with a sense of melancholic sympathy is a mistake. The extraordinary intensity that Mackintosh devoted to his early architectural commissions, most especially the Glasgow School of Art, was never lost. He embraced each facet of his career with the same seriousness of intent. His textile and furniture designs and finally his watercolours were treated with equal artistic vision and enthusiasm. His decision to devote himself to watercolour painting was perhaps not so surprising in the light of his life-long affinity with nature and sketching. The work that he produced, however, was astonishing and it is rarely afforded the critical acclaim that it deserves. Although his architecture had voiced an undeniably new language, his painting style was virtually unique. The difference being that the evolution of his architectural voice, though not derivative, is certainly traceable through different areas of influence, while his watercolour landscapes are singularly modern in expression.

What of the man behind the great name? 'Tosh' to his friends, or 'Uncle Toshie' to his younger admirers, was as flamboyant and complex as his formidable talent would suggest. As a student he enjoyed the wild, hedonistic days of the art school. He immersed himself in the progressive artistic culture synonymous with the school under the direction of Francis Newbery, a man who would be a life-long friend, patron and supporter to Mackintosh. The 'Glasgow Four', comprising of Mackintosh and his friend Herbert MacNair and the Macdonald sisters, Margaret and Frances, forged a name for themselves based on their similar artistic expression. Their studios became meeting points for long nights of discussions and parties, swapped ideologies and shared artistic aims. Mackintosh was pivotal to the group, admired for his talent and extrovert personality amongst the students. Attractive, warm-hearted, generous and proud, but also prone to violent tempers, arrogance and inflexibility, he was a complex individual, irascible and with a legendary attention to every miniscule detail. Undoubtedly, aspects of his character were significant in the crumbling of his architectural career. Accounts indicate he was difficult to work for and with – his working methods were fluid and creative, and his architectural plans a point of departure for him rather than a concrete projection of design. Frustrated by lack of recognition and the inability to change the ideas of those around him, he suffered increasingly from depression and loss of self-confidence resulting in his first move away from Glasgow, to Walberswick, in an attempt to heal old wounds.

The one constant in Mackintosh's life was an extraordinary woman without whom one must wonder what might have befallen him. Margaret Macdonald was four years older than Charles and won his heart in the late 1890s when he was still engaged to Jessie Keppie, sister to John Keppie, Mackintosh's business partner. By 1900 Charles had broken Jessie's heart and married Margaret, sealing a relationship of immense stability and mutual respect. Margaret provided the even keel to Charles's temperament. The couple were popular amongst their circle and on their move to London they immersed themselves in the local culture, throwing spectacular parties and becoming involved in theatre and arts

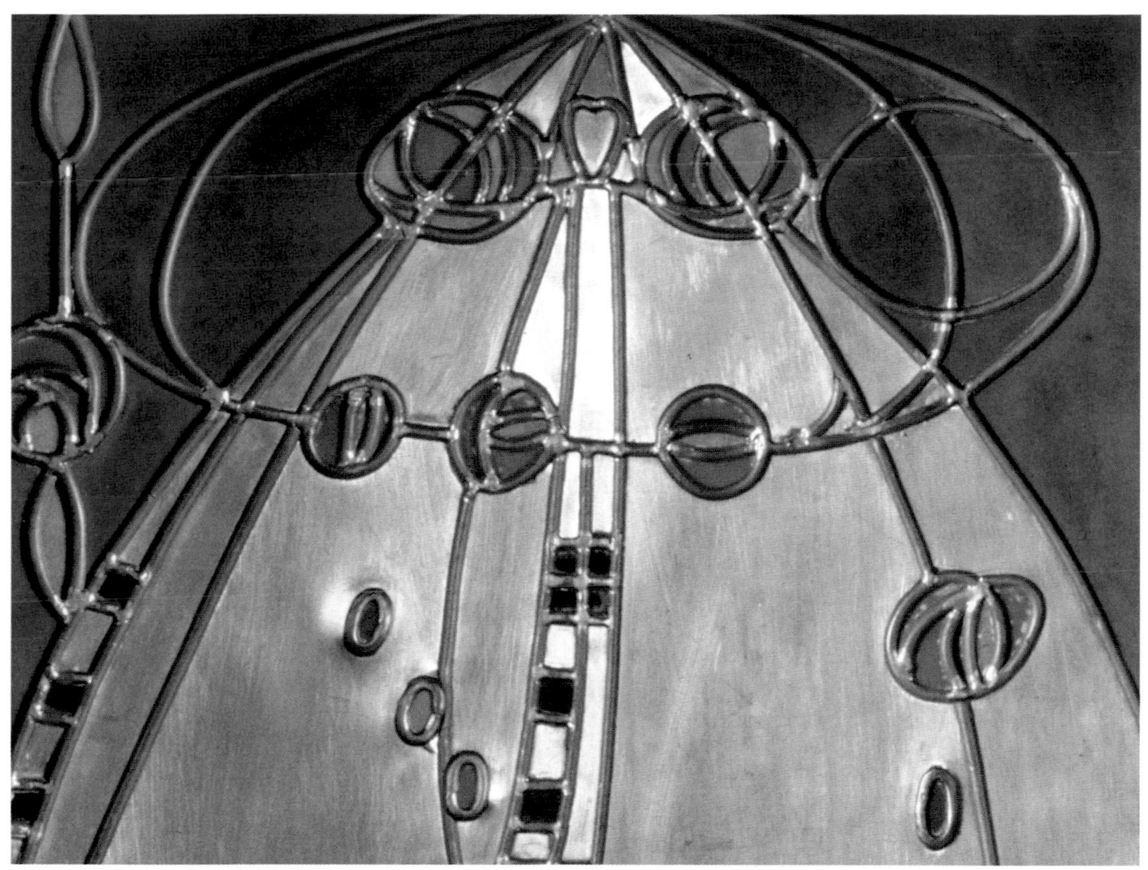

Charles Rennie Mackintosh, Detail from an ebonized mahogany writing cabinet

groups. The intensity of their symbiotic relationship was never diluted by children – they never had children of their own, although they were both extremely fond of them and Margaret would often throw elaborate children's parties for their friends' youngsters. Margaret was a member of the Four and was a highly talented artist and craftswoman, working in a similar style to her sister Frances and Herbert MacNair. Margaret's influence on Charles is often scathingly referred to. Her work was distinctively mystical and ethereal, often associated with the Symbolist and Aesthetic movements, and was of a romantically decorative nature. She is held responsible by some for holding Charles back artistically, the conjecture being that he would have gone on to a greater degree of Modernism without her influence. The more decorative aspects of his work are cited as being reflective of Margaret's hand and as being detrimental to his work as an architect and designer. To believe this is to misinterpret Mackintosh completely. The decorative element to his style was of great importance to Mackintosh, inextricable from his architecture and treatment of form. His work was far deeper than simple ornament and manipulation of space – every aspect of his designs had some meaning or significance to him. Invariably the sheer wonder at his work, and its unique decorative aesthetic, overshadows the significance of every detail that he created. In a relationship as close as that of Charles and Margaret, both personal and working, it is inevitable that they shared inspiration and ideas. Charles referred to Margaret as a 'genius' in the face of his mere 'talent'. She was his rock and stalwart, steadfastly guiding them both through periods of extreme difficulty. The Mackintosh style is surely a collaboration, an artistic joining and flowering from a relationship of mutual artistic respect and talent.

Charles Rennie Mackintosh, *Collioure*

Mackintosh's greatest architectural work came at the beginning of his career, seen in the domestic commission for The Hill House (1902) and, of course, the Glasgow School of Art (1896–99 and 1907–09). His productive working career was incredibly short, and by the time the Glasgow School of Art was completed his fortunes were already on the decline. It is the greatest irony that the triumph of his career also signalled its demise. Mackintosh's vision for a new way forward was misunderstood and largely ignored by his countrymen and it was on the Continent that he finally achieved some measure of distinction. Mackintosh's work and that of the Four was widely acclaimed by their contemporaries in Vienna, whose own artistic language had developed along similar routes to that of the young Scots. Mackintosh did not execute a vast number of commissions abroad despite his popularity, probably due to his large workload at that time in Glasgow. By the time he would have been in a position to work extensively abroad, the First World War had begun and his close relationship with the Continent was effectively severed.

Charles Rennie Mackintosh, Detail of a wall stencil for The Hill House

On his death his estate was valued at a paltry £88, four chairs being valued at £1, and yet he is now regarded as one of the greatest designers of modern times. Some years ago one of his writing desks sold for the princely sum of £720,000 and his furniture is widely sought after and collected. His death passed virtually unnoticed in 1928 and by a typically twisted hand of fate, the following year a group of Austrian architects wrote to invite Mackintosh to Vienna, to honour his prodigious influence on the evolution of their architecture and design. Unrecognized during his lifetime and forgotten for years, the spirit of Mackintosh has at last been rekindled. Finally the true measure of his genius is starting to be understood, the mystery of his artistic evolution detangled and his unique artistic language comprehended.

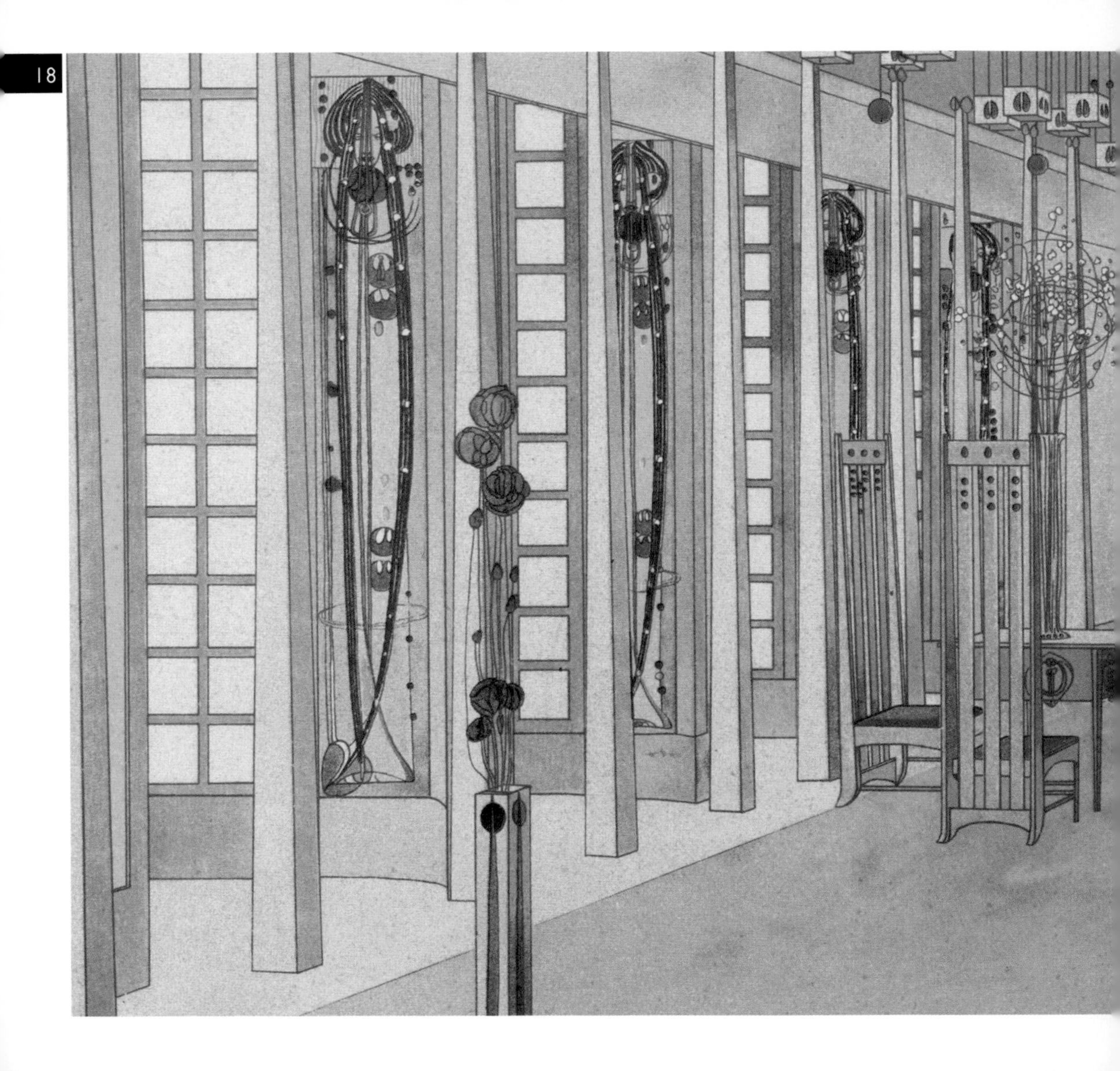

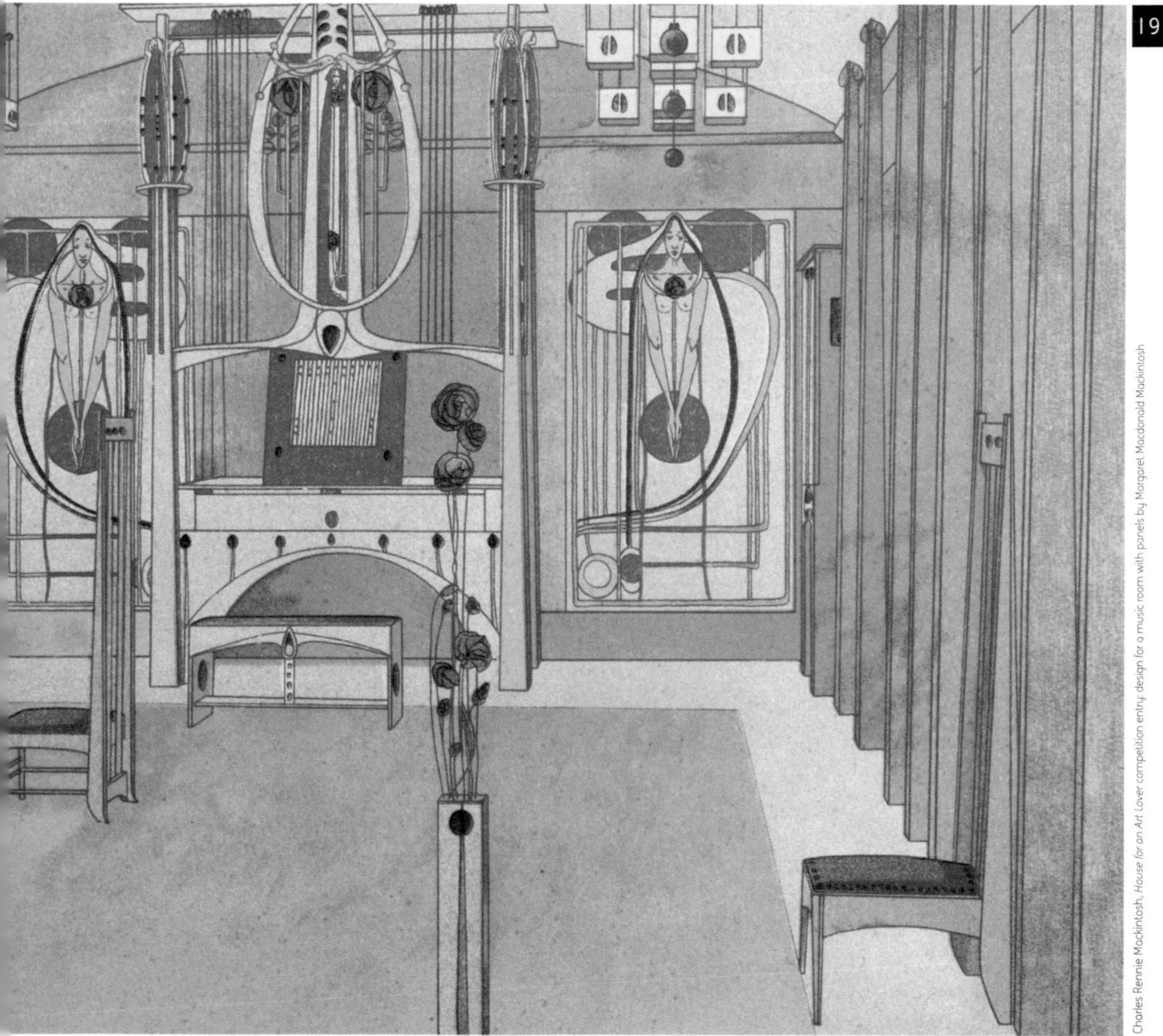

Charles Rennie Mackintosh, *House for an Art Lover* competition entry: design for a music room with panels by Margaret Macdonald Mackintosh

THE W
GREAT

Mackintosh

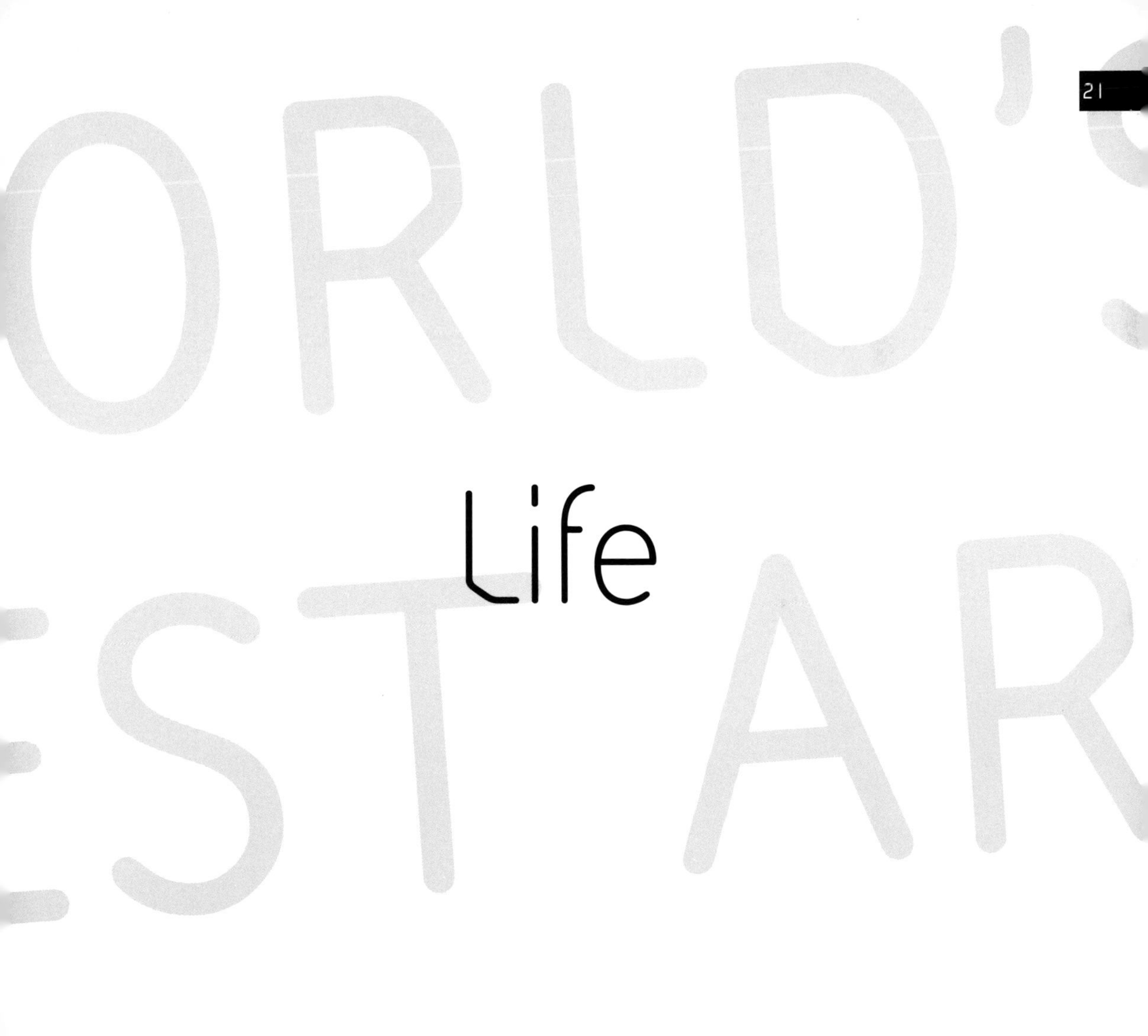

Life

Study of a Jesuit altar, Certosa di Pavia, 1891

Charles Rennie Mackintosh was the son of a police superintendent, and one of 11 siblings. His early life was spent in Dennistown a community on the fringes of Glasgow. There his father, who was a keen gardener, planted the 'Garden of Eden' on a plot of land next to the Mackintosh family home. This was to instil and inspire a love for nature in the young Charles, something he would refer to his whole life. At the age of 16, in 1884, Mackintosh was apprenticed to a local architectural firm run by John Hutchison and enrolled for night classes at the Glasgow School of Art. His prodigious talent and conscientious attitude were quickly recognized. In 1890 he won a competition to design 'A Public Hall', run by the Alexander Thomson Travelling Scholarship. He used the prize money to fund a trip to Italy in 1891 where he produced many drawings and watercolour sketches. His *Study of a Jesuit altar* shows his strong architectural allegiance, softened with a subtle handling of colour that superimposes an interesting asymmetrical balance upon the classical symmetry of the structure.

CREATED

On a tour of Italy

MEDIUM

Pencil and watercolour

SERIES/PERIOD/MOVEMENT

Italian tour

SIMILAR WORKS

Colourful Pavements, Studies, Sicily by John Singer Sargeant, *c.* 1901

Charles Rennie Mackintosh *Born* 1868 Glasgow, Scotland

Died 1928

IHS
GRA

Photographic portrait of Charles Rennie Mackintosh, 1893

Mackintosh joined the architectural firm of Honeyman and Keppie in 1889. John Honeyman (1831–1914) and his younger partner John Keppie (1862–1945) ran the successful and respected business that had a reputation for versatile and accomplished designs. Keppie was closer in age to Mackintosh and the pair struck up a strong, but brief, friendship. Some years later Mackintosh left Keppie's sister Jessie brokenhearted and, although Keppie and Mackintosh continued to work together, their relationship was irrevocably damaged. On joining the firm Mackintosh quickly became acquainted with Herbert MacNair (1868–1955), an employee and a like-minded artist, who would go on to become a member of the Glasgow Four. MacNair and Mackintosh became great friends and spent many weekends sketching together in the surrounding countryside. Mackintosh was the epitome of the flamboyant, artistic dandy, summarized succinctly in this photograph. MacNair too, favoured the floppy neckties and creative style of his friend Mackintosh. This was in some contrast to the conservative dress of the more formal John Keppie. All three men appear together in a recently discovered photograph at the Glasgow School of Art, along with Jessie Keppie (1868–1951) and Frances (1874–1921) and Margaret Macdonald (1864–1933).

PHOTOGRAPHED

Glasgow

MEDIUM

Photograph

SERIES/PERIOD/MOVEMENT

Photographs from the 1890s

SIMILAR WORKS

John Keppie, date/photographer unknown

Mackintosh, MacNair, John and Jessie Keppie, Margaret and Frances Macdonald, photographer unknown, 1890s

Conversazione Programme, designed for the Glasgow Architectural Association, 1894

In 1885 Francis Newbery (1855–1946), an Englishman, had been appointed head of the Glasgow School of Art. He inaugurated himself within the Scottish culture making few waves and was readily accepted. He quickly recognized Mackintosh's talent and modernity and introduced him and MacNair to Margaret and Frances Macdonald. The Macdonald sisters were also students at the school and were developing a style along similar lines to Mackintosh and MacNair. The four quickly formed a close friendship and began to work together, becoming known as the 'Glasgow Four'. They exhibited together and their unique vision became the foundation for the emergence of the Glasgow style. In 1893 Mackintosh delivered a lecture urging his fellow architects to 'go straight to Nature', to 'clothe modern ideas with modern dress', a suggestion contrary to the conservative view of many academics. The Glasgow Four built their style around fluid organic shapes, sinewy tendrils and stylized forms of leaves, trees, branches and stalks. Their figures were as lean and willowy as the foliage they depicted. *The Conversazione Programme* is typical of this period in Mackintosh's work and combines the boldness of architectural line with a curvilinear sweep of organic form.

CREATED

Glasgow

MEDIUM

Lithograph in black and green on blue paper

SERIES/PERIOD/MOVEMENT

Poster designs of the 1890s

SIMILAR WORKS

Glasgow Institute Poster by Herbert MacNair and the Macdonald sisters, *c.* 1896

THE GLASGOW ARCHITECTURAL ASSOCIATION
CHAS. R. MACKINTOSH

Wareham, Dorset, 1895

Mackintosh left the Glasgow School of Art at the end of the session in 1893–94. He had spent 10 years as a part-time student there and was familiar with every drawback of the building's design. During his time there he forged strong and enduring friendships, amongst which was his bond with Francis Newbery, head of the school. In 1895 Mackintosh set up his own studio where he was able to work on small decorative commissions between his architectural projects with Honeyman and Keppie. MacNair had by now left the firm and set up on his own, specializing in furniture design and craftwork, and the Macdonald sisters had graduated from the school and opened their own studio. These studios were frequented by young artists and designers and became a forum for sharing progressive ideas and designs. Mackintosh was busy with architectural work, but found the time for several sketching trips to the Cotswolds in 1894 and to Wareham in Dorset in 1895. *Wareham, Dorset* is a softly coloured painting that indicates his interest in poster and decorative work. He used a thin stylized line and faintly outlined each individual pictorial element, a technique that would evolve into a stunningly modern approach with his late watercolours.

CREATED

Dorset

MEDIUM

Watercolour

SERIES/PERIOD/MOVEMENT

Sketching trips of the 1890s

SIMILAR WORKS

Grez from the River by David Gauld, *c.* 1896–97

Casket, *c.* 1895

Jessie Keppie had enrolled at the Glasgow School of Art in 1889, the same year that Mackintosh joined the firm of Honeyman and Keppie. The two met shortly thereafter, possibly when Mackintosh was staying at the Keppie family home in Ayrshire while working on one of his many competition designs. It is thought that Jessie and Mackintosh embarked on a tumultuous affair, during which time he designed the metal jewellery box for her seen here. The casket is strikingly simple in design, with an asymmetrical frontal hinge lock and decorative glass inserts. Mackintosh would continue to use balanced asymmetry throughout his designs to maximum aesthetic effect. Jessie's name is engraved on a plaque on the underside of the lid and within the box there is a velvet lined removable tray, with another wooden one below it. The pair were engaged for a short time before Mackintosh started to pursue Margaret Macdonald, whom he later married. After their break-up Jessie was left heartbroken and never married. Although the split did not immediately obviously affect the relationship between John Keppie and Mackintosh, it undoubtedly sowed the first seeds of resentment.

CREATED

Glasgow

MEDIUM

Repoussé brass, mounted on wood, with glass inserts

SERIES/PERIOD/MOVEMENT

Early craft work

SIMILAR WORKS

A casket in repoussé metal by De Courcy Lewthwaite Dewar, *c.* 1900

Montacute House, Somerset, 1895

The early 1890s were a period of intense architectural activity for Mackintosh, during which time he designed three significant buildings, the *Glasgow Herald* building (1893), Queen Margaret's Medical College (1894) and the Martyrs' Public School, designed *c.* 1895. For each one he produced fine perspective drawings, including both the architectural structure and natural features. He was even criticized by some parties for making his architectural studies too ornate and decorative. Today, in the wake of a rekindled interest in Mackintosh, he is most commonly remembered as an architect or furniture designer and yet he was an extraordinarily accomplished draughtsman. When he enrolled at the Glasgow School of Art great emphasis was placed on drawing and painting classes, summarized in the words of the chairman at a meeting in 1885, 'All our industries – whether of ship-building or house building, whether of engineering or machine making, whether of pattern-making or the higher art of painting – must first have their origin in drawing ...'. This premise of all artistic endeavours having their roots in solid drawing skills is well demonstrated in this sketch of Montacute House.

CREATED

Somerset

MEDIUM

Pencil

SERIES/PERIOD/MOVEMENT

Architectural drawing

SIMILAR WORKS

Sketch of Blackwell, Cumbria by M. H. Baillie Scott, 1898–1900

MONTACUTE HOUSE.
CHAS. R. MACKINTOSH

Armchair, dining chair and occasional table, 1897 and 1896

Tea rooms enjoyed a huge increase in popularity through the end of the nineteenth century and the first decade of the twentieth century. They were closely associated with Glasgow and were the product of an upsurge in the city's economy and industry, combined with a need for acceptable social venues. Miss Catherine Cranston (1849–1934) was a shrewd mover in the business circles of the day and was the proprietress of several well-established tea rooms by the time Mackintosh made her acquaintance. His first commission for Miss Cranston was shared with the notable designer George Walton (1867–1933). Mackintosh was in charge of designing mural decorations for the Buchanan Street Tea Rooms (for which the table pictured here was made) and Walton produced the furniture. The pair worked together again at the Argyle Street Tea Rooms, but here Mackintosh designed the furniture (including the armchair and dining chair shown here) and Walton the wall treatments. This marked the beginning of a long association between Mackintosh and Miss Cranston, which saw the realization of many of Mackintosh's unique design ideas. His chairs combine the utilitarian necessity of continual use with a strong geometric form and they dominate Walton's slender table.

CREATED

Glasgow

MEDIUM

Oak wood

SERIES/PERIOD/MOVEMENT

Tea rooms

SIMILAR WORKS

Rush-seated ladder-back chair by George Walton, *c.*1896

Glasgow School of Art: view of the exterior, built 1897–99

In 1896 the Glasgow Four were invited to exhibit at the Arts and Crafts Society Exhibition in London. They failed to get the recognition that they deserved, but their work was spotted by Gleeson White of *The Studio* magazine. He would go on to feature the artists' work, frequently in the respected art journal and was significant in publicizing the work of the Four across England and the Continent. The same year a competition was announced to draw up designs for a new building to house the Glasgow School of Art. Eleven firms entered and Honeyman and Keppie won with Mackintosh's plans. There was an immediate outcry. The strong friendship between Mackintosh and Francis Newbery, head of the school, was no secret and it was rumoured that that was why Mackintosh had secured the commission. Mackintosh's plans were also criticized for being Art Nouveau in style and for failing to register the importance of historic traditions of architecture. His plans were, in fact, an extraordinary accomplishment for a young architect and addressed the difficult site parameters head-on and creatively.

CREATED

Glasgow

MEDIUM

Architecture

SERIES/PERIOD/MOVEMENT

Glasgow School of Art

SIMILAR WORKS

10-12 Palace Court, Bayswater by James MacLaren, 1890

Glasgow School of Art: Director's Room, 1897–99

The Glasgow School of Art was built in two stages separated by a number of years. The initial stage, which was budgeted at £14,000 was completed by 1899, but had run over the costing by more than a third. The school in its final state stands as the summation of Mackintosh's design articulation and is a singularly brilliant synthesis of function through form. Mackintosh's concern with detail, down to the smallest element, provided the school with a completely unified artistic statement, from the interior to the exterior and all the fittings and furnishings in between. The Director's Room is a classic example of Mackintosh's use of simple form made dramatic through light and carefully placed decoration. The room is at first austere, but the light from the deep arched window recess reflects from the white panelling to bathe the entire room. This is one of the first examples of Mackintosh's 'white rooms', something he would return to in later interiors. The clean, simple lines of the room call to mind the traditional stone interior walls of Scottish castles.

CREATED

Glasgow

MEDIUM

Interior design

SERIES/PERIOD/MOVEMENT

Glasgow School of Art

SIMILAR WORKS

Café Museum by Adolf Loos, 1899

Design for a cabinet for H. Bruckmann, 1898

On completion of his designs and drawings for the Glasgow School of Art, Mackintosh embarked on a project for the Queen's Cross Church, Garscube Road, and parallels between the buildings have often been made. Queen's Cross is now, fittingly, the headquarters for the Charles Rennie Mackintosh Society. By 1898 Mackintosh was working on a number of different projects, including furniture designs for the Argyle Tea Rooms and plans for the interiors of a dining room for H. Bruckman, editor of the *Dekorative Kunst*, in Munich. This would be Mackintosh's first commission outside Scotland and it marked the beginning of a strong relationship with the Continent, which was sadly ended by the onset of the First World War. Between 1898 and 1905 Mackintosh received several commissions from the Continent, most significantly becoming involved with the Secessionists in 1900. His affiliations with the Secessionists and his friendships in Germany and Vienna would come back to haunt him when he was arrested on charges of espionage in 1914. Mackintosh's designs were always a synthesis of form and function, two qualities that can be seen in this simple but effective cabinet designed for H. Bruckmann.

CREATED

Glasgow

MEDIUM

Pen and ink

SERIES/PERIOD/MOVEMENT

Furniture commissions of the 1890s

SIMILAR WORKS

Sideboard, The Miraculous Draught of Fishes by Koloman Moser

Four-poster bed at 120 Mains Street, Glasgow, 1900

Photos © Hunterian Museum and Art Gallery, University of Glasgow, Mackintosh Collection

By 1899 MacNair had married Frances Macdonald and the couple moved to Merseyside where he was appointed Instructor in Decorative Design at Liverpool University. Mackintosh married Margaret Macdonald in 1900, signalling an immensely satisfying conclusion to the tight-knit Glasgow Four. The same year Mackintosh and Margaret moved into their first home together, the studio flat at 120 Mains Street in Glasgow. At around the same time, Mackintosh was working on plans for Windyhill, attributed as being one of Mackintosh's first commissions independent from the firm of Honeyman and Keppie. The interior decorations at Mackintosh's Mains Street home are interesting because they are one of the first examples of the artist working completely free from the constraints of a patron's wishes. Mackintosh and Margaret were able to achieve the precise aesthetic quality that they sought. The four-poster bed combines Mackintosh's use of Scottish vernacular through its form, with a modern infusion seen in the clean lines and startling white paint. The rose pattern on the mantle of the bed was one of Mackintosh's favourite motifs.

CREATED

Glasgow

MEDIUM

Painted wood and textile

SERIES/PERIOD/MOVEMENT

120 Mains Street

SIMILAR WORKS

Bed by Gustav Serrurier Bovy, *c.* 1902

Designs for bedroom furniture and fireplace, 120 Mains Street, 1900

The Mackintoshes lived at 120 Mains Street for six years between 1900 and 1906, at which point they moved to a new house on Southpark Avenue. Mackintosh was responsible for the entire decorative scheme at the Mains Street house and designed everything from the cutlery to the fittings and furnishings. They took their furniture and fittings with them to Southpark Avenue, so the two dwellings were comparative in theme. Mackintosh used plain walls, floors and ceilings throughout with an uncluttered and simple interior arrangement. The drawing room of the 120 Mains Street house has a distinctive and exaggerated moulding, which divides the top one third of the wall space from the bottom two thirds. He used this design feature again in the drawing room of The Hill House and in their Southpark residence. Mackintosh's attention to detail is legendary and every feature of his interiors, down to the smallest element, was significant and artfully arranged, producing a cohesive totality in his rooms. These preliminary drawings for furniture demonstrate him exploring ideas within a set framework of design, with a strong emphasis on verticality.

CREATED

Glasgow

MEDIUM

Pencil

SERIES/PERIOD/MOVEMENT

120 Mains Street

SIMILAR WORKS

Dining room at The Orchard, Chorley Wood by C. F. A. Voysey, 1900

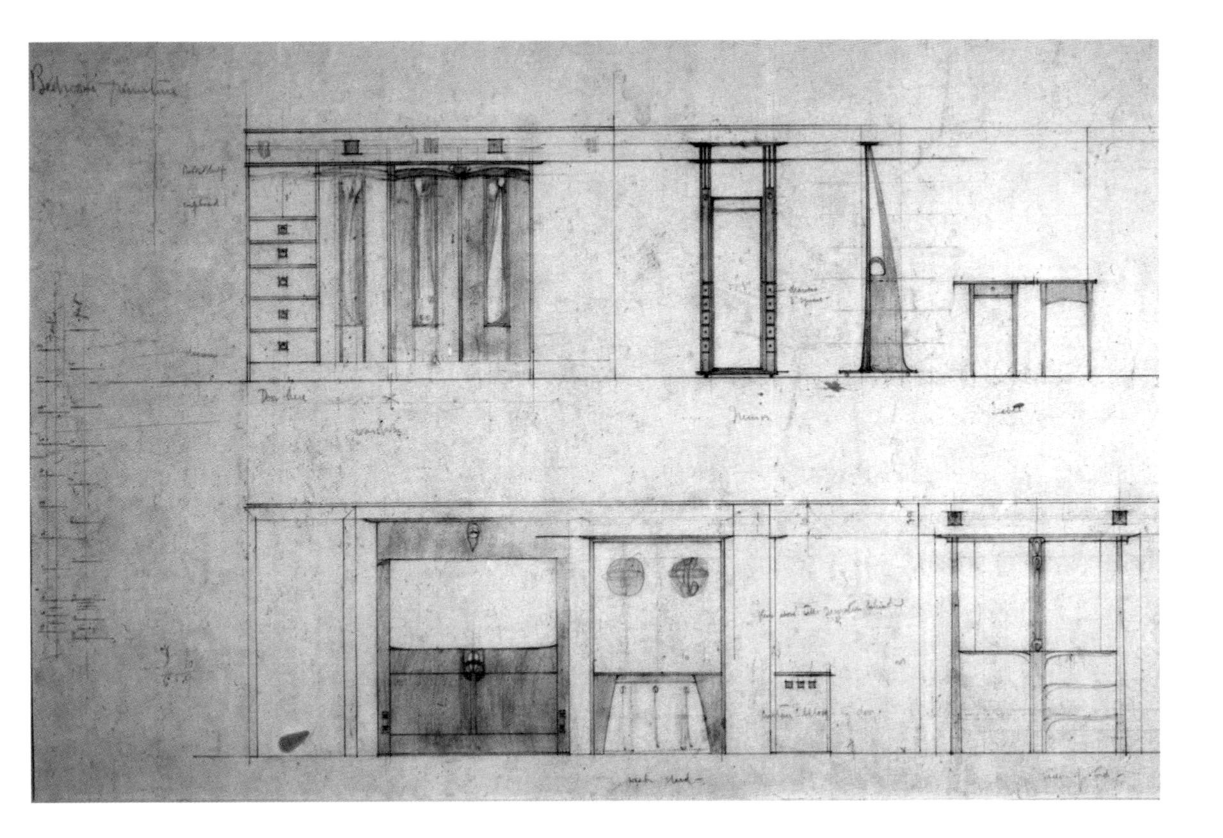

Stork's Bill, Holy Island, 1901

In the autumn of 1900 the Glasgow Four were invited to design an interior, including soft furnishings and furniture, for the Eighth Secessionist Exhibition in Vienna. The Secessionists were an avant-garde group of artists and architects whose work had been severely criticized by the conservative Viennese Academy. Most notable of the Secessionists were the artists Gustav Klimt (1862–1918) and Carl Moll (1861–1945), and the architects Josef Hoffman (1870–1956) and J. M. Olbrich (1867–1908). The Mackintoshes and the Secessionists formed close links based on a mutual appreciation and understanding of their respective artistic aims, many of which were on converging paths. During the same period Mackintosh worked on the Ingram Street Tea Rooms for Catherine Cranston and created designs for An Artist's Country Cottage, An Artist's Town House, and A Country Mansion. In 1901 he travelled to Northumberland to Holy Island where he sketched avidly, producing some delicate flower studies. In *Stork's Bill*, Mackintosh's distinctive linear style can be seen. When working 'from nature' he would invariably use his imagination to create a more aesthetic design, rather than remaining true to the natural form. Although the plant is recognisable, the exquisite arrangement and vibrant colour touches were undoubtedly Mackintosh's embellishments.

CREATED

Holy Island, Northumberland

MEDIUM

Pencil and watercolour

SERIES/PERIOD/MOVEMENT

Flower paintings

SIMILAR WORKS

Primrose Tile by William Morris, 1862–65

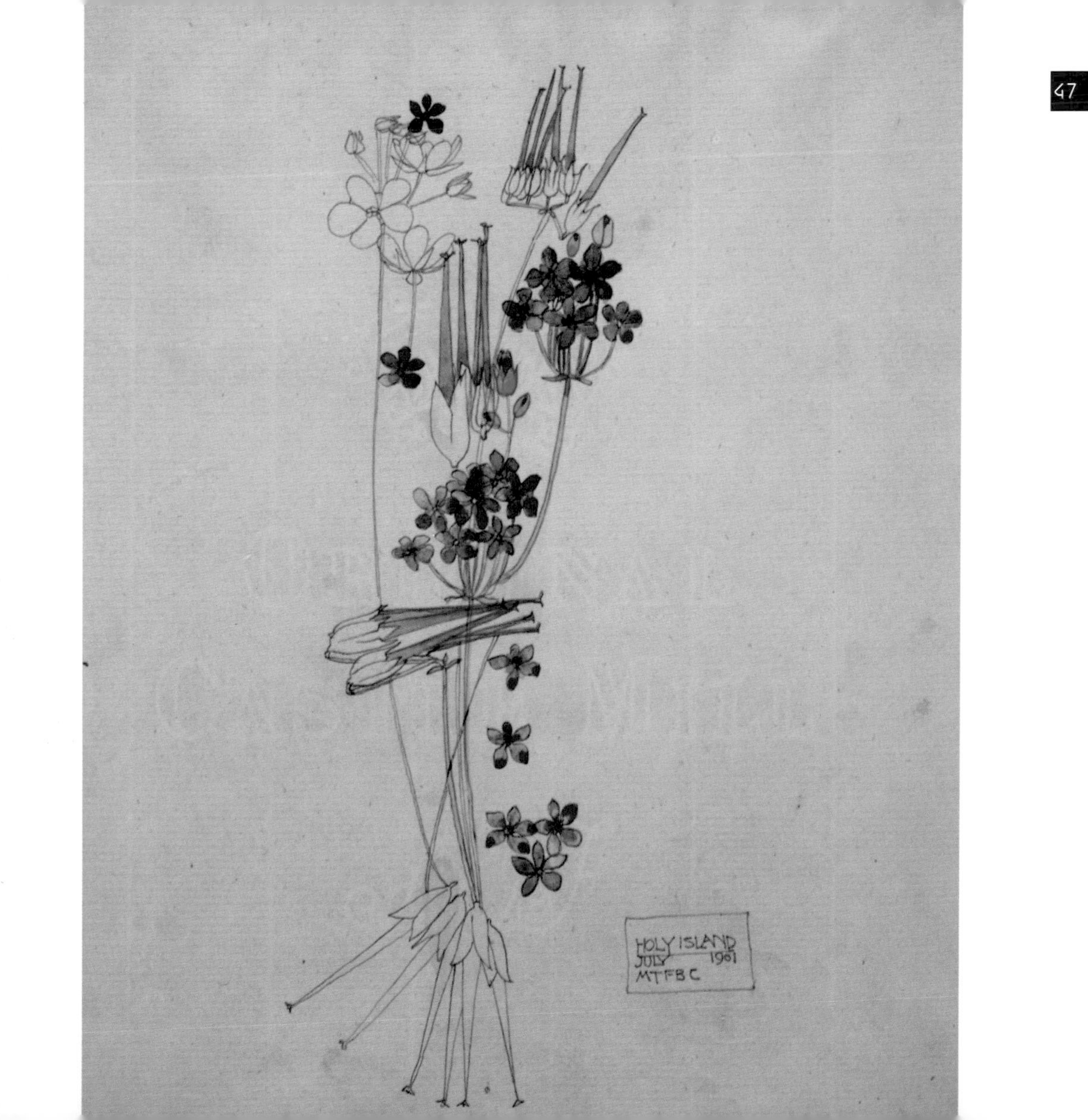
HOLY ISLAND
JULY 1901
MTFBC

Design for an exhibition stand for Francis Smith, 1901

Mackintosh finished his designs for the *Daily Record* building in 1900 although the project was not completed until 1906. He handled the constrictive, dark site with an innovative approach and overcame the substantial financial restrictions admirably. At the beginning of 1901 John Honeyman retired and Mackintosh was made a partner. The firm was renamed Honeyman, Keppie and Mackintosh. At this time Glasgow was the glowing city of the North. She was blossoming in industry and commerce, the economy was rising and the artistic culture taking off. Nowhere were these achievements better showcased than in the Glasgow International Exhibition, 1901. The exhibition ran from May until November, covering a staggering 73 acres in Kelvingrove Park. The main exhibition building was the temporary Eastern Palace, designed by the architect James Millar. His plans pandered to the public's demand for excessive exuberance, displayed through his Oriental extravaganza. With sixteenth-century Spanish-Renaissance influence, and topped with a golden angel of light, nothing could have been further from Mackintosh's artistic expression! Mackintosh designed this exhibition stand for Francis Smith and it was later illustrated in *The Studio* magazine.

CREATED

Glasgow

MEDIUM

Pencil, grey wash and watercolour

SERIES/PERIOD/MOVEMENT

Glasgow International Exhibition

SIMILAR WORKS

Design for a picture frame by Josef Hoffmann, 1898

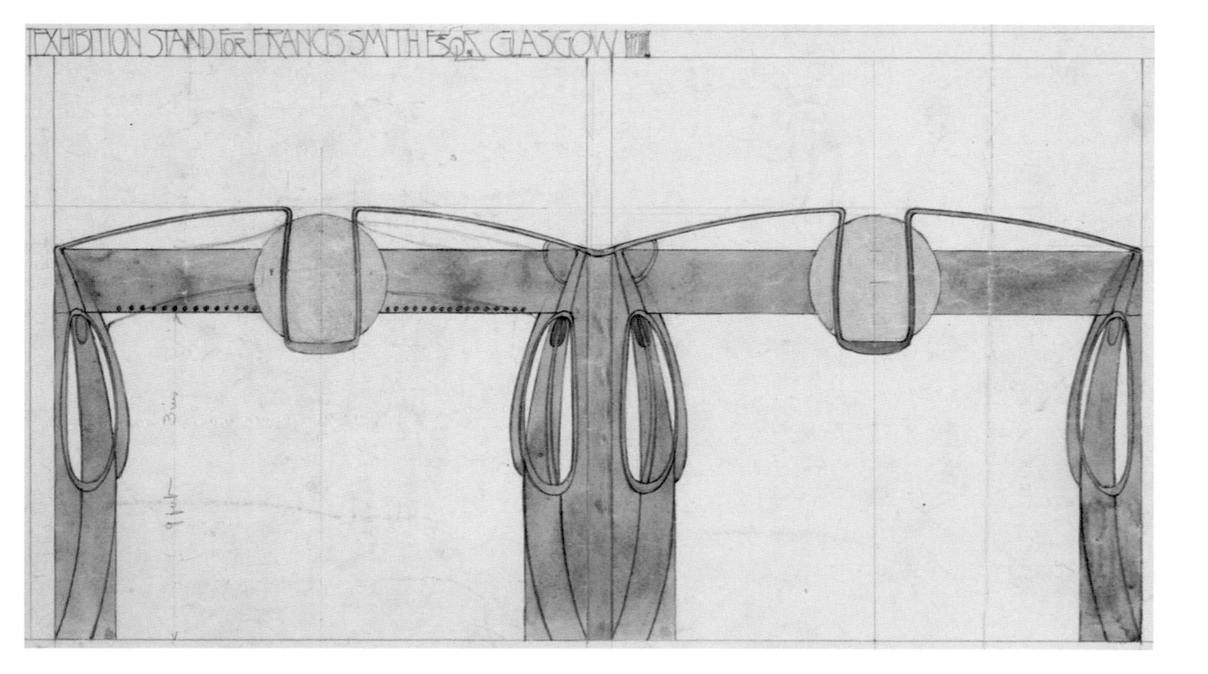
EXHIBITION STAND FOR FRANCIS SMITH ESQR GLASGOW

Glass panel, 1902

The Mackintoshes had been warmly received on the Continent following their inclusion at the Eighth Secessionist Exhibition in Vienna, 1900. In 1902 they were commissioned by Fritz Wärndorfer to design a music salon for his house. The finished room was held in high regard by many critics and was considered a masterpiece of unity. Sadly the room was later destroyed and nothing of it remains. The same year saw the International Exhibition of Modern Decorative Art in Turin, for which Mackintosh designed a series of three rooms. The most notable of these was the Rose Boudoir, panelled in white-painted woodwork and furnished with his high-backed chairs; the room was the result of both Charles and Margaret's artistic input. A characteristic of Mackintosh's style was the use of coloured glass and glass panels to highlight and enhance a visual plane, be it architectural or in furniture. Panels such as the one pictured, and another one of a stylized female form done in the same year, would be effective in filtering rich and varied light into a room.

CREATED

Glasgow

MEDIUM

Stained glass

SERIES/PERIOD/MOVEMENT

Glass panels

SIMILAR WORKS

The Enchanted Farm by Jessie M. King, 1904

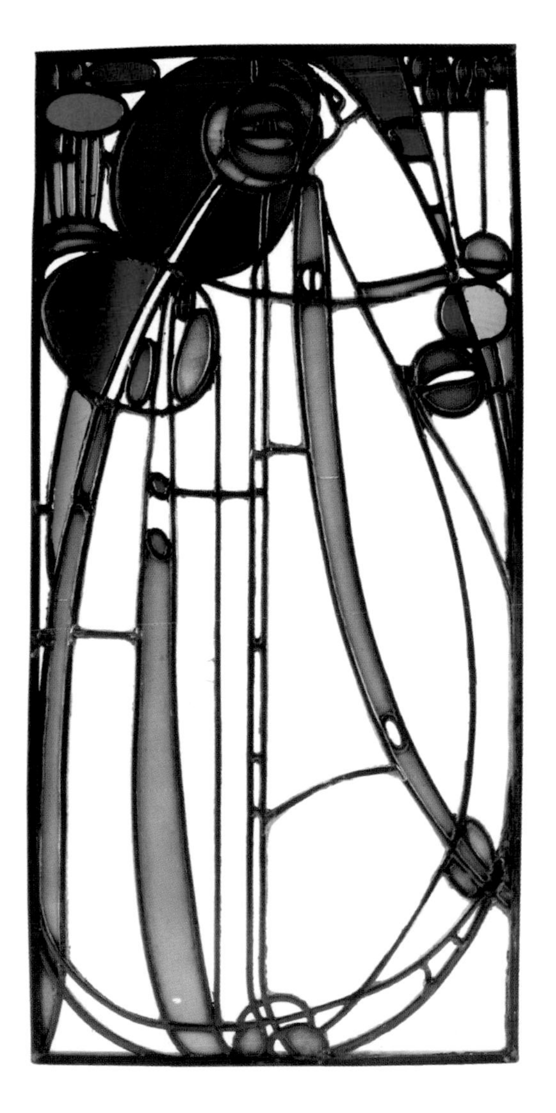

House for an Art Lover: perspective exterior view, 1902

Alexander Koch publicized a competition for *Haus Eines Kunstfreundes*, or House for an Art Lover, in December 1900 in his magazine, *Zietschrift für Innendekoration*. There were strict restrictions to adhere to, outlined in the competition brief, which stressed the need to look in new directions and to provide complete designs covering the exterior architecture, the interiors and the furnishing. Mackintosh's finished designs were published in 1902 and showed the artist at his most whimsical. Parallels can be drawn between his plans and the shape of an earthbound ocean liner. The critic David Brett has pointed out the significance of shipbuilding to Glasgow's economy at that time and Mackintosh's own relationship with the skilled craftsmen involved in this trade. Mackintosh's entry was eventually disqualified on a technical detail, namely that he had failed to include the required number of interior perspectives. The judges chose not to award a first prize and awarded second prize to the architect M. H. Baillie Scott (1865–1945). Mackintosh's entry was recognized with a 'special purchase prize' because he had captured the innovative spirit that the competition had hoped to inspire.

CREATED

Glasgow

MEDIUM

Pen and ink

SERIES/PERIOD/MOVEMENT

Competition entry

SIMILAR WORKS

House for an Art Lover by M. H. Baillie Scott, 1902

IDEEN·WETTBEWERB FÜR EIN HERRSCHAFTLICHES WOHNHAUS EINES KUNST·FREUNDES LI
5

Cabinet made for 14 Kingsborough Gardens, Glasgow, 1902

The early years of the 1900s were a period of intense activity for Mackintosh. He had several commissions at Kilmacolm, one for the Gate Lodge at Auchenbothie and another for a house in the area, details of which are now lost. He designed the House at Bridge of Weir for Alfred Todd, delivered the lecture 'Seemliness' and his work was illustrated in *Dekorative Kunst* and *Deutsche Kunst und Dekoration*. Also in 1902 he was commissioned by Mrs Rowat to complete a series of interior decorations for the family home at 14 Kingsborough Gardens, Glasgow. Mrs Rowat was the mother of Francis Newbery's wife Jessie. Mackintosh was responsible for the wall decorations, in the form of stencilling, and for designing fireplaces, fixtures, fittings and some furniture. The cabinet pictured here is one of a matching pair. Seen with the doors open the piece is simple, yet beautiful and includes a stylized female figure holding a rosebud on the inside of each door. His use of silver leaf and fine coloured glass adds an opulent note to the piece that was crafted from painted Scottish oak.

CREATED

Glasgow

MEDIUM

Painted oak

SERIES/PERIOD/MOVEMENT

Furniture design of early 1900s

SIMILAR WORKS

Daffodil Dresser by M. H. Baillie Scott, 1901

Sideboard for dining room of Henry Von Heiseler's House by Hermann Obrist, 1899

Detail from an ebonized mahogany writing cabinet, 1904

Mackintosh was introduced to Walter Blackie in 1902 when the publishing magnate had bought a plot of land to the north of Helensburgh, not far from Glasgow. After showing Blackie the Windyhill House, built in 1902 for William Davidson Junior, Mackintosh was commissioned to design The Hill House. The Hill House is widely regarded as the best example of Mackintosh's domestic architecture. During 1902 to 1903 Mackintosh created the interiors for the Moscow Exhibition of Modern Architecture and Design, further enhancing his growing reputation abroad. In 1903 his designs for Liverpool Cathedral were published and in the same year he returned to work for Catherine Cranston, embarking on the Willow Tea Rooms. Mackintosh worked on the interiors and furniture designs for The Hill House during 1904. He designed three similar writing desks, one of which he used himself. These cabinets were crafted from expensive materials: ebonized wood, mother-of-pearl and pear-wood inlays, and ivory and exotic stained-glass features. The interiors of the desks were as beautiful as the exterior with pigeon-hole divisions and a sliding writing surface.

CREATED

Glasgow

MEDIUM

Stained glass

SERIES/PERIOD/MOVEMENT

Furniture design of early 1900s

SIMILAR WORKS

Princess of the Red Rose, screen detail with pen and ink inset drawing by Jessie M. King, 1902

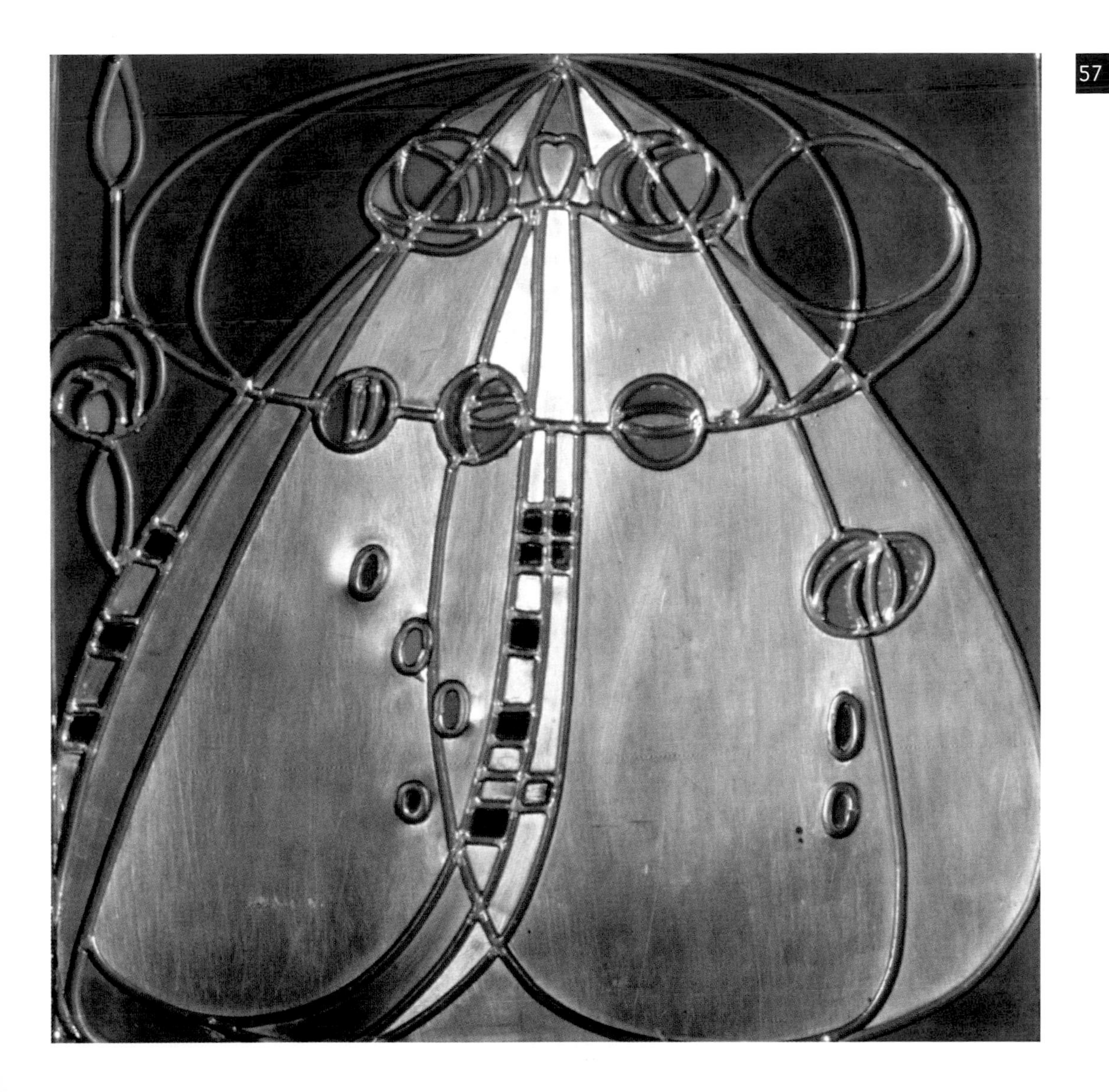

Elevation of a wall for the dining room of A. S. Ball, 1905

Catherine Cranston, who had been a long-standing patron to Mackintosh, commissioned him to redesign the interiors and furniture in her home, Hous'hill, Glasgow. Work began in 1903 and continued on to 1905 as Mackintosh ingeniously redefined the house within its existing architecture. He designed a significant amount of the furniture and all of the fixtures and fittings. Another of Mackintosh's great supporters was the attaché to the German embassy in London, Hermann Muthesius (1861–1927). Muthesius had left London in 1904 after serving seven years with the embassy. He was a prominent figure in architecture and design and was partly responsible for publicizing Mackintosh's skills on the Continent. He also secured Mackintosh's first overseas commission from Munich publisher H. Bruckmann for a dining room. Muthesius was again instrumental in Mackintosh being commissioned by the Berlin company A. S. Ball to produce a dining room. The regard with which Mackintosh held Muthesius emanates through his own words, 'I am afraid that there is little chance of our getting a Grand Prix at Torino (the International Exhibition of Modern Decorative Art, Turin, 1902), but when you say we should have it – we feel that we have got something we value much more'.

CREATED

Glasgow

MEDIUM

Pencil and watercolour

SERIES/PERIOD/MOVEMENT

Continental commissions

SIMILAR WORKS

Waller House dining room, Chicago by Frank Lloyd Wright, 1899

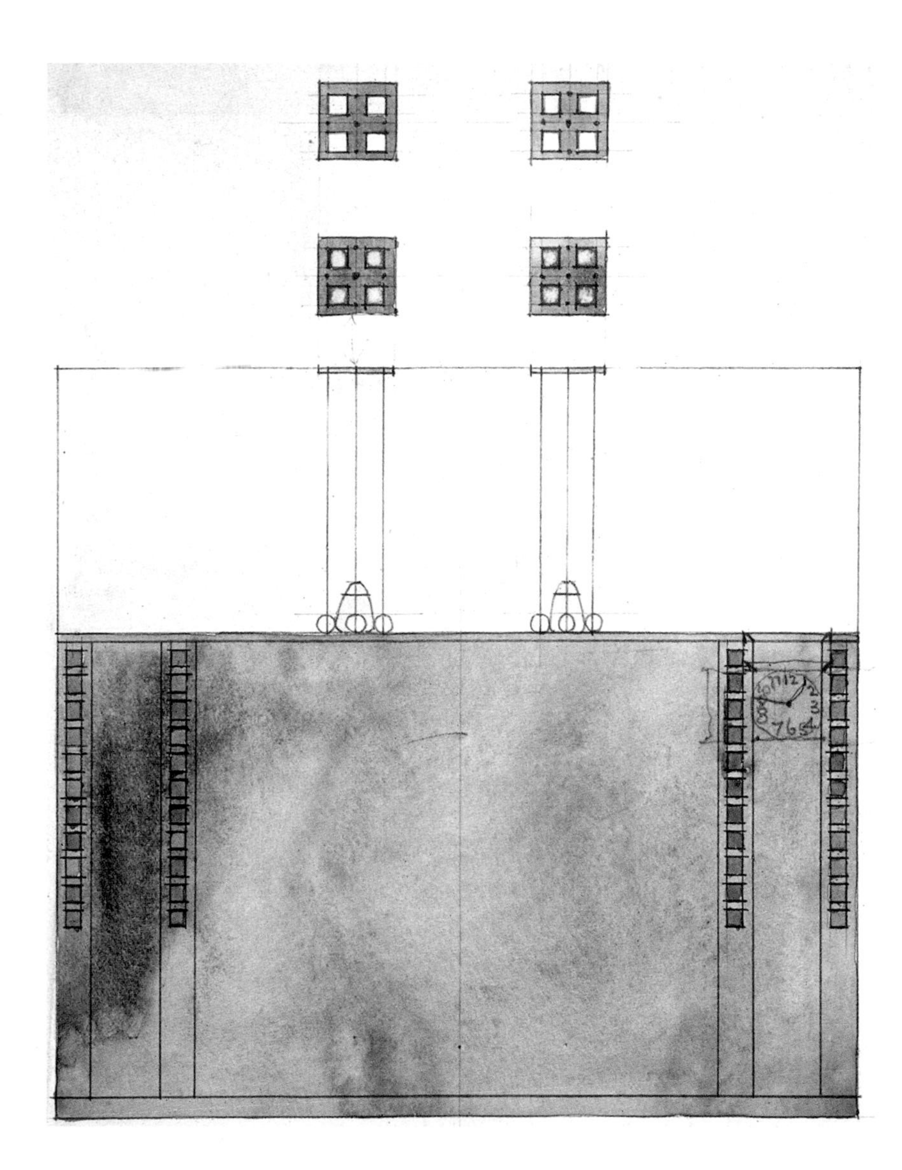

Sidechair, *c.* 1905–10

In 1906 the Mackintoshes left their Mains Street studio home and moved to 78 Southpark Avenue, taking their furniture, fixtures and fittings with them. Their Southpark home has been reconstructed and is on display at the Hunterian Art Gallery in Glasgow. The same year Mackintosh was elected a Fellow of the Royal Institute of British Architects and worked on the boardroom at the Glasgow School of Art. Between 1905 and 1906 he designed the Dutch Kitchen for the Argyle Street Tea Rooms and then from 1906 to 1907 worked on the Oak Room for the Ingram Street Tea Rooms. It was through his extensive work in the tea rooms that his reputation as a designer was widely established. His architecture was still relatively unknown outside Glasgow and he was recognized as much for his furniture design and interiors as anything else. The side chair is one of his low-backed designs that he returned to in different forms again and again. He has abandoned his earlier use of organic curvilinear form, seen in the chairs designed for the International Exhibition of Modern Decorative Art, Turin, 1902, and turned instead to a stout, geometric structure.

CREATED

Glasgow

MEDIUM

Ebonized wood

SERIES/PERIOD/MOVEMENT

Chairs

SIMILAR WORKS

Spindle-back chair with turned legs by George Walton, 1896

Photograph from *The Studio* of Miss Cranston's Tea Rooms, Glasgow, published 1912

The second stage of building and development on the Glasgow School of Art began in 1907. It is testament to Mackintosh's extraordinary talent that he was able to synthesize his new designs into the existing building, creating a unity of expression through the two stages whilst producing something new and innovative. Since the completion of the first stage in 1899, Mackintosh had defined his artistic vision through the designs of Windyhill, The Hill House and the numerous tea-room projects that he continued to manage. Between 1909 and 1912 Mackintosh was again employed by Catherine Cranston, this time with commissions for the Ingram Street Tea Rooms and the White Cockade Tea Room at the Glasgow International Exhibition, 1911. Margaret and Charles worked together on the latter, designing everything from the furniture to the cutlery and menu cards. Mackintosh's style was becoming more inventive and adventurous, seen especially in his designs for the Chinese Room and Cloister Room at the Ingram Street Tea Rooms.

The early collaboration between George Walton and Mackintosh was quite successful. Here in the Argyle Luncheon Room Walton provided the screens and decoration and Mackintosh the furniture.

CREATED

Glasgow

MEDIUM

Interior design

SERIES/PERIOD/MOVEMENT

Tea rooms

SIMILAR WORKS

Stuart Cranston's Buchanan Street Tea Room, opened 1889

Apple, 1915

In 1913 after a final terminal row with John Keppie, Mackintosh dissolved his partnership in the firm of Honeyman, Keppie and Mackintosh. The following year the Mackintoshes moved to Walberswick, a small village on the Suffolk coastline. Walberswick had a long artistic tradition and had been home to a succession of artists over a period of years. It was a difficult time for Mackintosh, who was suffering from a severe confidence crisis and was disillusioned with the reception of his work. Accounts indicate that he had become increasingly difficult to work with, was prone to bouts of drinking and would not have been sorely missed by the people of Glasgow. Often referred to as his greatest accomplishment, Mackintosh would tragically never see the Glasgow School of Art again. Nor would he live long enough to gain the recognition and praise that he so craved and deserved for his work. During his time at Walberswick he produced over 40 watercolour studies of flowers and several landscapes. These are considered some of his best watercolour work and the delicate colouring, assured handling and the skilful compositions belie the artist's depressed state of mind.

CREATED

Walberswick

MEDIUM

Pencil and watercolour

SERIES/PERIOD/MOVEMENT

Walberswick watercolours

SIMILAR WORKS

Sketch from Nature by Jessie Keppie, 1895

APPLE
WALBERSWICK
1915
CRMMMM

Larkspur, 1914

The Walberswick flower studies were originally intended for publication in Germany, until the onset of the First World War effectively severed Mackintosh's ties with the Continent. Mackintosh was never accepted into the small community of the fishing village and was viewed with suspicion. Extraordinarily he was arrested in 1914 on charges of espionage and appeared before a local magistrate. Correspondence between Mackintosh and members of the Viennese Secessionists may have contributed to his arrest, as did his thick accent that was unrecognizable to the Walberswick locals. He was finally released after the intervention of Lady Norah Mears who pleaded his case at the War Office in London. Naturally the incident was a massive blow to Mackintosh who had moved to Walberswick to recover his self-confidence. Despite the traumatic circumstances surrounding his stay, his flower studies show a harmony of expression that is quite remarkable. They bridge the divide of botanical correctness and decorative creativity in a seamless totality. In his own words, 'Let every artist strive to make his flower a beautiful living thing – flowers that are not dead; are not dying; not artificial; real flowers springing from your own soul...'.

CREATED

Walberswick

MEDIUM

Pencil and watercolour

SERIES/PERIOD/MOVEMENT

Walberswick watercolours

SIMILAR WORKS

April by Katharine Cameron

LARKSPUR
WALBERSWICK
AUGUST 1914
C.R.M.M.M.M

Design for W. J. Bassett-Lowke, 1916

The Mackintoshes moved to London in 1915, to Glebe Place in Chelsea. Chelsea was a centre of artistic activity in the capital at this time and was a favourite haunt of artists, poets and intellectuals. The couple rented adjacent studios and quickly settled into life in London. The Blue Cockatoo, a restaurant in their neighbourhood that was a hubbub of arty types, became a regular destination for the Mackintoshes. Around this time, Mackintosh met the successful businessman W. J. Bassett-Lowke. He became an important patron for Mackintosh and commissioned a number of pieces of furniture, some textile designs and most importantly the redecoration of his home No. 78 Derngate, in Northampton. The house was spatially restrictive and challenging to redesign. This was perfect for Mackintosh who was particularly intuitive in moulding interior space to appear larger than its physicality, something he had worked on in the tea-room projects. The end result was outstandingly original in design concept, from the wooden screen to the darkly painted walls and ceiling. He worked on many strong geometric patterns that were used throughout the dramatic interior scheme.

CREATED/DESIGNED FOR

Derngate, Northampton

MEDIUM

Pencil and body colour on oiled tracing paper

SERIES/PERIOD/MOVEMENT

Derngate designs

SIMILAR WORKS

Antimacassar from The Hill House by Margaret Mackintosh, *c.* 1904

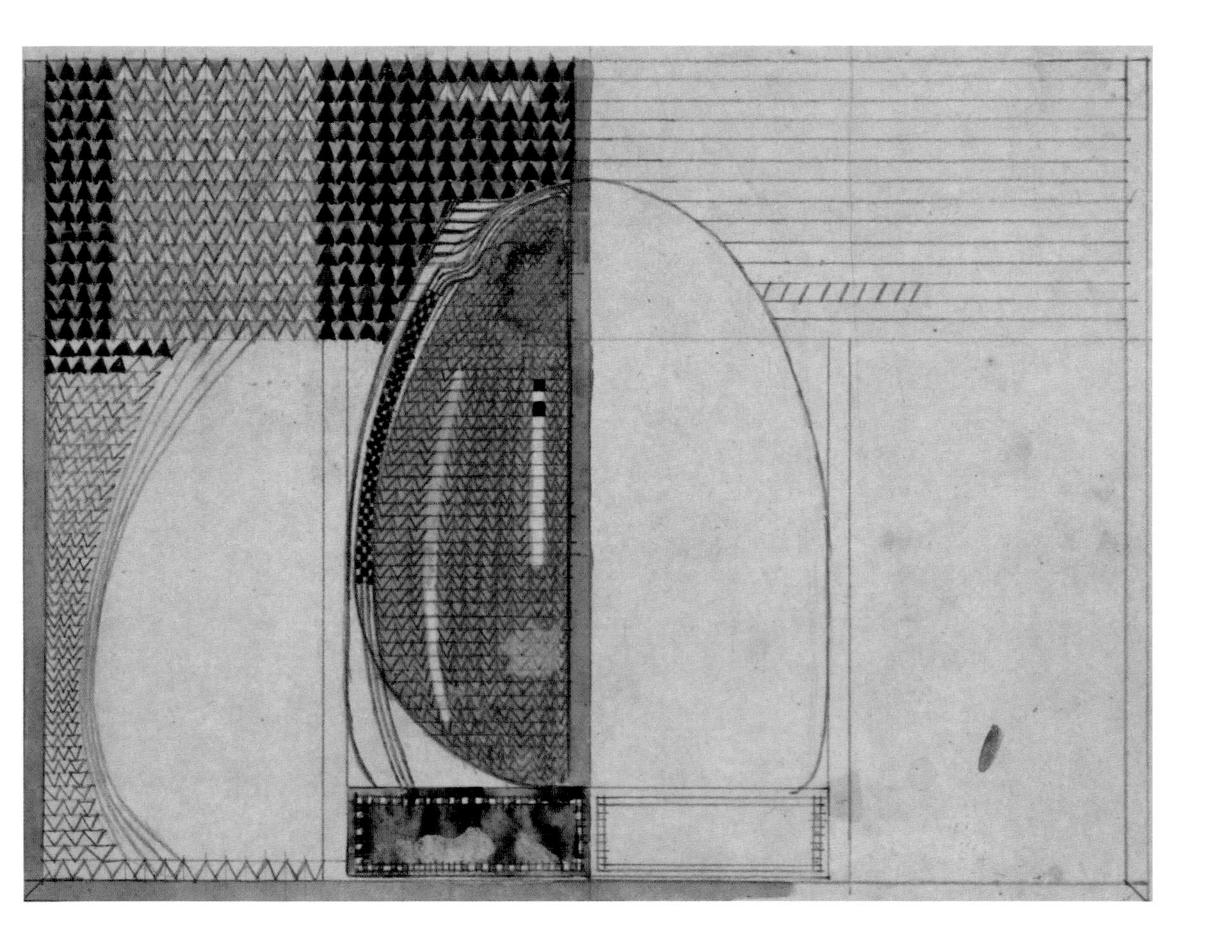

Domino Clock, 1917

Number 78 Derngate was the most significant of Mackintosh's sparse commissions at this time, along with the decoration for the Dug Out, in the basement of the Willow Tea Rooms. The Dug Out project was again to include all interior design, furniture, fixtures and fittings, and demonstrates Mackintosh's inexhaustible supply of innovative ideas. He used strong geometric forms that appear modern and Oriental in conception. The Willow Tea Rooms were the only tea rooms for which Mackintosh designed the exterior façade. This gave the rooms a continuation in handling and vision from the exterior to the interior, something that Mackintosh was greatly concerned with. The Domino Clock was designed for Bassett-Lowke in 1917 for the Derngate residence. The bold linear form and use of ebonized wood were typical of Mackintosh's designs at this time. The clock fitted perfectly within the scheme of the house, which was based around patterns of chequerboards, lines and triangles. Dominoes was a popular game at this time and the domino motif was one that Mackintosh often employed.

CREATED

Derngate, Northampton

MEDIUM

Ebonized wood with ivory and plastic inlay

SERIES/PERIOD/MOVEMENT

Derngate designs

SIMILAR WORKS

Telechron mantle clock by Paul Theodore Frankl, 1928–29

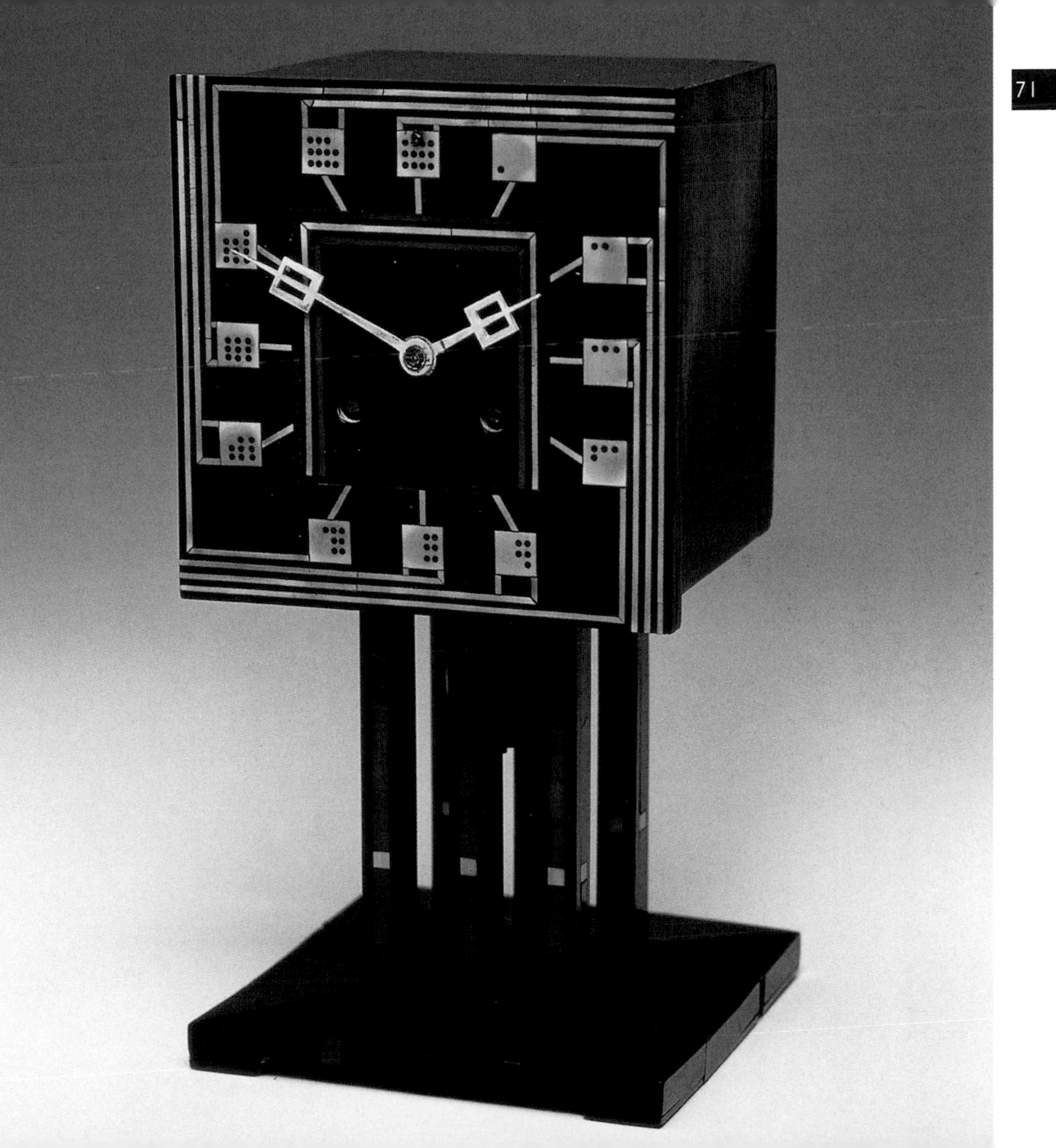

Repeating design with stylized flower and scale motifs

Derngate was the fruition of a great artistic output and terrific creative energy. It was the first large commission that Mackintosh had undertaken since leaving Glasgow and moving south. When Mackintosh arrived in London he was not particularly well known, the majority of his work being focused either in Scotland or on the Continent. The Derngate commission therefore was significant to the artist in highlighting his skills to a 'new' public. It was a thoroughly masterful manipulation of a small space and a singularly original decorative scheme. Disappointingly for Mackintosh it did not, however, lead to greater commissions. Some years after completion when Derngate was featured in *Ideal Home* magazine, Mackintosh's name failed to appear alongside his building, which must have been a bitter blow. Bassett-Lowke eventually chose the architect Peter Behrens (1868–1940) over Mackintosh, to build a bigger house in Northampton in 1922. Both Mackintosh and Margaret worked on textile designs during this period and this repeating flower design demonstrates the vivid use of colour, typical of their work at this time.

CREATED

London

MEDIUM

Body colour on paper

SERIES/PERIOD/MOVEMENT

London furnishings designs

SIMILAR WORKS

Trail furnishing fabric by John Henry Dearle, 1891

Design based on concentric circles

Mackintosh's short life and even shorter working career was plagued with misfortune and missed opportunity, poor timing and an increasingly irascible nature. It is a tragedy that he did not live to see his work finally appreciated. The First World War put an end to the growing reputation that he had established on the Continent and prevented any further commissions from overseas. When Margaret and Charles moved to London, they were able to integrate into their community, but due to war restrictions there was little demand for an architect. Architectural commissions were few and far between and the Mackintoshes had to look to other areas to make a living. In 1914 Mackintosh started to produce textile designs for Foxton's in London and Sefton's in Belfast. He is also believed to have worked for Liberty's, F. W. Grafton in Manchester and Templeton's in Glasgow. His concentric circle design, pictured, is one of a set of four and was probably produced for ceramic decoration. Mackintosh was the consummate designer, his ingenious sense of style extending from architecture through interiors, to posters, wall decorations, cutlery and textiles.

CREATED

London

MEDIUM

Pencil and watercolour

SERIES/PERIOD/MOVEMENT

London furnishing designs

SIMILAR WORKS

Lidded ceramic box by Bertold Löffler, 1912–13

Bowl with geometric and floral pattern by Josef Hoffmann, 1913

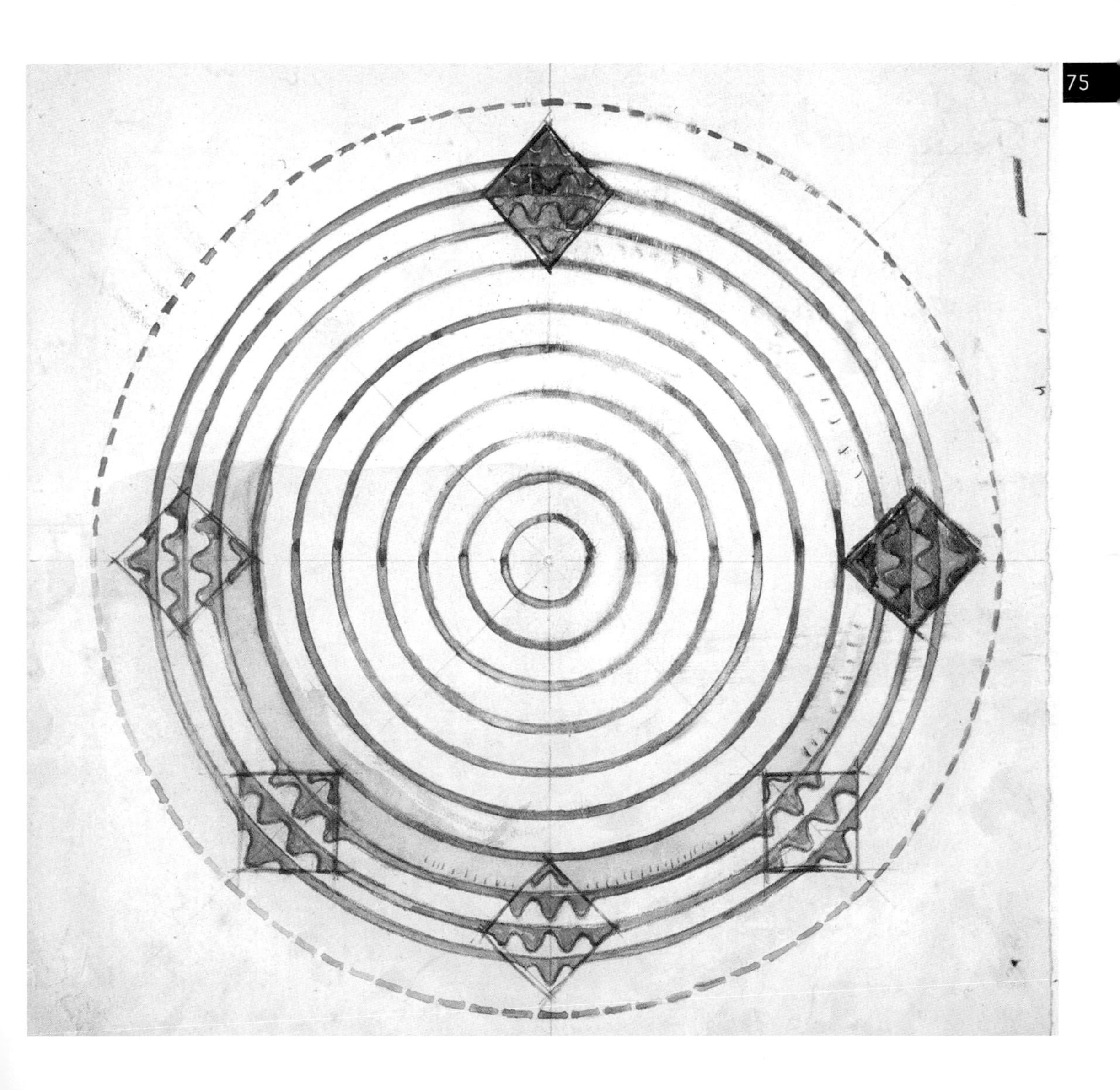

Textile design

Mackintosh had never designed printed fabric before. The fabrics that he had used in his interiors were almost always stencilled or embroidered in appliqué and would probably have been primarily executed by Margaret. He had also not designed in a commercial sense, having always produced his designs for specific interiors and clients. Working for the textile companies signified a step in an entirely new direction for the artist. Records show that Mackintosh was quite well remunerated for his designs. In 1920 he was paid approximately £200 for textile designs, which was not a paltry sum. Sadly there is little documentation surrounding his different designs and only two samples survive that can be accurately attributed to Mackintosh. The textile designs can be roughly divided into two groups, organic and geometric. The detail here is strongly organic and reminiscent of wave patterns, perhaps inspired by the beaches at Walberswick.

CREATED

London

MEDIUM

Pencil and watercolour

SERIES/PERIOD/MOVEMENT

London textile designs

SIMILAR WORKS

Matina by Dagobert Peche, 1911–12

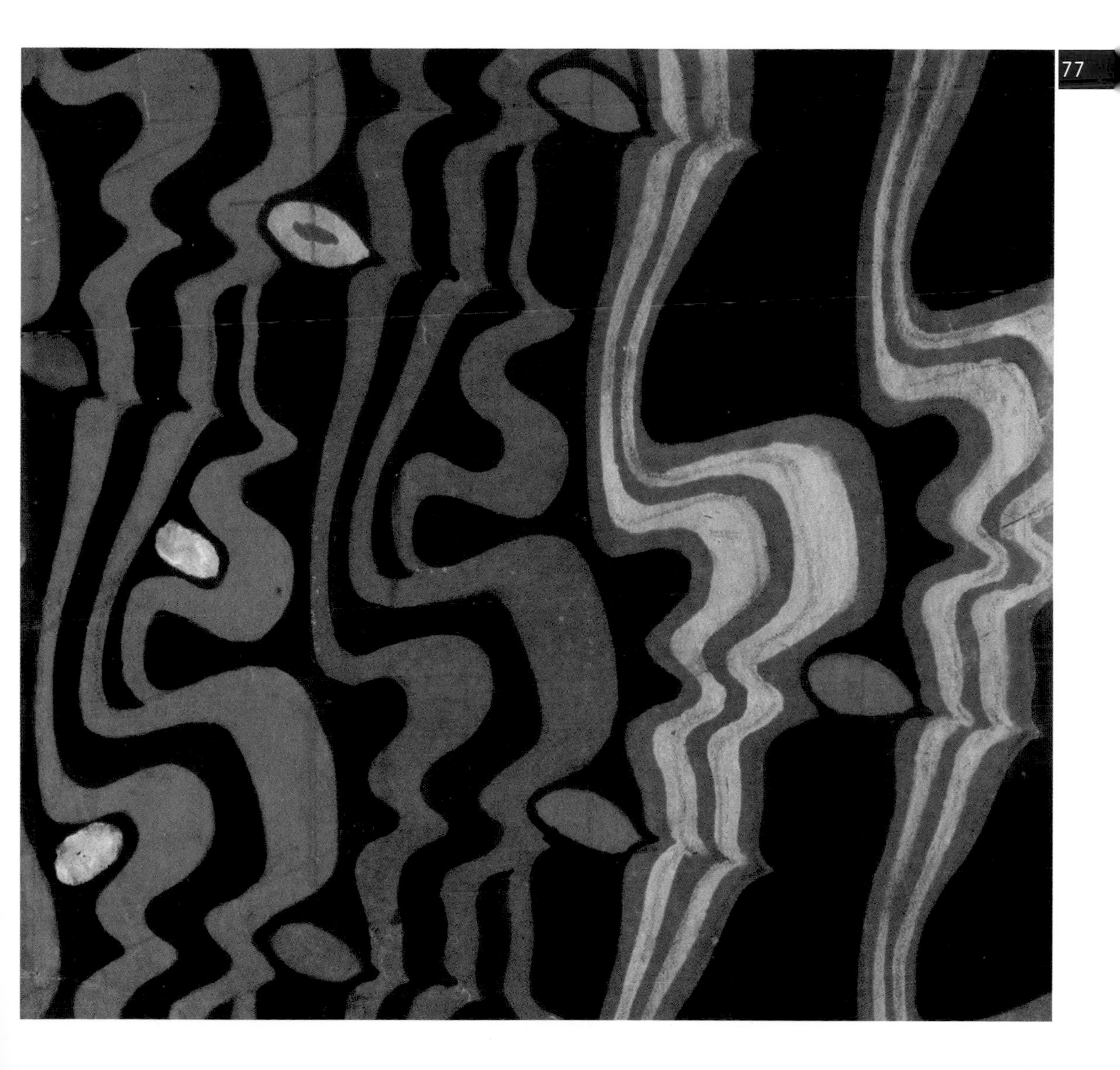

Washstand, *c.* 1917

Since their move to London the Mackintoshes had established themselves within a tight-knit circle of artists and artisans. Thomas Howarth, in his substantial reflection on the Mackintosh's life, refers to Margaret as an enthusiastic party thrower, especially children's parties even though the Mackintoshes had no children of their own. Her parties were planned and co-ordinated down to the last detail, a method not dissimilar to the design treatment of their interiors. Charles and Margaret were flamboyantly unconventional; Charles in his long academic-style cloak and Margaret in dresses that she designed and made herself. They became great friends with Margaret Morris, an accomplished dance teacher who had opened a studio in Chelsea the year before the Mackintoshes arrived in London. Margaret Morris's studio became a centre of performing arts and creative thinking, an atmosphere that the Mackintoshes were naturally attracted to. During this period Mackintosh worked on textile and furniture designs, producing pieces that truly foresaw the emergence of Modernism. The washstand, pictured, demonstrates his use of inlaid mother-of-pearl in simple squares, distinctly different from his earlier Glasgow style of curvilinear forms.

CREATED

London

MEDIUM

Mahogany, inlaid with mother-of-pearl and green erinoid, with glass backplate

SERIES/PERIOD/MOVEMENT

London furniture designs

SIMILAR WORKS

Full front desk in burl wood by Rene Prou, 1929

Design with dotted curvilinear element for textile

Margaret Morris's husband, the painter J. D. Fergusson (1874–1961) encouraged Mackintosh to get involved with the London Salon of the Independents. This society was similar to the Salon des Indépendants in Paris and was chiefly concerned with organizing 'open' exhibitions for painting, sculpture and crafts, in direct retaliation to the closed ranks of the Academy exhibitions.

Mackintosh and his wife collaborated to produce a series of paintings that were exhibited at the Arts and Crafts Society's Eleventh Exhibition, in 1916, under the title *The Voices in the Wood*. One of these, *Figures and Foliage*, was executed by Mackintosh alone and represents the only known oil painting in his oeuvre. A number of motifs from these paintings can be seen in his textile designs, especially the daisy design in *The Little Hills*, another of the *Voices in the Wood* panels. The development of Mackintosh's vibrant strong textile designs of his London days are in contrast to the spare, minimalist fabrics of his Glasgow period. The bold geometry and stylized flower designs anticipate Art Deco patterns seen in the mid-1920s.

CREATED

London

MEDIUM

Watercolour

SERIES/PERIOD/MOVEMENT

London textile designs

SIMILAR WORKS

Helena by C. F. A. Voysey, 1895–1900

Table with mother-of-pearl inlay, 1918

The London Salon of the Independents was instigated to give any artist the opportunity to exhibit. A small annual membership fee was charged because, unlike the Salon des Indépendants in Paris, the London group was not supported by the government. This put them at a huge disadvantage and the members struggled to keep the group going. Mackintosh was involved in trying to establish exhibition space for the society to get it up and running. Sadly nowhere was found and the group was eventually disseminated. At around the same time both Margaret and Charles became involved in the Plough, a performing arts group formed for, 'the purpose of stimulating interest in good art of an unconventional kind'. The Plough's innovative approach to play production was based on involving the author/composer closely in the artistic presentation of their work and the performances became very popular.

Mackintosh had first turned towards rigid geometric shapes in his designs for the furniture at The Hill House, *c.* 1904. This pattern of design was then further realized in his work at Derngate, 1916–17. The use of simple mother-of-pearl inlay was an aesthetic device that Mackintosh used frequently during this period.

CREATED

London

MEDIUM

Stained mahogany wood with mother-of-pearl inlay

SERIES/PERIOD/MOVEMENT

London furniture designs

SIMILAR WORKS

Dining room table exhibited at the Eighth Secessionist Exhibition, Vienna by Josef Hoffmann, *c.* 1900

Dress fabric, 1918

In 1917 Mackintosh had been commissioned by Sidney Horstmann to undertake the redecoration of a bedroom at his home in Bath. The following year he worked on Candida Cottage, the Northampton weekend retreat belonging to W. J. Bassett-Lowke. These small commissions were bread and butter to Mackintosh who was increasingly frustrated by the lack of a large-scale architectural venture. Charles and Margaret threw themselves into the activities of the Plough. They had been involved with the performing arts when they were both still students at the Glasgow School of Art and now, many years later, they were again immersed in the theatre culture. They worked on set designs and costumes, including the décor for Maurice Maeterlinck's *Joizelle*, staged in 1917. Mackintosh continued to work on his textile designs, creating astonishingly bold and Modernistic patterns. His use of strong line and colour would later be seen in the watercolours of his final years and show the enormous breadth of his artistic development over a short working career. The rhythmic pattern of yellow and black seen here in this dress fabric seems to anticipate the 'chain mail' fashion designs of Paco Rabanne in the 1960s.

CREATED

London

MEDIUM

Printed silk

SERIES/PERIOD/MOVEMENT

London textile designs

SIMILAR WORKS

Leaf pattern by Koloman Moser, 1899

Vine furnishing fabric by Richard Riemerschmid, 1905

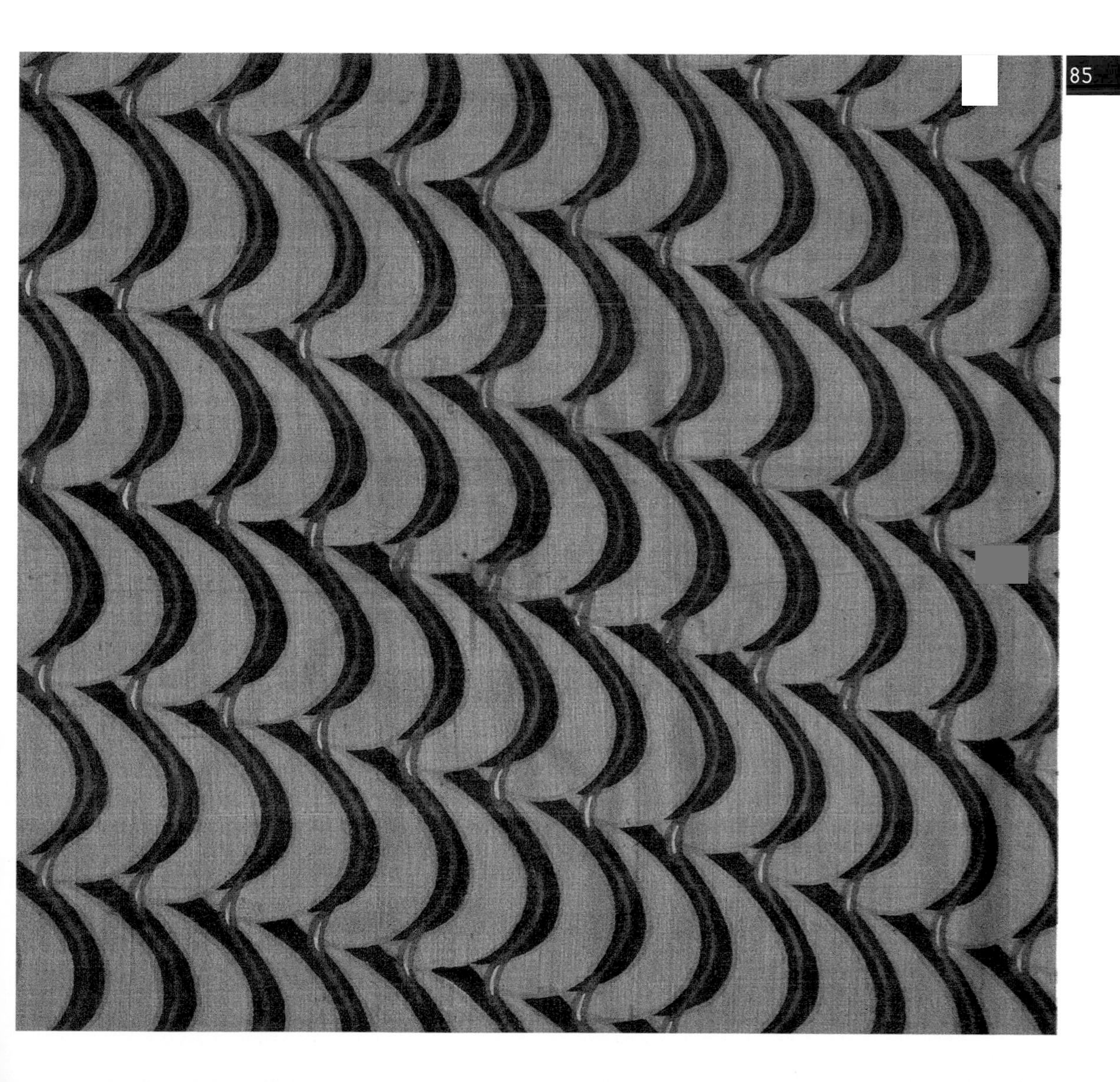

Dining room suite, *c.* 1918–19

Bassett-Lowke continued to provide Mackintosh with small commissions after the major redecoration of Derngate, 1916–17, and in 1919 he was commissioned to redesign the Derngate guestroom. The guest room would become the most original of the decorative schemes throughout the house and was startlingly modern in concept. The room has since been recreated as part of the Mackintosh House at the Hunterian Gallery in Glasgow. The twin beds in the room demonstrate Mackintosh's use of the square motif as his only decorative feature. This was something he employed frequently during this period, often using inlaid squares of mother-of-pearl, as seen in this dining room table and chairs. This dining room set that was commissioned by Harry Franklin, director of a prominent engineering firm, is sturdy and utilitarian in design. In 1919–20 Mackintosh worked on a studio cottage and pigeon house for the acclaimed photographer E. O. Hoppé (1878–1972), who was also involved with the activities of the Plough group. The studio cottage, which was created from the shell of an old gamekeeper's house at the Little Hedgecourt estate in Grinstead, Sussex, is not regarded as a particularly memorable piece of Mackintosh's work.

CREATED

London

MEDIUM

Wood, inlaid with mother-of-pearl and aluminium

SERIES/PERIOD/MOVEMENT

London furniture designs

SIMILAR WORKS

Dining room set by K. Bertsch, 1898

Elevation of proposed studio in Glebe Place and Upper Cheyne Walk, London, 1920

Surviving records indicate that 1920 was a relatively busy year for Mackintosh. He was commissioned to build a studio for the artist Harold Squire on a narrow site bordering Glebe Place to the north. Shortly afterwards he received two further similar commissions, from Francis Derwent Wood and Arthur Cadogan Blunt. The same year he was commissioned by the Arts League of Service to design a group of studio flats for artists and was then commissioned by Margaret Morris to design a theatre. Of these commissions, for which Mackintosh produced elaborate plans, only the Harold Squire project was built. The others remained unexecuted primarily due to financial restraints and difficulties with the local authorities. The original plans for Squire's studio proved too costly and Mackintosh had to revise them to bring the costs down to around £4,000. Although Squire was pleased with the finished building he only lived there for a short time. His staff complained of ghostly encounters with a man on a horse and then Squire himself allegedly saw the apparition. The building site had belonged to an eccentric doctor, Dr Phené, who had apparently buried his beloved horse somewhere beneath the newly erected Mackintosh studio.

CREATED

London

MEDIUM

Pencil, watercolour and body colour

SERIES/PERIOD/MOVEMENT

Late architectural plans

SIMILAR WORKS

25 Cadogan Gardens by A. H. Mackmurdo, 1899

The Fort, c. 1925–26

After the disappointment of unrealized architectural plans Mackintosh became increasingly frustrated. The local authorities had objected strongly to his proposed plans for Margaret Morris's theatre and the project eventually fell by the wayside. From 1920 to 1921 he was commissioned by Miss Brooks to make some alterations to her home, Little Ease in Burgess Hill, Sussex, and in 1921 he produced some book covers for his old patron Walter Blackie. Quite possibly the greatest blow for Mackintosh came in 1922 when Bassett-Lowke commissioned the German architect, Peter Behrens, to design New Ways, his inspiringly modern new house in Northampton. In 1923 Margaret and Charles went on an extended holiday, finally settling in Port Vendres, a small village on the Mediterranean side of the Franco-Spanish border. For the next four years Mackintosh devoted himself to watercolour painting. Their move abroad signalled the end of Mackintosh's career as an architect and designer with great finality, but was a period during which he produced some of his most stunning paintings. His work clearly shows his architectural heritage with its strong linear pattern and arrangement of bold planes of colour.

CREATED

Port Vendres

MEDIUM

Pencil and watercolour

SERIES/PERIOD/MOVEMENT

Late period watercolours

SIMILAR WORKS

Earth Home or *The Fortress* by Paul Nash, 1939

The Little Bay, 1927

Similar to the way in which he took on the mantle of textile designer, Mackintosh embraced his new 'career' as a watercolourist. His handling of paint and subject matter in an entirely original manner was astonishing and yet in reflection should be entirely expected from such an enormous talent. His paintings fall into two groups, still life and landscape. They appear to have been well received with reproductions of some appearing in *The Studio* magazine. During this time he painted approximately only 40 canvases, indicating a slow working process. He exhibited works at the Chicago International Exhibitions in 1923, 1924 and 1925, at the Duveen Invited Artists' Show in Paris in 1927 and at the Leicester Galleries in 1928. *The Little Bay* is regarded as one of his most accomplished works and is an extraordinary reflection of light and tranquillity.

At the end of 1927 he complained of a sore throat and was persuaded by his doctor to return to England to seek treatment. Margaret accompanied him and he was quickly diagnosed with cancer of the tongue and throat. He underwent radiation therapy, had a brief remission, but relapsed and died on 10 December 1928. Margaret was devastated and died four years later.

CREATED

Port Vendres

MEDIUM

Pencil and watercolour

SERIES/PERIOD/MOVEMENT

Late period watercolours

SIMILAR WORKS

Le Port d'Anvers by Othon Friesz, 1906

C.R. MACKINTOSH 1927

THE W
GREAT

Mackintosh

Society

Perspective drawing of Martyr's Public School, Glasgow, 1896

As Mackintosh embarked on his career as an architect, Glasgow was reaping the benefits of the industrial age, but was also suffering the inevitable consequences. Glasgow was rapidly becoming the gold mine of the north, not in actual gold, but in ships and shipping, and all the industries that survived on the peripherals of this. The shipbuilding trades were a major source of employment and people flocked to the city to earn more than they could in the country. This led to severe overcrowding amongst the working classes and property developers became rich from building poor-quality, cheap housing to cater for the increased low-income population. Coal mining and steel manufacturing thrived on the back of shipbuilding and by the end of the nineteenth century Glasgow and her surrounding areas were becoming leaders of industry in Britain. Mackintosh's designs for the Martyr's Public School (1896) were extraordinarily detailed, with this perspective drawing being especially beautiful. His artistic handling of this drawing would not have been well received in his day, however, and would have been considered too fanciful.

CREATED

Glasgow

MEDIUM

Ink on paper

SERIES/PERIOD/MOVEMENT

School designs

SIMILAR WORKS

Clouds by Philip Webb, 1881–86

Charles Rennie Mackintosh *Born* 1868 Glasgow, Scotland

Died 1928

THE SCHOOL BOARD OF GLASGOW
MARTYRS PUBLIC SCHOOL

Perspective drawing of the Scotland Street School, 1904

By the end of the nineteenth century Glasgow was a city riding the wave of progression and success. There had been a tremendous growth in the population based around the expansion of industry, most notably that of shipbuilding. Housing conditions for the majority were poor, consisting of tenements and squalid blocks of flats, the population growth having surpassed the natural expansion of the city and its facilities. In 1872 an Education Act was passed in Scotland requiring the formation of a school board in each district. The school board was responsible for ensuring that every child between the ages of five and 13 was provided with a set standard of education. This led to the construction of many new schools. Mackintosh, who had designed the Martyrs School (1895–98), was approached by the school board to design the Scotland Street School in 1903. The school board required a strict code of segregation between the boys and girls and allotted the project a tight budget. The eventual building was a great success in terms of planning, but ran over the budget considerably, causing consternation amongst the members of the board.

CREATED

Glasgow

MEDIUM

Black ink and pencil on thick woven paper

SERIES/PERIOD/MOVEMENT

School designs

SIMILAR WORKS

Extension to Stirling High School by James MacLaren, 1888

SCHOOL BOARD OF GLASGOW
SCOTLAND STREET PVBLIC SCHOOL.

Interior of the stair tower of Scotland Street School, 1904

Due mostly to the financial restraints of the commission, the Scotland Street School was supremely simple in design with ornamentation occurring only around the doors and windows. The required segregation of the co-educational system resulted in a design of symmetrical form, with separate entrances for the girls and boys, as well as separate stairways, cloakrooms, classrooms and playgrounds. Through the simplicity of the design, however, shines the brilliance of aesthetic realization. The soaring verticality of the stair towers lends a quasi-religious solemnity to the structure, enhanced by the bank of rhythmic vertical windows that anticipate Modernism. As is typical of Mackintosh's designs, the interior space is of equal or greater importance than the exterior. Every detail, even down to the arrangement of the staircase with its metal banisters echoing the verticality of the windows, was considered and executed with a brilliant synthesis of form. The detail, pictured, demonstrates Mackintosh's use of small insets of coloured glass and his geometric pattern of triangles and squares. Both of these were motifs that he would come back to again and again through his designs.

CREATED

Glasgow

MEDIUM

Stained glass

SERIES/PERIOD/MOVEMENT

School designs

SIMILAR WORKS

Staircase at Exhibition Building, Cologne by Walter Gropius, 1914

Extension to the *Glasgow Herald* Building, 1894

The *Glasgow Herald* building was one of the first projects that Mackintosh worked on after joining the firm of Honeyman and Keppie and the full extent of his input to the design is not clear. The firm was commissioned in 1893 by the *Herald* to provide extended premises for the flourishing newspaper. The building was to be used to house the production area and storage facilities for the paper and, although the structure remains, it is no longer used for this purpose. The plans were for an ordinary elevation in a Scottish Baronial Victorian style, with the notable inclusion of a significantly 'Mackintosh' tower. The rest of the building appears to have been heavily influenced by another hand, but the tower is a distinctive feature highly suggestive of Mackintosh's design. The use of tall pilasters at the corners of the building could have been influenced by Mackintosh's trip to Italy in 1891. Thomas Howarth noted the significance of a drawing of the tower on the back of one Mackintosh's Italian sketches and the fact that he had been very impressed with the Campanile in Sienna.

CREATED

Glasgow

MEDIUM

Ink on paper

SERIES/PERIOD/MOVEMENT

Early architectural designs

SIMILAR WORKS

Royal Insurance Building, Glasgow by the office of Honeyman and Keppie, 1894

THE HERALD
MITCHELL ST

Proposed hall of residence, Queen Margaret's Medical College, 1894

At the time of Mackintosh's involvement with Honeyman and Keppie, Glasgow was referred to as the 'Second City of the Empire'. Glasgow cut a leading edge in the arts and architecture and was recognized as the European pioneer in the use of cast iron and steel for commercial buildings. New materials allowed for innovative and progressive designs, seen in the work of the local architect John Baird, Charles Wilson and Alexander Thompson. It is indicative of the forward-thinking city that it became home to one of the first schools of medicine for women. In 1894 Mackintosh was commissioned to design the school, Queen Margaret's Medical College, on Hamilton Drive. The extent to which Mackintosh worked on the building has been questioned and much of the work has been attributed to John Keppie, although the perspective drawing that was published in *The British Architect*, 1896 is unmistakably by Mackintosh. To accompany the medical college Mackintosh drew up plans for a proposed hall of residence for the students. Here the basement plan appears rather more complicated than the layout for the ground and first floor of the medical college, which consisted of the main rooms spiralling from a central hall.

CREATED

Glasgow

MEDIUM

Pencil

SERIES/PERIOD/MOVEMENT

Early architectural designs

SIMILAR WORKS

North Court at Emmanuel College, Cambridge by Leonard Stokes, 1910–14

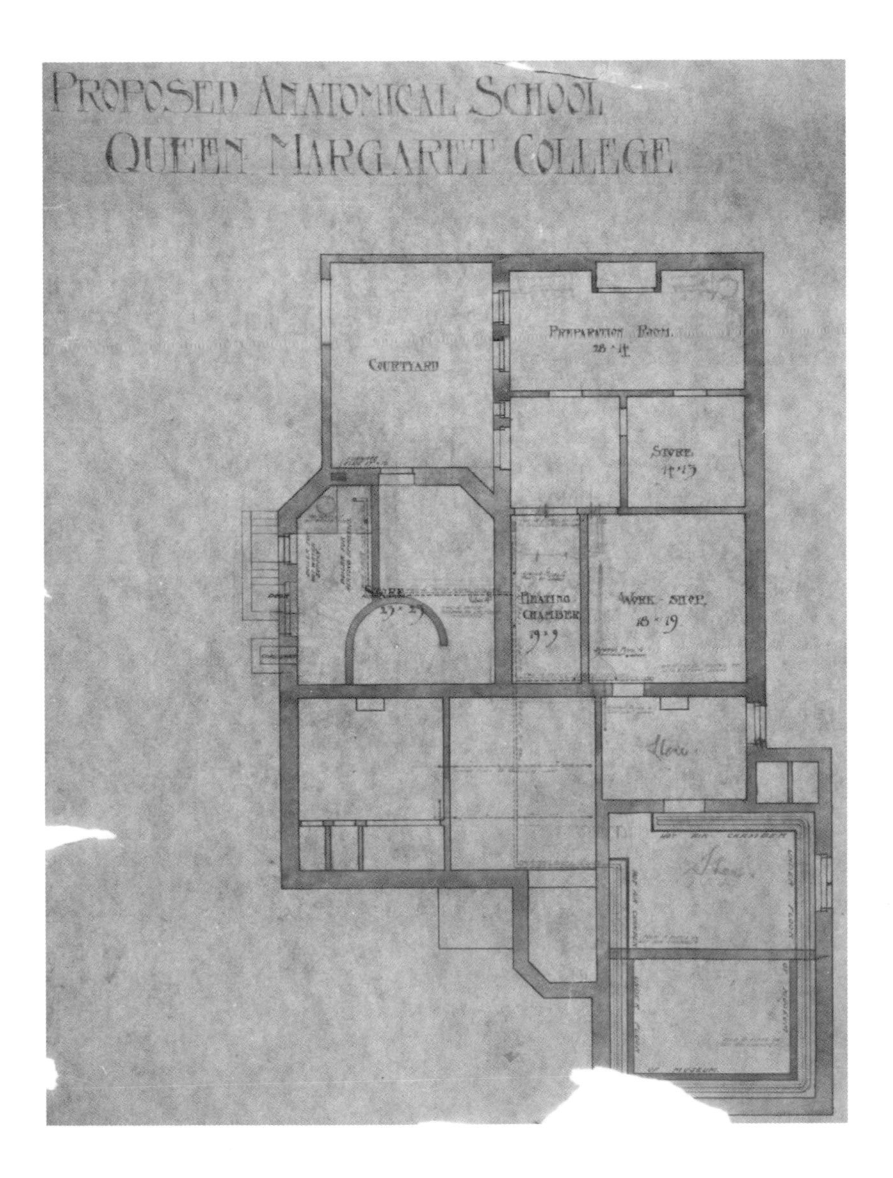
PROPOSED ANATOMICAL SCHOOL
QUEEN MARGARET COLLEGE
PREPARATION ROOM
28 × 14
COURTYARD
STORE
14 × 19
STORE
23 × 23
HEATING CHAMBER
9 × 9
WORK - SHOP
18 × 19
HOT AIR CHAMBER

South-east perspective of the *Daily Record* building, Glasgow, 1901

The death of Queen Victoria occurred in 1901 and was followed by the accession of Edward VII for his far shorter reign. The same year the mammoth Glasgow International Exhibition opened on 2 May. This was an exuberant festival of Victorian self-confidence that showcased the city and her accomplishments and was indicative of the new-found enthusiasm for arts and culture in the city. While Glasgow was being turned into a forum for arts, crafts, literature, music and sport, Mackintosh was working on plans for the *Daily Record* building. The site presented a series of problems, being long and narrow and enclosed on three sides creating a dark space of awkward proportions. Mackintosh developed an idea to use white glazed brick on the upper elevations of the building to increase the sense of light and he emphasized the upward surge of movement through the structure in a sculptural manner. His inclusion of projecting bricks in the form of a basic tree pattern alleviates the façade, creating interest and drawing the eye from the street level to the fourth storey. The building was a long ongoing project that was built in stages and was not finished until 1906.

CREATED

Glasgow

MEDIUM

Pencil, ink and watercolour on paper

SERIES/PERIOD/MOVEMENT

Early architectural designs

SIMILAR WORKS

Sanderson & Sons Factory, Chiswick by C. F. A. Voysey, 1902

DAILY RECORD BUILDINGS

Four spoons for Miss Cranston's Tea Rooms

The economic swelling of Glasgow saw the emergence of a wealthy middle class with the captains of industry reaping the benefits. Although the poor remained poor and the workers continued to live and labour under horrifying conditions, those at the top of the ladder skimmed the cream. The increased revenue was reflected in the abundant architectural commissions at this time; Glasgow was revelling in an age of expansion and construction. On the back of financial success, increased leisure time and a reduction in the tax on tea, the tea-room phenomenon exploded on to the social scene, at the helm of which stood Miss Cranston. Tea rooms were big business and, although they would fade with the onset of the First World War and all but disappear by the Second World War, they provided Mackintosh with a good source of commissions. Mackintosh's work on Miss Cranston's tea rooms encompassed all details of interior design, from the furniture to the cutlery and the façade of the Willow Tea Rooms. The cutlery, pictured, was used at the Ingram Street Tea Rooms in the Oak Room.

CREATED

Glasgow

MEDIUM

Metal

SERIES/PERIOD/MOVEMENT

Tea room designs

SIMILAR WORKS

Tableware designed by the *Wiener Werkstätte*, 1955

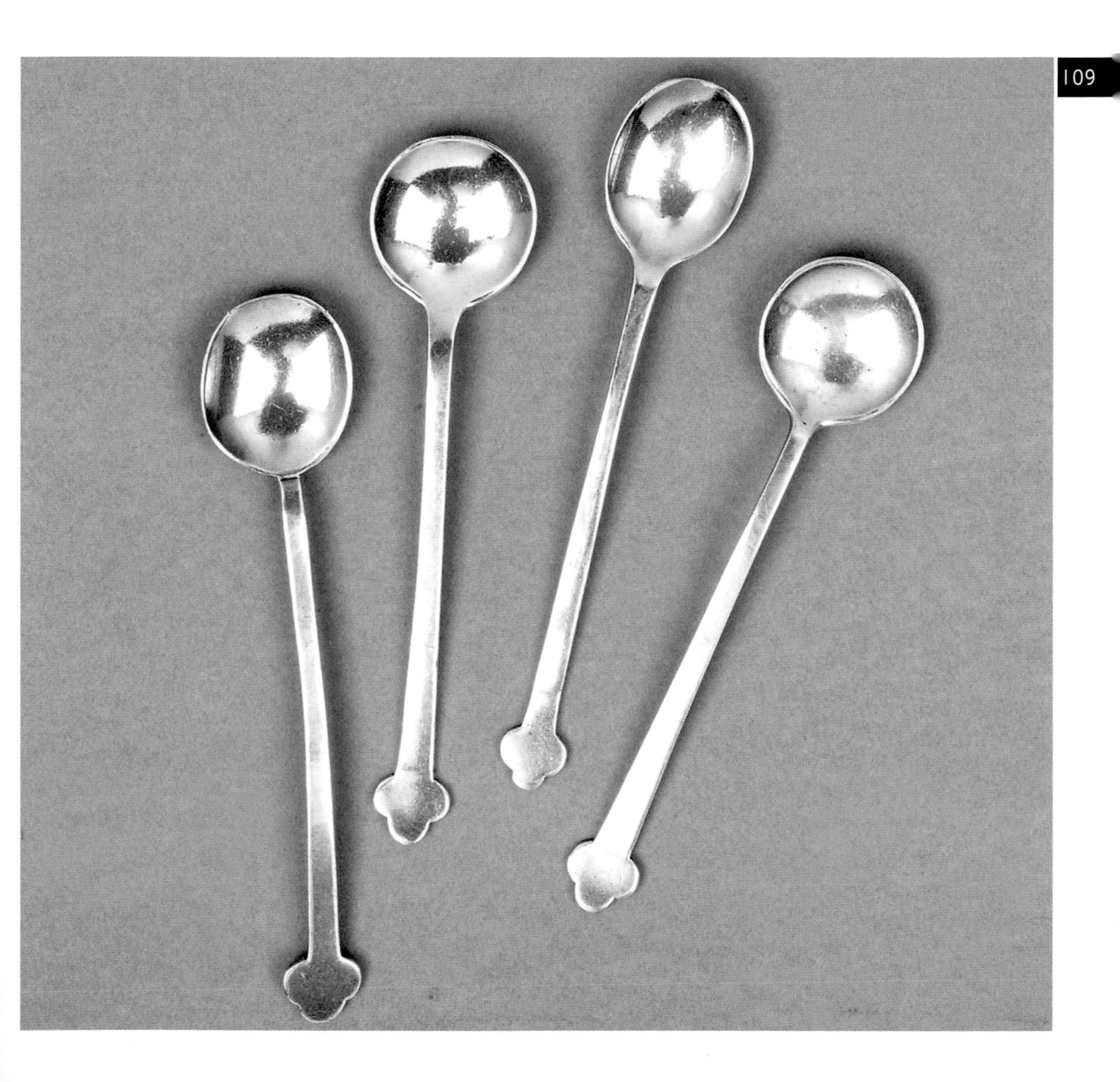

The White Cockade: illustration for a menu, 1911

King Edward died in 1910 and was succeeded by his son George V. He was greeted by a political maelstrom begun in 1909 with 'the people's budget', instigated by the Liberal Welshman Lloyd George. The Lords were bitterly opposed to the increased taxes and the ensuing rivalry peaked in 1911 with the 'Parliament Bill'. This effectively removed power from the Lords resulting in the Commons becoming virtually the sole legislative body. The same year saw the first Post-Impressionist exhibition in London, described by the harshest critics as 'the negation of civilisation'. This was also the year of another Glasgow International Exhibition, as the city continued to demonstrate its success. Miss Cranston opened a restaurant, The White Cockade, at the exhibition and commissioned the Mackintoshes to design the layout and furnishings. Margaret and Charles often collaborated on the tea-room designs, although in this instance the menu card for The White Cockade is attributed to Margaret herself. At the same time, the Mackintoshes were also working on designs for the Cloister Room and the Chinese Room at Miss Cranston's Ingram Street Tea Rooms.

CREATED

Glasgow

MEDIUM

Lithographic print, poster colour on white paper, white, red and green laid on paper

SERIES/PERIOD/MOVEMENT

Tea room designs

SIMILAR WORKS

Design for a menu card for The Red Lion by Frances Macdonald MacNair, 1911

Margaret Macdonald Mackintosh *Born* 1864 Tipton, Wolverhampton

Died 1933

THE WHITE COCKADE
MISS·CRANSTONS·
LUNCH + TEA·ROOMS·
91·93·BUCHANAN·ST·
114·ARGYLE·ST·
205·215·INGRAM·ST·
217 SAUCHIEHALL·ST·
GLASGOW
MARGARET MACDONALD MACKINTOSH INV·ET·DELT·
THE·PRINCIPAL·SUPPLIES·USED·IN·
MISS·CRANSTONS:
EXHIBITION·CAFES:
ARE·FROM·THE·FOLLOWING·
WELL·KNOWN·SOURCES·
TEA + COFFEE
AND·MELROSE + Co
39· GEORGE·ST
EDINBURGH
BREAD
WM·BEATTIE
DENNISTON BAKERY
GLASGOW
CAKES
MISS·CRANSTONS BAKERY
292·ST·VINCENT·ST
GLASGOW
BISCUITS
McFARLANE LANG + CO
VICTORIA·WORKS
GLASGOW
FISH + POULTRY
THOS·ANDERSON
58·60·WEST·NILE·ST
GLASGOW
COLD MEAT SPECIALTIES
R·D·WADDELL
NAPIERSHALL·ST
GLASGOW
MILK + CREAM
HUGH·HAMILTON
HIGH·JOHN·ST
GLASGOW
CHOCOLATES
CAILLERS
BROC
SWITZERLAND
THE WHITE COCKADE

Fireplace from the Salon De Luxe in the Willow Tea Rooms, Glasgow, c. 1904

The turn of the twentieth century was a time of political change and massive advancements in technology and science. In 1902 A. J. Balfour passed the Education Act and 1903 saw the Conservative party's strength start to crumble. Joseph Chamberlain split the party with his campaigns for Tariff Reform and Imperial Preference, and by the elections of 1906 the Liberals had gained 220 seats over the Conservatives. The Wright brothers demonstrated the first man-carrying aeroplane flight in 1903 and around the same time H. G. Wells wrote animatedly about *The First Men in the Moon*.

Catherine Cranston continued to expand her tea-room empire, commissioning Mackintosh to undertake her last major commercial venture, the Willow Tea Rooms. This project would be the most cohesive of all, with Mackintosh having total design control from the façade of the building through to the interiors. The Salon De Luxe was the heart of the scheme, an opulent room of mirrors and glass set against a white-painted background and intended to evoke an alley of willow trees. The fireplace sat at one end of the room, opposite a gesso panel painted by Margaret.

CREATED

Glasgow

MEDIUM

Iron with ceramic tile surround

SERIES/PERIOD/MOVEMENT

Tea room designs

SIMILAR WORKS

Library fireplace by H. Davis Richter, 1909

Rare ladder-back chair for the Willow Tea Rooms, 1903

Miss Cranston's tea rooms enjoyed their great success based in part on the variety of facilities that they offered. In true entrepreneurial spirit she used the 'tea room' as her point of departure and added to it: billiard rooms, ladies rooms, smoking rooms and restaurants. Her tea rooms provided every available source for relaxation and spending money and catered to a wide section of society. She was herself known as a singularly unusual and striking woman and these qualities she sought to utilize in her tea rooms. Mackintosh, as one of the most innovative designers of his time was the ideal champion of her cause. For the Willow Tea Rooms he created three separate areas, without the use of partitioning walls: a front saloon decorated mostly in white, the rear saloon, which was much darker, and the gallery from which an open stair led to the ground floor. The ladder-back chair design was intended to symbolize the willow tree. On first glance the multiple chair backs in the dining room (rear saloon) would appear as a forest of willows. This heavy, darker furniture was in direct contrast to the white-painted high-backed chairs in the Salon De Luxe.

CREATED

Glasgow

MEDIUM

Ebonized oak

SERIES/PERIOD/MOVEMENT

Tea room designs

SIMILAR WORKS

Ladder-back chair with rush seat, Buchanan Street Tea Rooms by George Walton, 1897

Sign for the Willow Tea Rooms

The Willow Tea Rooms were built on Sauchiehall Street, a popular and fashionable area of Glasgow. 'Sauchiehall', translating to 'alley of the willows', provided the foundation for the entire decorative scheme throughout which Mackintosh alluded to and evoked the willow tree. Although he was able to design the façade and interior arrangement of the building, he had to work with an existing structure situated on a narrow and restrictive site. His solution to the scheme was a brilliant display of startling Modernism, far ahead of its time. He created a building that rests easily between its neighbours and yet also stands alone in its harmonious asymmetry. One of the most striking features of the exterior was the first-floor expanse of glittering window spanning over six metres (18 feet). This marked on the exterior the jewel-like room of the Salon De Luxe on the interior. The façade was white and divided by a narrow projecting hood, below which the first-floor window sat in a gently curving plane. Above, the façade curves on one side and is punctured by recessed grid-like windows. The black-and-white chequerboard design on the sign is continued through the façade, running up each side of the building and decorating the window surrounds.

CREATED

Glasgow

MEDIUM

Iron

SERIES/PERIOD/MOVEMENT

Tea room designs

SIMILAR WORKS

Night wall sconce by Marion Henderson Wilson, early 1900s

THE
WILLOW
TEAROOM

Design for chairs for the Salon De Luxe in the Willow Tea Rooms, 1903

The Salon De Luxe became a talking point for the socialites of Glasgow and attracted great interest and attention, though not from the art journals of the day. Remarkably little was written about the room by national critics, especially in view of its originality, and even *The Studio* magazine that favoured the Mackintoshes made little or no comment. However, in April 1905 the journal *Dekorative Kunst* devoted almost the entire issue to the room, which was an indication of the Mackintoshes growing reputation on the Continent. One of the most distinctive features of the room was Mackintosh's use of the 'willowy' high-backed chair. The slender silver-painted chairs with their inset panel of nine purple squares of coloured glass are amongst the most famous of his early furniture designs. The high backs evoked the willow tree and created a natural division in the room, although they were to prove too fragile for the continued hard use of a tea room chair. They were a direct contrast to his use of the ladder-back chair in the darker dining room. These were more solid and sturdy, less decorative, more natural and just as aesthetic.

CREATED

Glasgow

MEDIUM

Pencil, watercolour, traces of body colour on oiled tracing paper

SERIES/PERIOD/MOVEMENT

Tea room designs

SIMILAR WORKS

Oak chair at Oak Park, Illinois by Frank Lloyd Wright, 1904

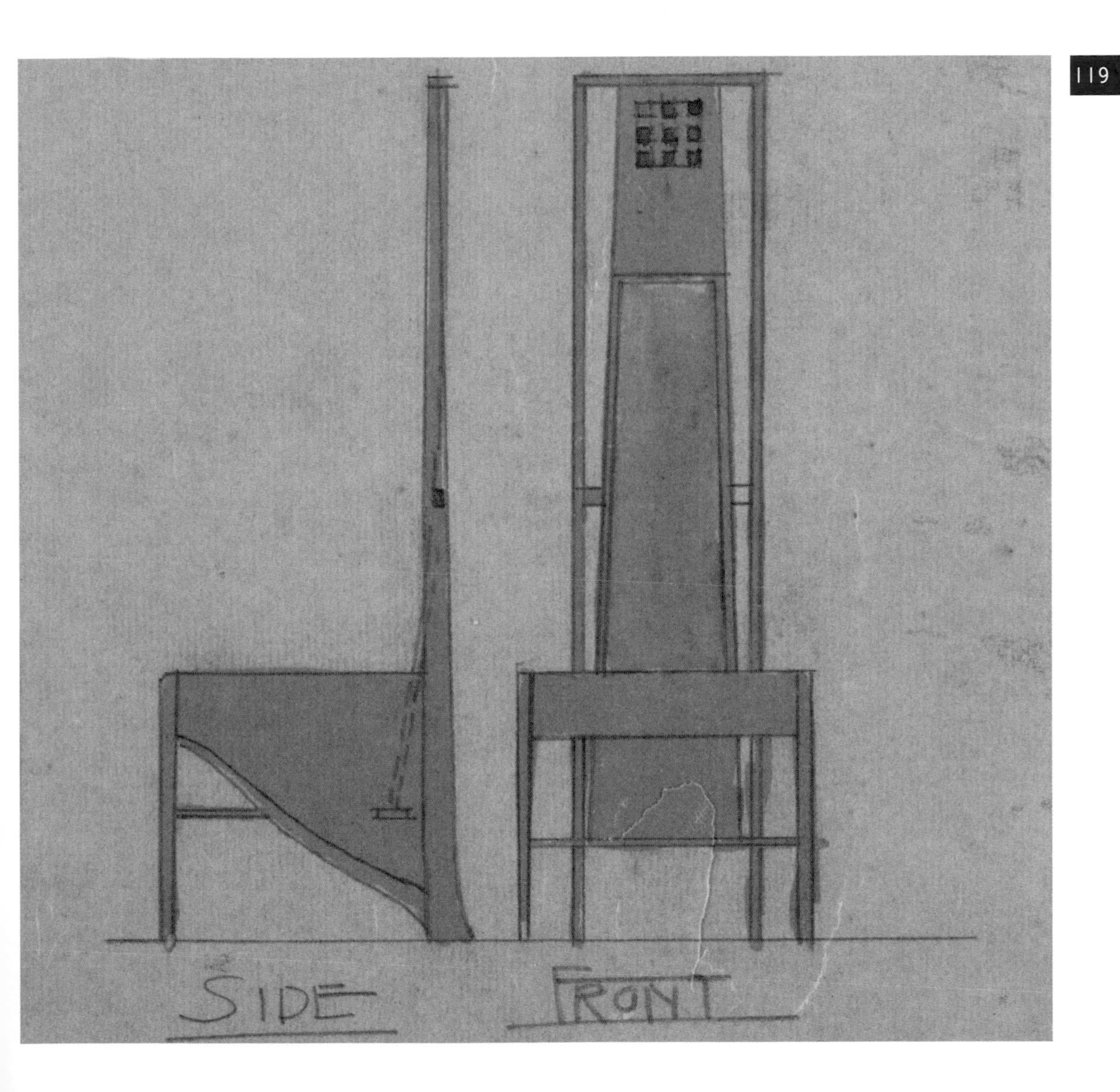
SIDE
FRONT

Settle from The Dug Out, Miss Cranston's Willow Tea Rooms

Glasgow was famous for its tea rooms and Miss Cranston virtually single-handedly turned the concept of the humble tea room into something altogether larger, grander and more popular. The tea rooms evolved into much more than simple social gathering places, functioning as art galleries, exhibiting works by local artists the Glasgow Boys and epitomizing the upwardly mobile atmosphere generated through Glasgow's burgeoning industries. Inevitably, however, all good things come to an end and the staggering effects of the First World War saw the demise of the tea room. Miss Cranston struggled to keep her edge and opened the Dug Out in the basement of the Willow Tea Rooms during the war years. The Mackintoshes had by now settled in London, but Charles undertook the commission for the decorative scheme, producing designs for a memorial fireplace in a patriotic style, two canvases and some furniture, fixtures and fittings. The strongly geometric settle was typical of his later style, having moved away from the Art Nouveau-inspired forms seen in the Salon De Luxe. Miss Cranston sold the Willow Tea Rooms in 1919, two years after the death of her beloved husband.

CREATED

Glasgow

MEDIUM

Painted wood

SERIES/PERIOD/MOVEMENT

Tea room designs

SIMILAR WORKS

Armchair for the Pürkersdorf Sanatorium by Koloman Moser, 1903

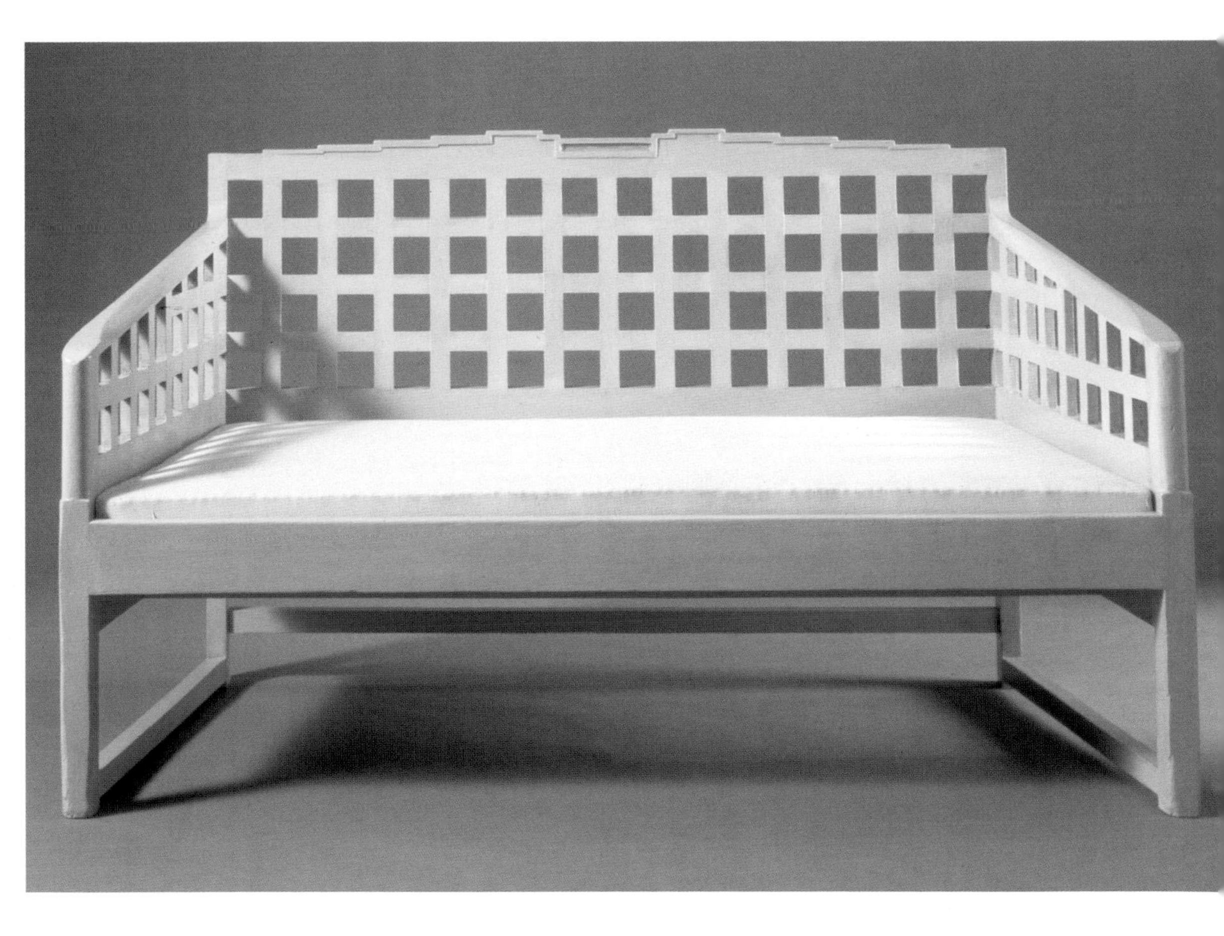

Hat, coat and umbrella stand for the White Dining Room, Ingram Street Tea Rooms, Glasgow, 1905

Mackintosh began work on the Ingram Street Tea Rooms in 1900, the same year that he married Margaret Macdonald. The turn of the century also marked the deaths of John Ruskin and Oscar Wilde and saw the enlightening and sharply witty plays of George Bernard Shaw published. Dante Gabriel Rossetti and his aesthetic followers had formed their Pre-Raphaelite circle, Aubrey Beardsley's macabre and sinuous illustrations for Wilde's *Salome* had come out and the architecture of Philip Webb and Norman Shaw was becoming popular. In the same year Margaret and Charles designed and furnished a room at the Secessionist Exhibition in Vienna, marking the start of their Continental relationship.

Work on the Ingram Street Tea Rooms involved redesigning and decorating the interiors and designing the furniture, fixtures and fittings. The White Dining Room was another striking example of Mackintosh's 'white rooms' of this period. He used white enamelled paint to emphasize the lofty interior and to provide a backdrop for his use of coloured-glass details. The coat stand was typical of Charles's designs, being functional and aesthetic. It stood in the White Dining Room and was characteristically elegant and simple.

CREATED

Glasgow

MEDIUM

Wood with metal detailing

SERIES/PERIOD/MOVEMENT

Tea room designs

SIMILAR WORKS

Coat stand for the Buchanan Street Tea Rooms by George Walton, 1897

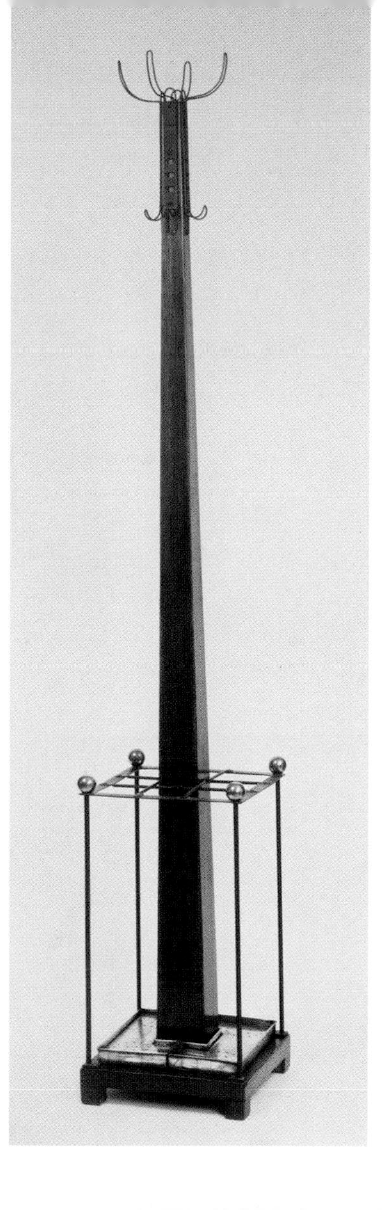

Designs for writing desks for the Ingram Street Tea Rooms, 1909

Mackintosh worked on the Ingram Street Tea Rooms for a number of years, first completing the dazzling White Dining Room and then moving on to work on the Willow Tea Rooms in Sauchiehall Street. He came back to Ingram Street and produced designs for the richly dark and intimate Oak Room, which bears some similarity in feel to the Glasgow School of Art Library. His designs for writing desks reflect the dark sobriety of the Oak Room, in stark contrast to the bright dining room. The designs, demonstrating his working process, show his simplistic form and outline with a minimum of decorative detail. The pared-down design of the writing desk is indicative of the serious nature of their purpose and again illustrates his interest in form for function. Some years later when Mackintosh returned to Ingram Street, this time to realize his plans for the Chinese Room, his approach had changed again. The Chinese Room was as richly ornate in its lavish Oriental spirit, as the Oak Room was quiet and natural. Oriental art and artefacts had become increasingly popular since 1855 and their influence was widely seen through the arts at this time.

CREATED

Glasgow

MEDIUM

Pen and black ink, brown wash on linen

SERIES/PERIOD/MOVEMENT

Tea room designs

SIMILAR WORKS

Washstand by Ford Madox Brown, 1860

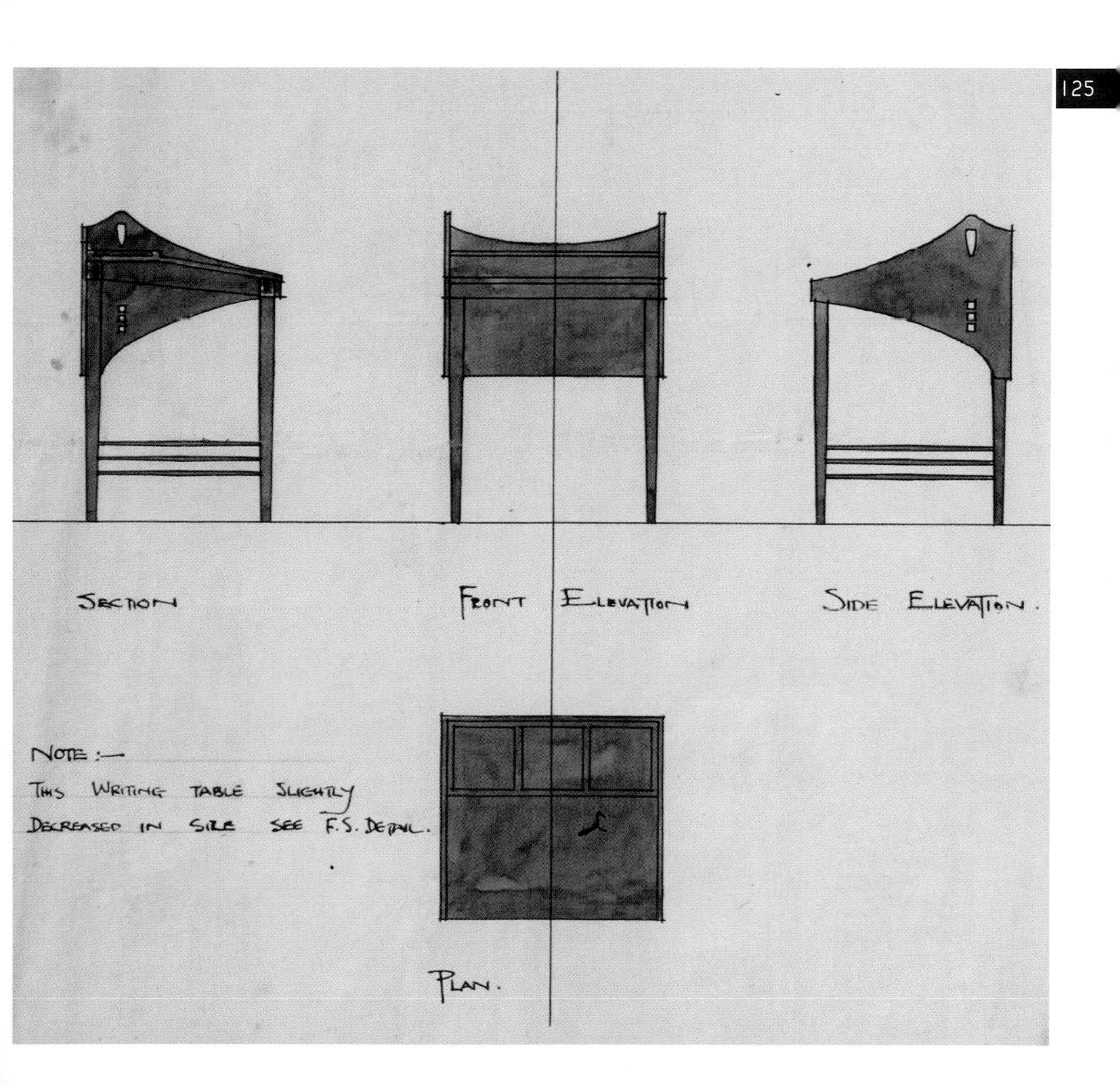
SECTION
FRONT ELEVATION
SIDE ELEVATION.
NOTE :—
THIS WRITING TABLE SLIGHTLY
DECREASED IN SIZE SEE F.S. DETAIL.
PLAN.

Domino table and chairs from the Ingram Street Tea Rooms, *c.* 1907

The establishment of the tea room as a phenomenon was not confined to Glasgow, although by some peculiar cycle of events, the Glasgow tea rooms were trailblazers and became famous for their spirit of congenial decadence. It took almost 20 years from the inception of the first tea room in Glasgow in 1875 for the idea to materialize in London under the guidance of Joe Lyons; now one of the most famous names associated with tea. Part of the success of tea rooms was to do with timing: Glasgow's wealthy middle classes were booming, women were suddenly enjoying greater freedoms and people had more time on their hands. The tea rooms provided a respectable and enjoyable place for women to gather, but equally offered suitably masculine areas for men.

The Domino Table was a design that Mackintosh had used at the Argyle Street premises, before using it again at Ingram Street. The simple and solid piece was used for playing dominoes, a popular game in Glasgow at this time. Mackintosh made use of structural details for decorative purposes, such as the pattern formed by the exposed square tenons that attach the table legs to the top.

CREATED

Glasgow

MEDIUM

Stained oak

SERIES/PERIOD/MOVEMENT

Tea room designs

SIMILAR WORKS

Round table by George Edmund Street, *c.* 1854

Chair for the Chinese Room at the Ingram Street Tea Rooms, 1911

Although Miss Cranston was amongst the most famous of the tea-room owners, she was not alone. Such was their popularity that tea rooms lined the fashionable streets of Glasgow in a manner similar to the coffee houses in Vienna. Each and every tea room strived to outclass its neighbours and to offer a unique slant to entice the customers in.

In 1911 Mackintosh undertook a commission to redesign two rooms at Miss Cranston's Ingram Street Tea Rooms. This saw the development of one his most unusual interiors so far, that of the Chinese Room. Distinctly masculine in feel the room encompasses an Oriental theme emphasized by the extensive use of square latticing and brilliant blues and reds. This was his first instance of using such vibrant colours, which would again be seen in his later work at 78 Derngate, his textile designs and the furniture he produced for Miss Cranston's Dug Out in 1919. This chair reflects the strong geometric modelling of the interior of the room and is striking in its modern look. When finished the room had a mysterious, exotic appeal that Mackintosh was very satisfied with.

CREATED

Glasgow

MEDIUM

Black-lacquered pine and horsehair

SERIES/PERIOD/MOVEMENT

Tea room designs

SIMILAR WORKS

Red lacquer chair by Marcello Piacentini, 1933

Detail of preliminary design for a mural decoration at Miss Cranston's Buchanan Street Tea Rooms, 1896–97

The economic boom of Glasgow based on shipping and heavy industries had a profound effect on the city, promoting great growth and expansion, but also creating severe social problems. Quite apart from the overcrowding of the working classes and related issues, there was a massive increase in alcoholism leading to petty crimes and disorderly behaviour. The initial rise of the tea room in the late 1870s played a major part in combating this. They offered cheap, sociable places for people to congregate and pass the time. The splendid tea rooms typified by those of Miss Cranston evolved from the first humble tea shops.

Mackintosh worked on the Buchanan Tea Rooms with George Walton, an accomplished, though underrated designer who has never quite received the accolade he deserves. Walton undertook the majority of the commission, with Mackintosh being primarily responsible for the wall decorations. The design here formed a highly stylized frieze that ran around the walls of the general tea room on the first floor. Mackintosh's decorative scheme impressed Gleeson White, editor of *The Studio* magazine, who described it as 'an honest attempt at novelty'.

CREATED

Glasgow

MEDIUM

Pencil and watercolour on tracing paper

SERIES/PERIOD/MOVEMENT

Tea room designs

SIMILAR WORKS

Album Von Dresden und Sächsisches Schweiz, bookcover by Jessie M. King, 1899

Windyhill, Kilmalcolm: detail of plan of west elevation, 1900

The shipping industry and the expansion of the steel industries led to an increase in revenue and opened up opportunities for entrepreneurial endeavours. At the turn of the century Glasgow was a place ripe for success and people were enjoying financial freedom that afforded indulgence in art and architecture. Wealthy individuals were able to patronize the arts and collect and support their home-grown artists. Glasgow was enjoying a renewed spirit of nationalism and this was reflected through all areas of the town's culture.

William Davidson Senior was a prominent local businessman and collector of the Glasgow Boys' art. Mackintosh and Davidson had first been introduced by Francis Newbery in the early 1890s and had immediately become friendly. The Davidson family were keen admirers of Mackintosh's work and in 1900 William Davidson Junior commissioned Mackintosh to design him a house on a steep plot of land at Kilmacolm, about 20 miles from Glasgow. The west elevation of Windyhill, shown here, shows Mackintosh's nationalistic sympathies in his use of Scottish vernacular, but by simplifying and paring it down he evoked a spirit of Minimalist Modernism.

CREATED

Glasgow

MEDIUM

Pencil on paper

SERIES/PERIOD/MOVEMENT

Windyhill

SIMILAR WORKS

Perrycroft, Herefordshire, north elevation by C. F. A. Voysey, 1893–94

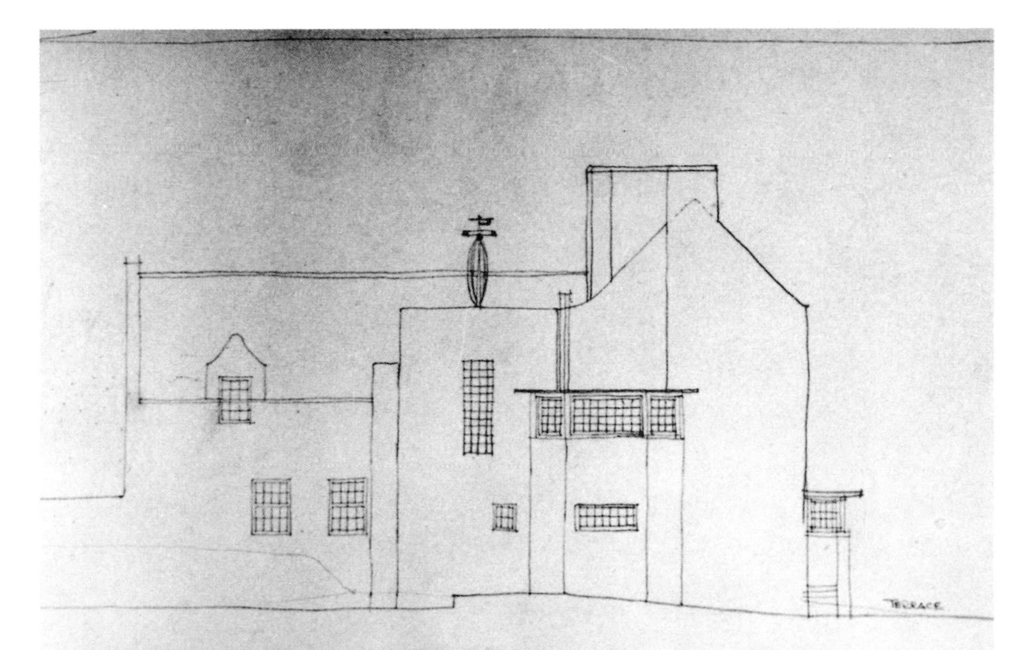
WEST ELEVATION
TERRACE
1900

Design for a couch for the drawing room at The Hill House, Helensburgh, 1904 (detail)

The Hill House is considered to be Mackintosh's most successful domestic architectural commission and corrects areas that were less successfully realized in the earlier Windyhill. Walter Blackie was, like the Davidsons, another product of the prospering Glasgow economy. Blackie and his family bought a hillside plot of land with stunning views over the Clyde and then began their search for an architect. Talwin Morris (1865–1911), a friend of the Glasgow Four but also art director at Blackie's publishing house, recommended Mackintosh to Walter.

The couch that was developed from these preliminary sketches sat in the large drawing room at The Hill House. Mackintosh split the room into summer and winter quarters, the summer end denoted by the expansive windows offering extensive views out across the countryside, the winter end was centred on the fireplace. This couch, with its high back and enveloping arms, sat at a right angle to the fire and shielded its occupants from draughts. It formed a spatial division between the winter and summer ends of the room. Mackintosh often used his furniture in this way, a method that was particularly effective at the Willow Tea Rooms through the use of high ladder-back chairs.

CREATED

Glasgow

MEDIUM

Pencil and watercolour on paper

SERIES/PERIOD/MOVEMENT

The Hill House

SIMILAR WORKS

Settle by Philip Webb, 1860

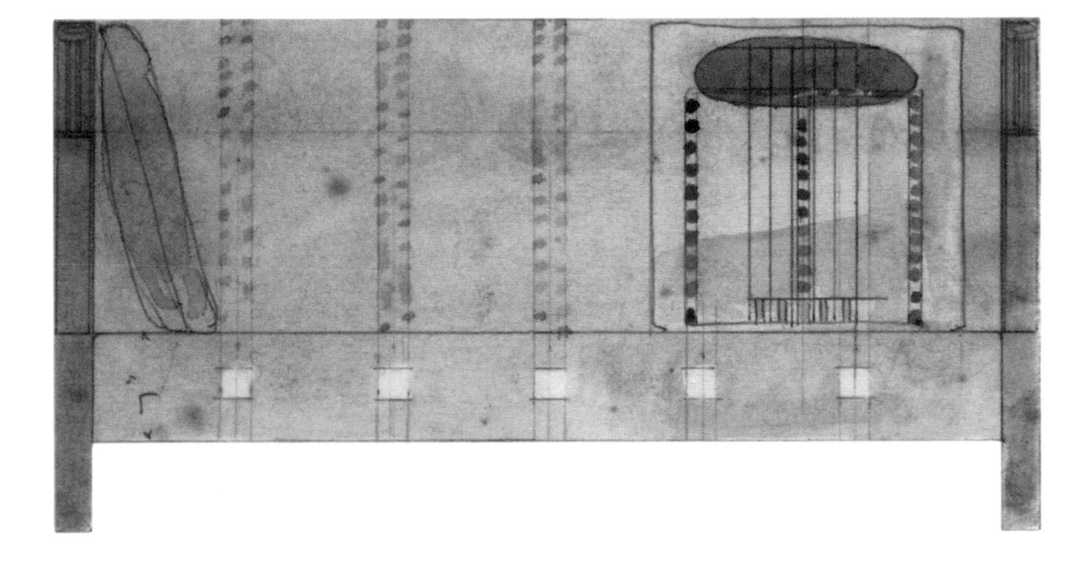

Photograph from *The Studio* of Miss Cranston's Tea Rooms, published 1912

Kate Cranston, who took Glasgow by storm with her innovative tea rooms, is the figure most commonly associated with them, but it was her brother Stuart Cranston (1848–1921) who initially set the ball rolling. Stuart was first and foremost an astute businessman, and secondly a tea dealer. Glasgow's fortunes had been built on the tobacco trade, and when this collapsed, the city turned to the tea and sugar trades. By the 1890s, Glasgow was second only to London in the tea and coffee industry, and had established strong links with India and the Far East. Stuart Cranston opened his first tea room in 1875 in conjunction with his tea trading, offering people the chance to taste his tea and indulge in some pâtisseries. The growth of the tea-room phenomenon went hand in hand with the increased temperance propaganda, aimed primarily at the working classes but also the middle classes, to reduce the instances of alcohol abuse.

Stuart expanded his tea room empire and in 1876 floated his company, Cranston's Tea Rooms Ltd. The following year Kate opened her Buchanan Street Tea Rooms, and was an instant success.

CREATED

Glasgow

MEDIUM

Interior design

SERIES/PERIOD/MOVEMENT

Tea rooms

SIMILAR WORKS

Gordon Street Tea Room, Smoking Room by James Carruthers, *c.* 1933

Arts League of Service Studios, Chelsea: elevation to Cheyne House Garden, *c.* 1920

Charles and Margaret moved to London from Walberswick in 1915. Mackintosh was little known in the capital and struggled to find work. London itself was reeling from the effects of the First World War, money was in short supply and architectural commissions were few and far between. In the years following the war there was a sudden increase in the formation of benevolent associations, many of which were concerned with the arts. One such group was the Arts League of Service, founded with the principle of 'bringing the Arts into everyday life'. One of the problems facing struggling and unknown artists was lack of decent studio space and so the Arts League proposed a scheme to build a block of studio flats on a co-operative basis. In this way each tenant would become a part shareholder in the building.

Mackintosh, who was closely involved with the Arts League, drew up plans for the studio project. The Arts League approved them immediately, but the local authorities heavily criticized the proposed building and the plans were rejected.

CREATED

London

MEDIUM

Pencil and wash on tracing paper

SERIES/PERIOD/MOVEMENT

London architectural designs

SIMILAR WORKS

House on the Michaelerplatz, Vienna by Adolf Loos, 1910

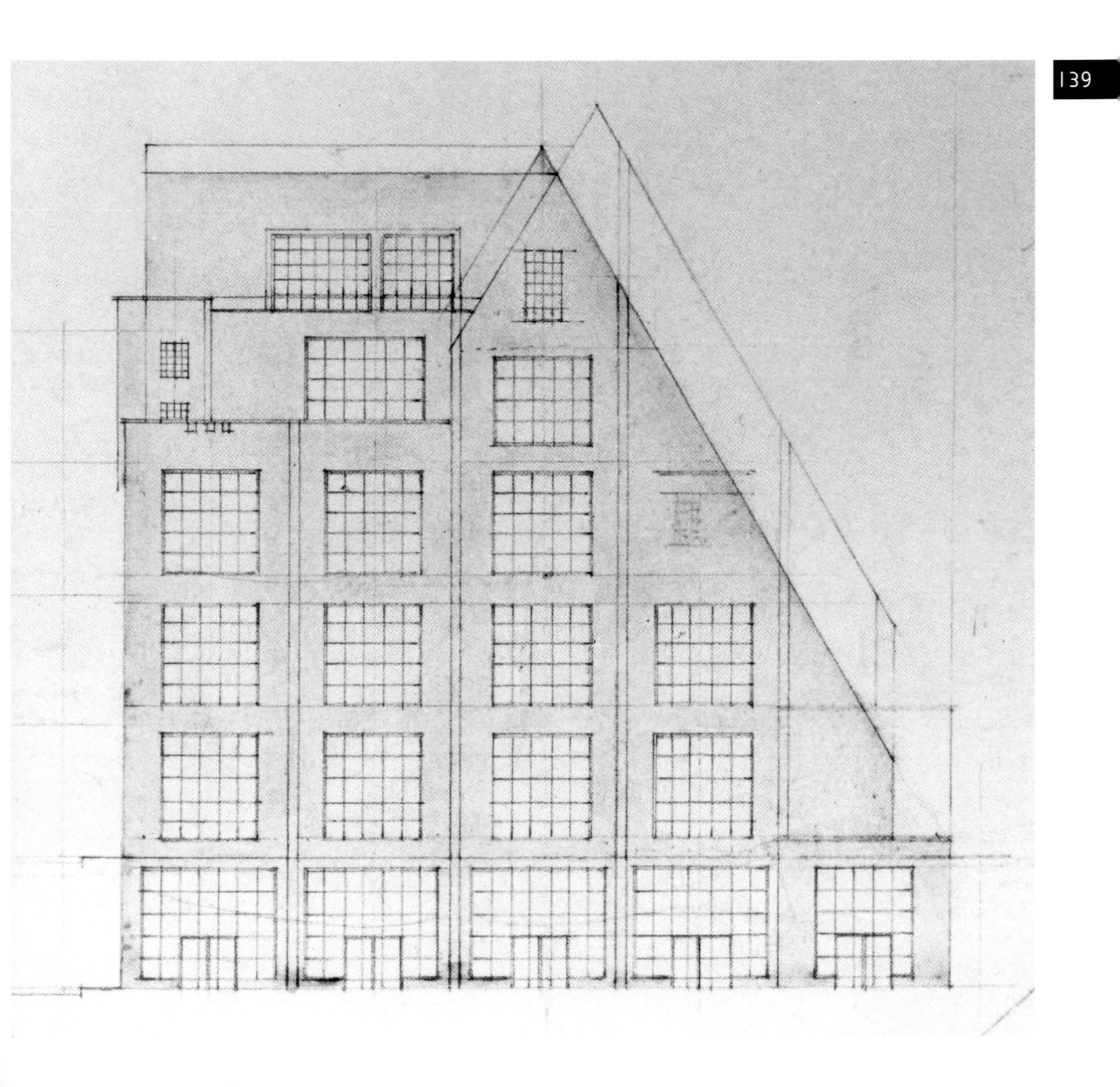

Design for proposed theatre in Chelsea for Margaret Morris, 1920 (detail)

In spite of his plans for the Arts League studios being so heavily criticized, Mackintosh refused to alter them. After lengthy wranglings with the authorities they were finally accepted, although the scheme was never realized, most likely due to lack of funds. This pattern would then repeat itself with the Margaret Morris theatre project. The Mackintoshes had met Margaret Morris and her husband J. D. Fergusson through their involvement in the local artist scene and all four of them were connected with the Arts League of Service.

In 1920 Mackintosh was commissioned by Margaret to design a theatre for her performing arts group. This was one of the few formal designs that he produced and was rigidly symmetrical throughout. The heart of the project was the auditorium, which focused on the revolving stage. The local authorities rejected Mackintosh's plans out of hand and he never revised them; eventually the project fell by the wayside. He received a number of small commissions and in 1921 worked for his old patron Walter Blackie designing covers for a series of booklets.

CREATED

London

MEDIUM

Pencil, ink and wash on paper

SERIES/PERIOD/MOVEMENT

London architectural designs

SIMILAR WORKS

Plans for a Concert Hall by Charles Rennie Mackintosh, 1901

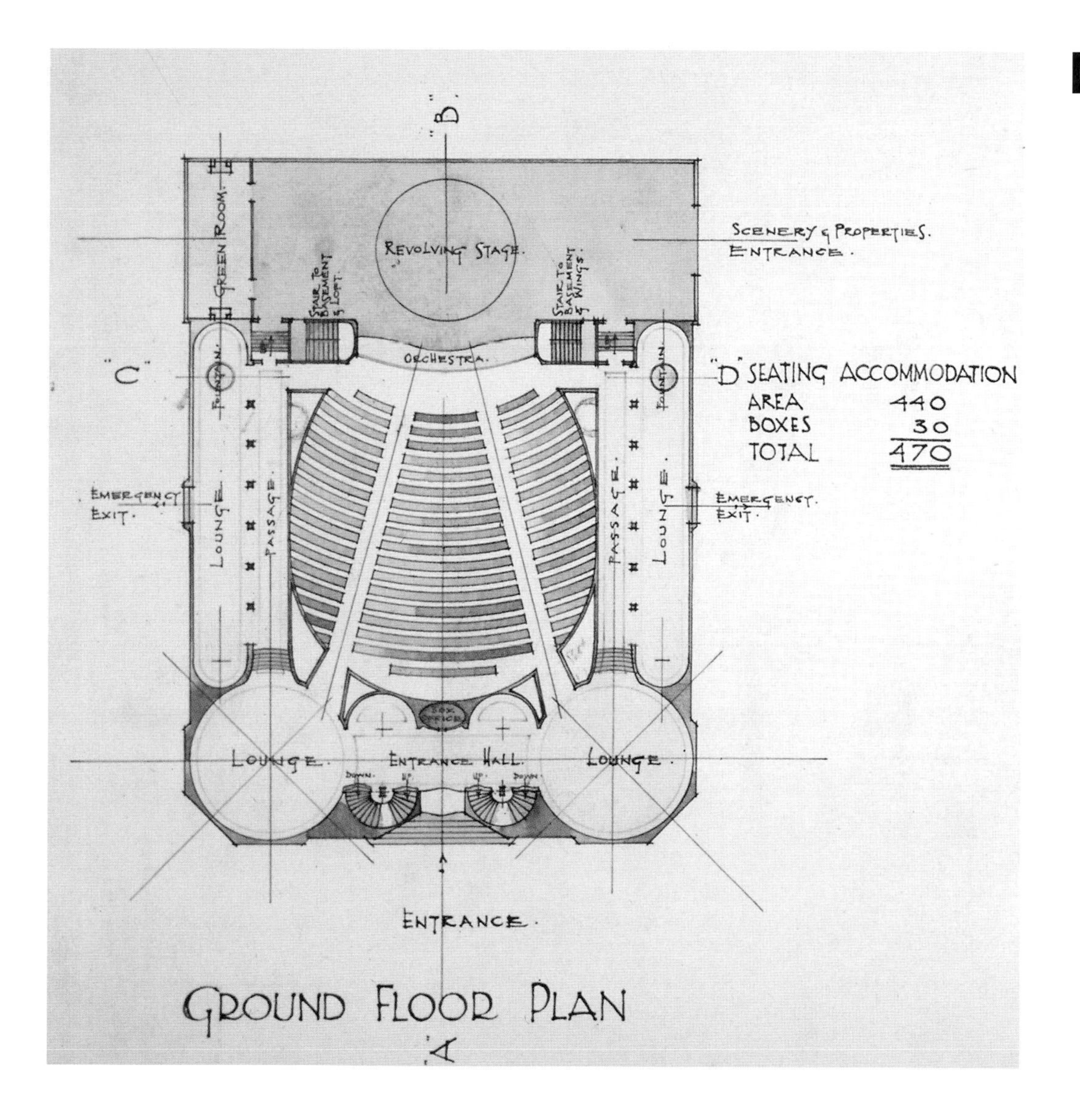
"D"
GREEN ROOM.
STAIR TO BASEMENT & LOFT.
REVOLVING STAGE.
STAIR TO BASEMENT & WINGS.
SCENERY & PROPERTIES.
ENTRANCE.
ORCHESTRA.
"C"
FOUNTAIN.
FOUNTAIN.
"D" SEATING ACCOMMODATION
AREA 440
BOXES 30
TOTAL 470
EMERGENCY EXIT.
LOUNGE.
PASSAGE.
PASSAGE.
LOUNGE.
EMERGENCY EXIT.
BOX OFFICE
LOUNGE.
ENTRANCE HALL.
LOUNGE.
DOWN.
UP.
UP.
DOWN.
ENTRANCE.
GROUND FLOOR PLAN
'A'

Stylized chrysanthemums, textile design, 1915–23

After moving to London Charles and Margaret supplemented their income by producing commercial designs for printed textiles. In the post-war years the textile industries in London started to increase their production and expand their designs in an effort to recover from the inevitable slump of the preceding years. Mackintosh was far from alone in turning to textile designing; he was one of a large number of artists and architects who tried this in the absence of other commissions. The architect C. F. A. Voysey (1857–1941) and the designer George Walton, with whom Mackintosh had worked in Glasgow on Miss Cranston's Tea Rooms, both worked for textile companies producing fabric designs. At this time many textile companies had a progressive attitude towards their designs, embracing a new approach to pattern that Mackintosh was able to reach and surpass.

Many of his designs show an awareness of the work of German and Austrian designers of the time. In spite of losing the close relationship he had had with the Continent prior to the war, Mackintosh continued to follow the work of his friends closely.

CREATED

London

MEDIUM

Pencil and watercolour on wove paper

SERIES/PERIOD/MOVEMENT

London fabric designs

SIMILAR WORKS

Designs for carpets for Alexander Morton & Co. by Ann Macbeth and Jessie Newbery, 1914

Photograph from *The Studio* of Miss Cranston's Tea Rooms, published 1912

Kate Cranston's tea rooms quickly overtook those run by her brother Stuart, and she rose to become the 'queen' of this domain. In part her extraordinary character, flamboyant, attractive and determined, drew the punters in and also her great understanding of business. In 1892 she married John Cochrane, a wealthy engineer and owner of Grahamston Engineering Works. His wedding gift to Kate was the lease on a building on Argyle Street and in 1897 she opened her Argyle Street Tea Rooms. The Argyle Street premise was decorated primarily by George Walton, while Mackintosh designed most of the moveable furniture. The smoking room was furnished entirely by Mackintosh as was the billiards room.

This photo was taken of the Dutch Kitchen at Argyle Street. In 1906 Kate commissioned Mackintosh to redecorate and furnish the basement at the tea rooms and they developed the idea for the Dutch Kitchen. He used a strong black-and-white chequerboard pattern and contrasted against this bright green chairs. An article in *The Studio* magazine referred to the room, writing, 'Nowhere has the modern movement in art been entered upon more seriously that at Glasgow'.

CREATED

Glasgow

MEDIUM

Interior design

SERIES/PERIOD/MOVEMENT

Tea rooms

SIMILAR WORKS

Bar room at the Kabarett Fldermans by the *Wiener Werkstätte*, *c.* 1907

La Rue du Soleil, 1927

Mackintosh had become increasingly despondent through his years in London, suffering from self-doubt and the frustration of ambitions never realized. J. D. Fergusson encouraged Margaret and Charles to spend some time in the warm sun of the Mediterranean, where the couple stayed for five years. The climate suited them and the cost of living was cheap at this time. Mackintosh made the decision to focus solely on his watercolour painting and during this period produced some of the most innovative and stunning paintings of his time. The light and atmosphere of Port Vendres and the surrounding area was translated through Mackintosh's vivid paint.

La Rue du Soleil is one of the most vibrant paintings he produced and is a remarkable study of reflections. The strong pattern across the canvas and the stylization through the static ripples of the water is abstract in its conception with the canvas being a curious combination of real and surreal. Mackintosh failed to sign the picture on completion and later did so after moving to a London nursing home in the last few months of his life.

CREATED

Port Vendres

MEDIUM

Watercolour

SERIES/PERIOD/MOVEMENT

Watercolour paintings, Port Vendres

SIMILAR WORKS

Le Canal Saint-Martin by Georges Braques, 1906

C.R. MACKINTOSH 1927

Mackintosh

Places

Studies of the ceiling decoration, Certosa di Pavia, 1891

Mackintosh joined the firm of Honeyman and Keppie in 1889 as a junior draughtsman and the following year entered and won the prestigious Alexander 'Greek' Thompson Travelling Scholarship. The competition was to produce 'the best original design of a public hall to accommodate one thousand persons (seated)'. The scholarship awarded a £60 prize and enabled the architect to travel to Italy for a period of months. During his tour he visited all the major Italian cities and produced a large volume of sketches and watercolours. He left Glasgow in February 1891, travelled to London and then on to Naples. In July he set off for Pavia, where he made these sketches of the ceiling decorations at the Certosa di Pavia. He was clearly drawn to the jewel-like colours and decorative design of the ceiling, which he reproduced in vibrant blue, gold and red. Mackintosh had a great interest in Celtic imagery and design and it is interesting to note the similarity of aspects of the Certosa di Pavia decoration with Celtic designs that he and MacNair had seen at the abbey on Iona two years previously.

CREATED

Pavia

MEDIUM

Watercolour

SERIES/PERIOD/MOVEMENT

Italian tour

SIMILAR WORKS

Decoration from Blythburgh Church, Suffolk, drawing by George Wardle, 1865–66

Charles Rennie Mackintosh *Born* 1868 Glasgow, Scotland

Died 1928

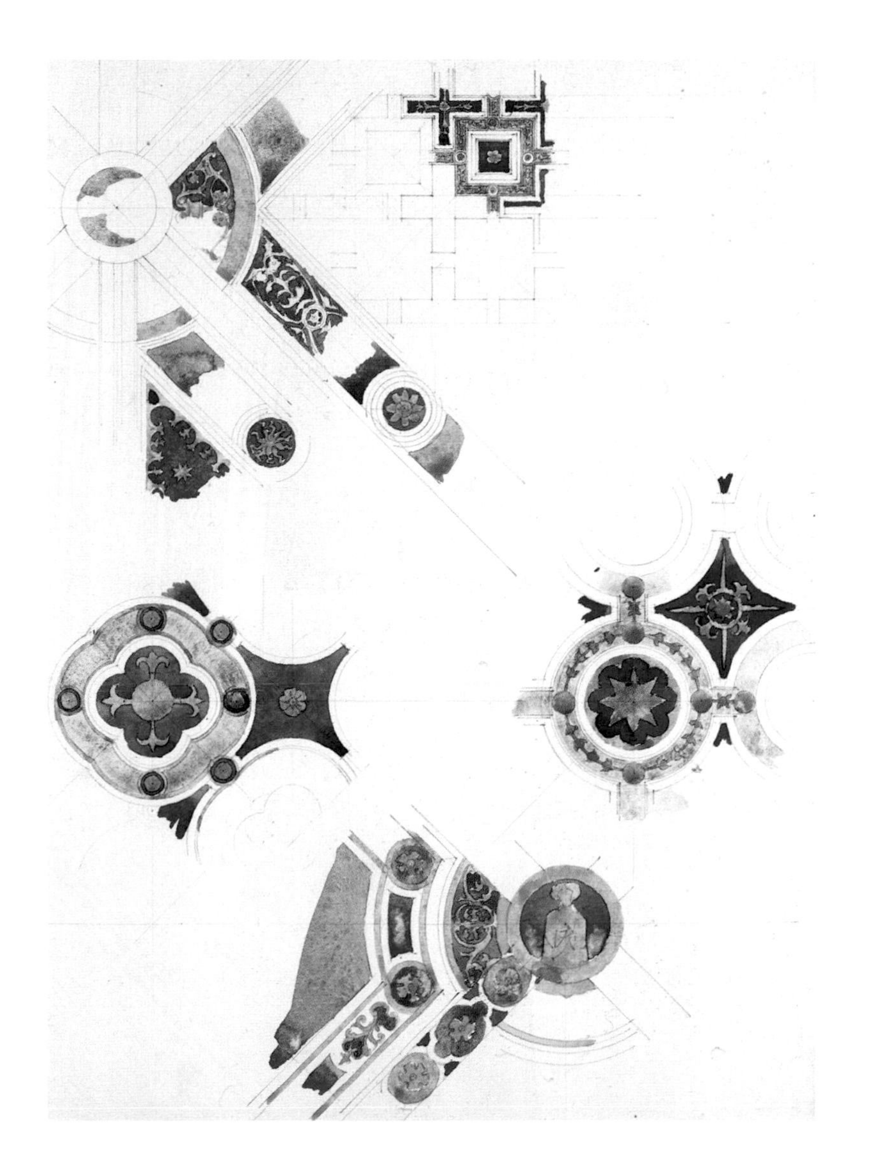

Study of an angel statue, Certosa di Pavia, 1891

During Mackintosh's years of evening classes at the Glasgow School of Art he had developed prodigious skills in drawing and painting, as well as geometry, perspective, building construction and architectural design. His comprehensive and broad artistic training was to stand him in great stead throughout his life, culminating in the eventual turn towards watercolour painting as his sole artistic expression. The quality of his Italian sketches reflects his early studies. When he sent a selection of them home from Italy for inclusion in the Students' Club Annual Exhibition at the Glasgow School of Art, his accomplishments were recognized and were awarded first prize. He was greatly impressed by the architectural details as much as the buildings as a whole, an approach that he applied to his own decorative and architectural schemes. His study of an angel at the Certosa di Pavia is not without a certain inflection of Pre-Raphaelite handling and this assimilation of 'ancient' into 'modern' would be seen in his use of the Scottish vernacular reformulated into his innovative architectural style.

CREATED

Pavia

MEDIUM

Pencil and watercolour

SERIES/PERIOD/MOVEMENT

Italian tour

SIMILAR WORKS

Boboli by John Singer Sargeant, 1907

Studies of decorative ceiling panels, San Miniato, 1891

It is symptomatic of the artist's appreciation for decoration and detail that his Italian sketchbooks were so full of patterns and stylized motifs. The drawing that he made here, taken from studies of decorative ceiling panels at San Miniato in Florence, focuses on the geometry of the design; the triangles and squares that he would later turn to in his late decorative style that was so beautifully expressed through his textile designs of 1916 to 1920. The bright squares of pure colour anticipate his use of stained-glass insets for which his interiors became so recognizably 'Mackintosh'. The vitality and energy of his Italian sketches relate the enthusiasm with which Mackintosh embraced his trip and his work on his return to Glasgow was imbued with a greater sense of confidence and assertiveness. Shortly after his return to Glasgow he submitted his classically inspired designs for a chapterhouse to the Soane Medallion Competition. He was unsuccessful in the competition although his design was later reworked and used in construction of the Pettigrew and Stephens Warehouse.

CREATED

Florence

MEDIUM

Pencil and watercolour

SERIES/PERIOD/MOVEMENT

Italian tour

SIMILAR WORKS

Design for the decoration of the cornice of the Green Dining Room by Philip Webb, 1866

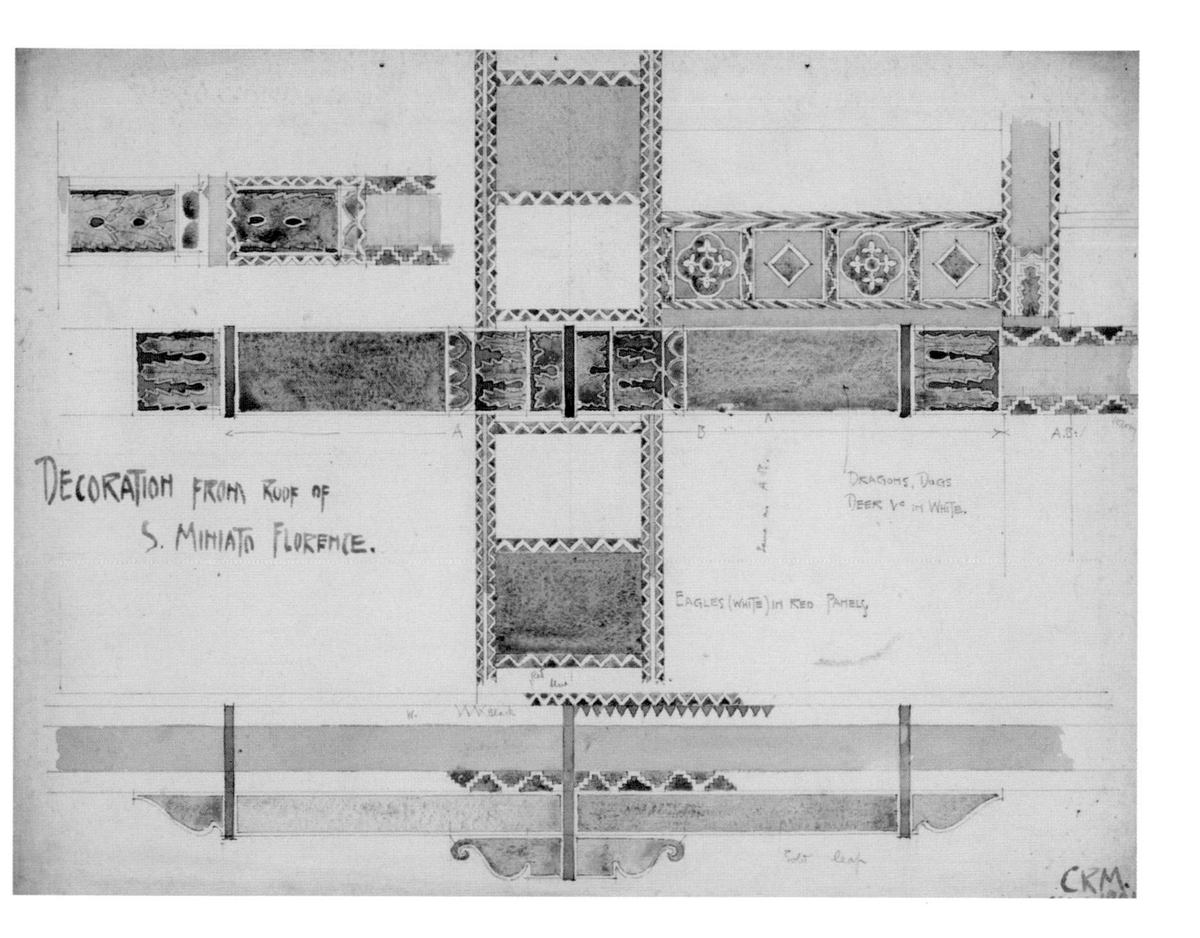
DECORATION FROM ROOF OF
S. MINIATO FLORENCE.
DRAGONS, DOGS
DEER &c IN WHITE.
EAGLES (WHITE) IN RED PANELS
CRM.

Study of the tomb of Carlo Marsuppini, Santa Croce, 1891

Mackintosh was particularly impressed with Florence and spent hours wandering through the Uffizi and the Pitti Palace. For the man from relatively humble beginnings and a life so far spent in the largely bilious, industrial Glasgow, the sudden immersion in Italy was a profoundly moving experience. He was especially struck by the colours around him, illuminated by the brilliance of the Italian sun and lending a startling clarity to moulded form. Of Florence Cathedral Mackintosh wrote, 'Not a ray of light enters the sacred enclosure but through the medium of narrow windows high up in the dome and richly painted. A sort of yellow green tint predominates which gives additional solemnity to the altar and paleness to the votary before it. I was conscious of the effect and obtained at least the colour of sanctity'. The watercolour sketch of the tomb of Carlo Marsuppini has a flatness of approach that melds the stylized form of an illustrator with the natural object before him. The delicate hue of the colour wash evokes an aesthetic response at the expense of depth and substance.

CREATED

Florence

MEDIUM

Pencil and watercolour

SERIES/PERIOD/MOVEMENT

Italian tour

SIMILAR WORKS

A Window at the Palazzo Foscari, Venice by John Ruskin, 1845

TOMB OF CARLO MARSUPPINI
SANTA CROCE, FLORENCE

A sheet of studies of mosaic bands, Orvieto Cathedral, 1891

The aura of Venice affected Mackintosh as it had the procession of artists whose trail he followed and those who followed him. Her unique combination of waterways and soft light was a source of wonder to the young man. He was fascinated by the gondolas and the life on the waterways, so far removed from the grimy shipping industries along the banks of his familiar river Clyde. Orvieto, the ancient town that had flourished since the beginning of the sixth century BC with an economy based largely on the production of ceramic and bronze, was another of Mackintosh's destinations. The famous Romanesque-Gothic cathedral of Orvieto that soared seven storeys into the sky made an impression on Mackintosh who was drawn to the strong decorative façade of polychromatic mosaic. The sketches Mackintosh made from the mosaics reflect his keen sense of the geometry of the design that was hundreds of years old but appeared contemporarily modern. The precision with which he executed the study is typical of his architectural training and, although only a study, it is minutely and accurately drafted.

CREATED

Orvieto

MEDIUM

Pencil and watercolour

SERIES/PERIOD/MOVEMENT

Italian tour

SIMILAR WORKS

Design for wall decoration by E. W. Godwin, *c.* 1870–86

MOSAIC BANDS.
ORVIETO CATHEDRAL. INTERIOR.

Rome, Arch of Titus, 1891

Although Mackintosh was clearly taken with Italy he was not impervious to the less salubrious side of Italian life. In his diaries he extolled the virtues of the peculiarly 'Italianesque' colours emphasized by the bright sunshine and unlike any he had experienced before, but he was quick to point out that parts of Rome were not dissimilar to the grimy realism of Glasgow's industrial backstreets. He was distracted from his watercolour studies by the thronging Italians and found himself surrounded by Italian peasants, intrigued by the foreigner with the strange accent and the beautiful drawings and hopeful no doubt of small handouts. His study of the Arch of Titus reflects the architect in him through the strong lines and accurate perspective. However, the subtle use of colour washes and the strong sense of total design indicate the 'painterly' qualities that would later become his sole artistic focus. When Mackintosh sent a collection of his Italian studies to the Glasgow Students' Club Competition, one of the judges, Sir James Guthrie (1859–1930), on hearing Mackintosh was an architectural student, exclaimed, '... this man ought to be an artist'.

CREATED

Rome

MEDIUM

Pencil and watercolour

SERIES/PERIOD/MOVEMENT

Italian tour

SIMILAR WORKS

The Library in Venice by John Singer Sargeant, 1904

CRM. 1891.

Study of an entrance porch, Palermo Cathedral, 1891

As part of his tour Mackintosh travelled to the island of Sicily off the toe of Italy and visited the capital city, Palermo. Palermo was often referred to as the 'Garden City' based on the large number of beautifully designed public gardens that the city boasted. For Mackintosh, who had had a love of gardens since his childhood, Palermo must have been one of the most inspirational stops on his trip. Significantly the National Exhibition of Palermo that ran from 1891 to 1892 would have afforded the young artist the opportunity to view the major artistic and architectural movements, and cultural history of the area, within one frame. The city's cathedral was particularly riveting to Mackintosh who made several studies of it. He was fascinated by the intricate detail on the façade and the unusual combination of styles reflected through the building's long history. The cathedral dates back to the twelfth century and was originally built on the site of an Arab mosque. Much of the decorative detail that Mackintosh captured in his studies was inspired by the Islamic period, which is in contrast to the Norman apse.

CREATED

Palermo

MEDIUM

Pencil and grey wash

SERIES/PERIOD/MOVEMENT

Italian tour

SIMILAR WORKS

Porta San Marco, Venice by John Marin, 1907

PALERMO CATHEDRAL.
ENTRANCE PORCH.

Palermo, Campanile Martorana, 1891

Palermo has a strong tradition of artistic and cultural progression and during the time Mackintosh visited the city Art Nouveau was developing as a conscious style of design. Ernesto Basile (1857–1932), the architect and designer, was producing exquisite Art Nouveau furniture from the Golia furniture factory, which was also exhibiting at the National Exhibition of 1891–92. The same year that Mackintosh was in Palermo, Ernesto Basile took over the architectural commission for the city's Teatro Massimo on the untimely death of his father, the architect Giovan Battista Basile (1825–91). The city was undergoing a period of expansion and construction on a scale similar to Glasgow.

The study of the Campanile Martorana is one of several studies of Italian and Sicilian campaniles that Mackintosh drew. The form of 'the campanile' would soon be utilized in his designs for the *Glasgow Herald* building. By and large, however, the influence of Italian and Sicilian architecture on his later development as an architect was fairly minimal. His exposure to Art Nouveau furniture and interior, on the other hand, had a more significant effect on his development as designer.

CREATED

Palermo

MEDIUM

Pencil and watercolour

SERIES/PERIOD/MOVEMENT

Italian tour

SIMILAR WORKS

S. Francescodi Paolta, by Edward Lear

The Piazza and the Old Campanile, Venice by Walter Richard Sickert, *c.* 1901

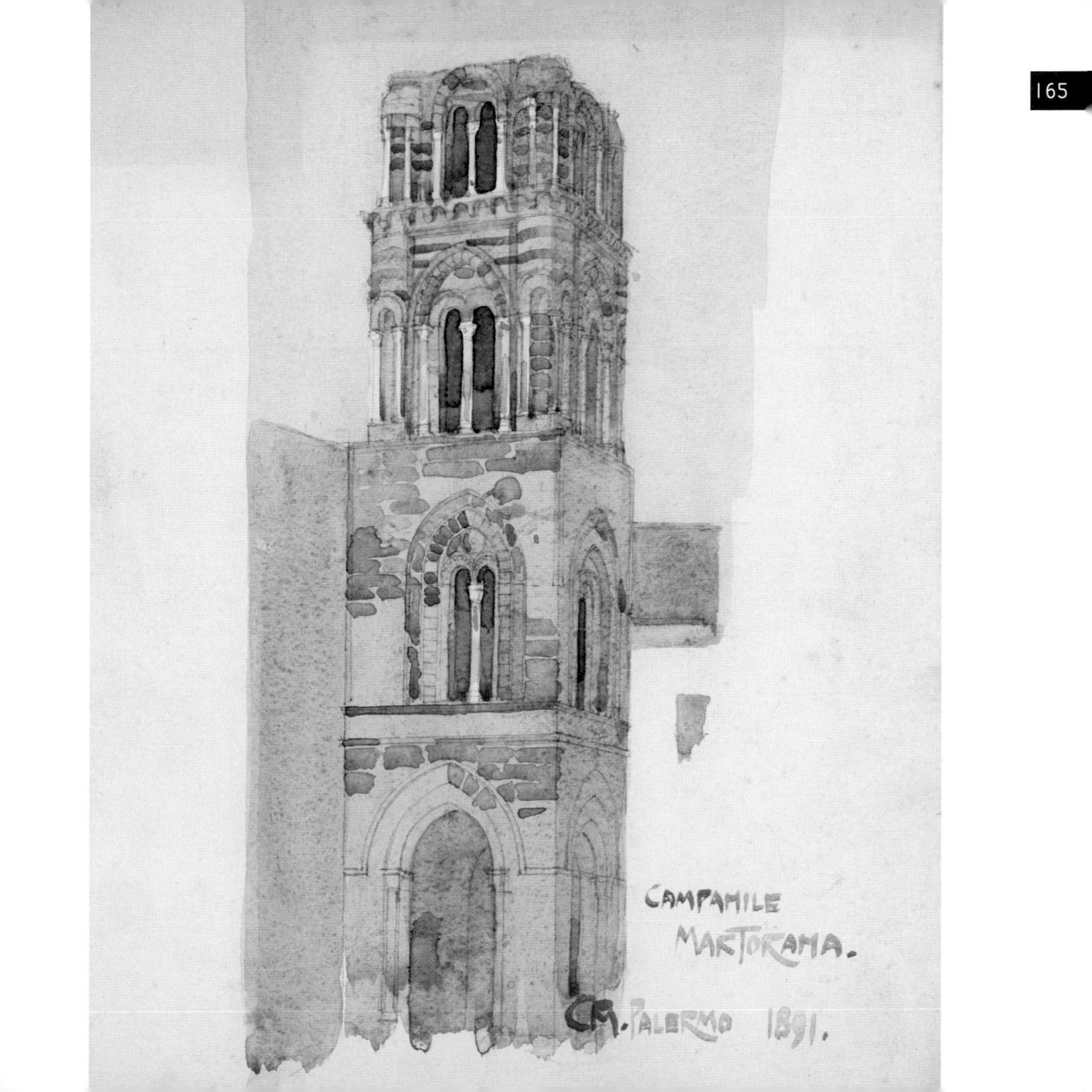
CAMPANILE
MARTORAMA.
CM. PALERMO 1891.

A sheet of studies, Pompeii, 1891

As a student at the Glasgow School of Art Mackintosh had had extensive training in drawing, which included working from casts of ancient statuary and drawings of Italian monuments. By the time he visited Italy he had already won a series of prizes for his drawings of historic ornament and was clearly knowledgeable about ancient art and architecture. In his tour diary he wrote that in the Uffizi gallery he had seen, 'the originals of many old and well known friends'. Similarly, while walking through ancient Rome he noted that 'it is intensely interesting to wander over those ruins and see for yourself all you have read about and much that you have drawn…'. It was, however, the Byzantine architecture that seems to have had the greatest impact on Mackintosh during his trip and he enthused over this and examples of Norman, Romanesque, Gothic and Early Renaissance, instead of the ancient ruins.

Diary entries indicate that Mackintosh visited Pompeii during April, shortly after his arrival in Naples. He made little comment about the ancient city and unfortunately the majority of his Pompeii sketches have been lost.

CREATED

Pompeii

MEDIUM

Pencil

SERIES/PERIOD/MOVEMENT

Italian tour

SIMILAR WORKS

Design for a tea house sundial by Sir Edwin Lutyens, 1898

SKETCHES FROM POMPEI
PEDESTAL.
CRM.
APRIL 7TH
1891

Study of a doorway, Naples, S. Trinita Maggiore, 1891

Naples was the first stop on Mackintosh's Italian itinerary and, according to an amusing account in his diary his first experience of Italy was to have his tobacco seized at the custom house. He went on to describe his first Italian meal, 'we tried Macaroni but couldn't manage to turn it round the fork in the most magnificent manner of the Italians ...'. His diary notes, of a more intellectual character, went on to provide the material for a lecture he delivered in Glasgow in 1892 appropriately called, 'A Tour of Italy'. In this he discussed his impressions of the country's architecture and referred to the sixteenth-century tombs of *S. Anna dei Lombardi* and *S. Domenico Maggiore* as 'the best in Naples'. A few days after his arrival he visited the Church of *Trinita Maggiore*, which he described as, 'not much outside but really magnificent inside, the decoration surpassed anything I had seen before'. The picture here shows a sketch he made of the doorway into the church, unfinished and hurried, but still capturing the architectural details that so fascinated him.

CREATED

Naples

MEDIUM

Pencil and watercolour

SERIES/PERIOD/MOVEMENT

Italian tour

SIMILAR WORKS

Villa D'Este, Tivoli by Henry Tonks, 1920

TRINITA MAGGIORE NAPLES
ENTRANCE DOOR.
9TH APRIL 1891
CRM.

Glasgow School of Art: exterior from the north-west, 1899

Glasgow was a city teeming with life, culturally, artistically, economically; the city was alive and poised on the brink of commercial success and artistic awakenings. This was an opportune moment for a young artist embarking on his architectural career. Mackintosh's relationship with Glasgow, from the place of his birth and childhood to finding his niche in the professional world, was one that bloomed young and soured early. It was a depressed and embittered man who finally turned his back on Glasgow for good in 1914. Prior to this he executed what is generally considered to be his finest work in the shape of the Glasgow School of Art. One of the most significant happenings in Glasgow at this time was the election of the young Englishman, Francis Newbery, as Director of the School of Art in 1885. Not only was Newbery to become a life-long friend and supporter of Mackintosh, he was also responsible for a singularly innovative and fresh approach to the art school, which nurtured the up-and-coming artistic talent of its pupils.

CREATED

Glasgow

MEDIUM

Architecture

SERIES/PERIOD/MOVEMENT

Glasgow School of Art

SIMILAR WORKS

10-12 Palace Court, Bayswater, London by J. M. MacLaren, 1889–90

Glasgow School of Art: view of a roof arch from the west, 1897–99

It was primarily to Newbery's credit that the art school established itself as one of the leading schools of art in the country, offering one of the most comprehensive artistic educations covering all areas of the arts and associated crafts. Newbery recognized Mackintosh's prodigious talent and that of the Macdonald sisters and Herbert MacNair, and he encouraged the young artists to foster their talents. The Four, as they became known, exhibited together, worked together and eventually cemented the group further with the marriage of Margaret Macdonald to Charles Rennie Mackintosh and that of Frances Macdonald to Herbert MacNair. Mackintosh's early days at the art school were full of optimism and growth. Photographs of the flamboyant artists depict the Four and other friends in the full grip of the halcyon days of being a student. It would not be until later that Mackintosh struggled with insecurities, loss of self-confidence and a lack of substantial commissions. He was a great proponent of the Scottish tradition of architecture and looked to the Scottish Baronial vernacular as a point of departure, although he believed in synthesizing this within a modern context.

CREATED

Glasgow

MEDIUM

Architecture

SERIES/PERIOD/MOVEMENT

Glasgow School of Art

SIMILAR WORKS

Linlithgow Palace, *c.* 1504

Northwest entrance arch to Glenbeigh Towers by E. W. Godwin, 1867–70

Glasgow School of Art: design for display and bookcase for the Ladies' Common Room, 1897–99

Mackintosh suffered from a drooping eyelid, the result of an illness during childhood, and had a contracted sinew in one foot that left him with a slight limp. To remedy both afflictions he was advised to take plenty of exercise and throughout his life walked frequently in the countryside, escaping with his sketchbook and drawing the nature around him. His love of nature, gardens and flowers would be reflected through his work and was a constant source of stimulation and inspiration to him. The unnecessary though beautiful inclusion of flowers in this design for a display case was a method he often used. Many of his architectural plans featured foliage and trees in delicate pencil lines. This would have been at odds with the traditional approach to plans and drafts practised by architects of the day. MacNair and Mackintosh frequently went on sketching trips together in the countryside surrounding Glasgow, or joined John Keppie at his home in Ayr, often with the other members of the Four. Through his sketching Mackintosh developed a sinuous organic language of expression, stepping away from naturalism towards stylized form and experimenting with imaginary shapes.

CREATED

Glasgow

MEDIUM

Pencil and watercolour

SERIES/PERIOD/MOVEMENT

Glasgow School of Art

SIMILAR WORKS

Cabinet displayed at the Secessionist Exhibition, Vienna by Josef Hoffmann, 1900

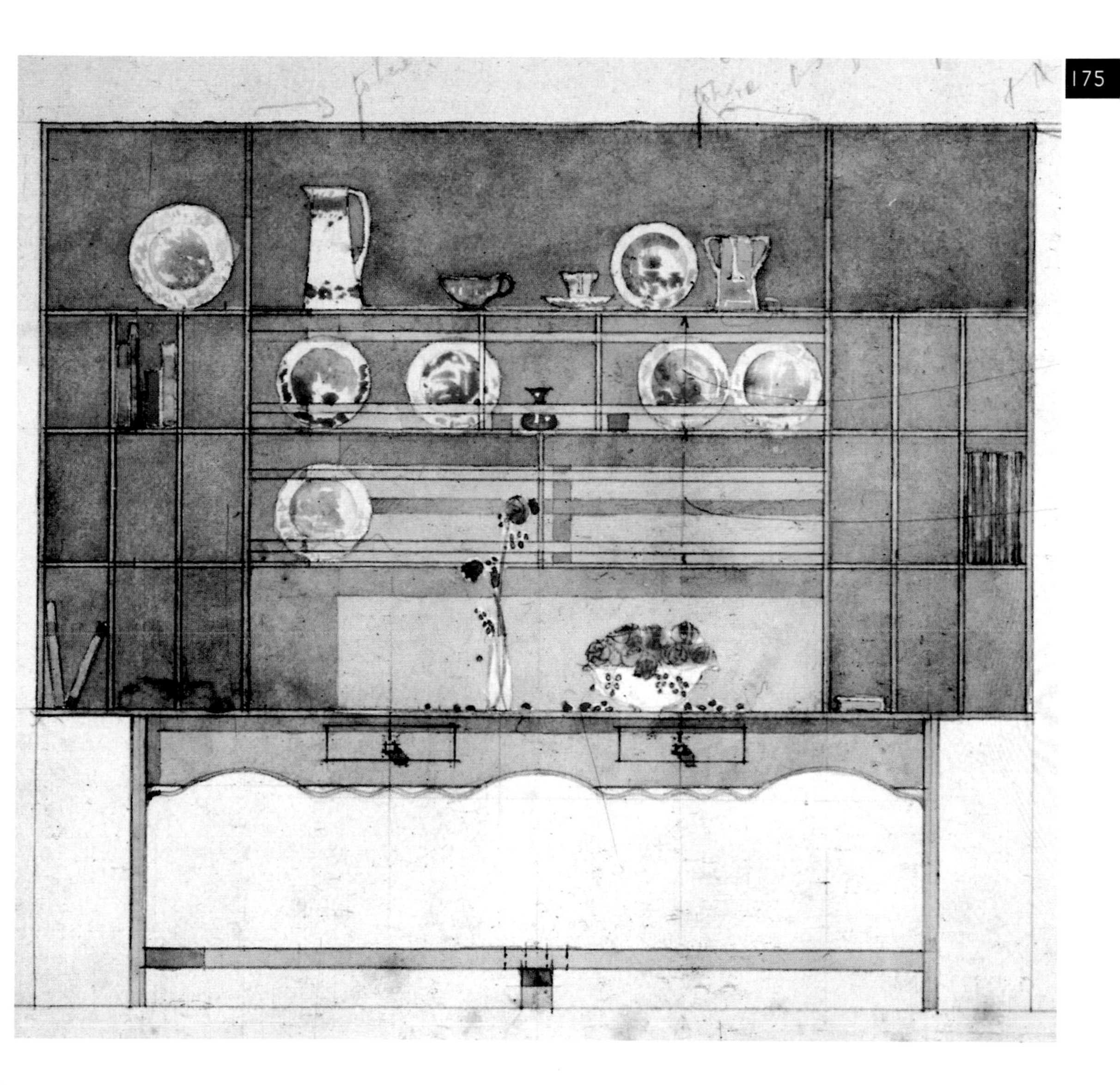

Glasgow School of Art: view of a studio

Mackintosh left the School of Art at the end of the 1893–94 session after 10 years of part-time studying there. The school had occupied a central role in his life, artistically obviously, but also socially through the strong friendships he had made. When the competition to design the new building was opened, Mackintosh was well qualified to understand the particular requirements and facilities of the school. Mackintosh's designs were stunningly new in concept and a far cry from the traditional styles of Gothic or pseudo-Classical, which were associated with significant public commissions. The close friendship between Newbery and Mackintosh did not go unnoticed and Newbery was accused of weighing the odds in Mackintosh's favour. The first stage of the designs took place from 1897 to 1899. Mackintosh was a young man of only 29 years of age and standing at the threshold of a glittering career that tragically never quite materialized during his lifetime. At the beginning of 1914 Newbery painted Mackintosh before he left Glasgow, portraying a sad and anxious man; the flamboyant, confident youth a distant memory of 20 years before.

CREATED

Glasgow

MEDIUM

Interior design

SERIES/PERIOD/MOVEMENT

Glasgow School of Art

SIMILAR WORKS

Hayaski House, living room by Arata Isozaki, 1976

Glasgow School of Art: library, 1897–99

At the time of submitting the designs for the School of Art Mackintosh was a junior architect with the firm Honeyman and Keppie. John Keppie was at first publicly credited with the project. This was in spite of the design having clearly been drawn by Mackintosh and, during the laying of the foundation stone on 25 May 1898, Mackintosh remained very much in the background. By the time of the second phase of building from 1907 to 1909 Mackintosh had become a partner in the firm and his name appeared alongside his plans. The library is quite possibly Mackintosh at his most brilliant. Soaring oak posts support substantial beams holding up the gallery and rhythmically dividing the room into a space of unequalled harmony. There is an undeniable parallel between the physicality of the room and the concept of the tree of knowledge seen through the heavy oak posts reaching towards the central grouping of 13 lights suspended from the ceiling on tendril-like cords. The symbol of the tree was one that Mackintosh used repeatedly through his career and in all areas of his art.

CREATED

Glasgow

MEDIUM

Interior design

SERIES/PERIOD/MOVEMENT

Glasgow School of Art

SIMILAR WORKS

Palais Stoclet, central hallway by Josef Hoffmann, 1905–11

ARCHITECTURE
INTERIOR

Glasgow School of Art: glass detail, 1896–99

Although Mackintosh was dogged by bad luck and poor timing throughout his career, a certain amount of his eventual disenchantment with Glasgow was self-inflicted. By all accounts he was inclined to bouts of temper and petulance, even as a small child, and it seems that his particularly fiery temperament continued on into adulthood. He was described on occasion as being difficult to work with and would frequently change his plans partway through a project. His initial drawings for a commission would identify his intentions, which would then mature and grow throughout the course of the building work. While this practice of a fluid artistic approach towards his architecture undoubtedly produced some of the finest works of the early twentieth century, it could also prove highly irritating to his patrons. The first phase of the Glasgow School of Art, which was to be built under a strict budget, suffered from a large overrun in expenses causing great consternation amongst the board of commissioners. It was possibly as frustrating for Mackintosh to be so tied financially, as it was for the board who saw their budget disappearing.

CREATED

Glasgow

MEDIUM

Stained glass

SERIES/PERIOD/MOVEMENT

Glasgow School of Art

SIMILAR WORKS

Screen with stained-glass inset by Van Eyck

Glasgow School of Art: the boardroom, 1897–99

The second phase of building from 1907 to 1909 was run under similar financial restraints as the first, against which Mackintosh battled fiercely. On completion the building was met with the predictable divided criticism. Mackintosh's greatest work was harshly criticized on some fronts, although the governors declared its form was perfectly suited to the function of an art school. The first step towards Modernism, the brilliant synthesis of form and the evocation of a new way forward, all seemed to be largely overlooked. It was perhaps one of the greatest tragedies that Mackintosh never lived to see his masterpiece properly appreciated.

The boardroom with its innovative steel beams, lofty windows and clean, spare lines allegedly made the members of the board uncomfortable. More accustomed to the traditional cluttered Victorian interiors, they probably thought the boardroom too sparse and a new boardroom was constructed in a large studio room to the left of the entrance. Panelled and rich in atmosphere and natural colour the new boardroom has eight carved pilasters topped with Mackintosh's interpretation of an egg and dart moulding, set between narrow Ionic volutes.

CREATED

Glasgow

MEDIUM

Interior design

SERIES/PERIOD/MOVEMENT

Glasgow School of Art

SIMILAR WORKS

The dining room, Pürkersdorf Sanitorium by Josef Hoffmann, 1904

Design for a smoker's cabinet, 1899

Mackintosh never received the accolade that he expected, or deserved, from his home town of Glasgow, a fact that led to his eventual loss of self-confidence and his rejection of the city altogether. The same could not be said for him or his reputation on the Continent where he fostered strong ties within the culture of artists and architects. In 1900 the Four were invited to exhibit at the Eighth Secessionist Exhibition in Vienna and were responsible for furnishing and decorating an entire room, 'The Scottish Room'. It was a brave move on behalf of the Four to take up the gauntlet and go to Vienna. They were still reeling from their poor reception at the Arts and Crafts Exhibition in London, 1896, and were popular only amongst their own circles. The Viennese, however, were delighted with the work of the Four and it is believed that they were welcomed with open arms and transported through the city in a flower-decked carriage. The design for the Smoker's Cabinet represents one of the pieces that were exhibited in their Scottish Room.

CREATED

Glasgow, for display in Vienna

MEDIUM

Pencil and watercolour on laid paper

SERIES/PERIOD/MOVEMENT

Continental designs

SIMILAR WORKS

Secretaire, exhibited at the 1900 Secessionist Exhibition, Vienna by C. R. Ashbee, *c.* 1900

SKETCH DESIGN FOR SMOKERS CABINET

Design for a wall with a table and doors for A. S. Ball, 1905

In spite of Mackintosh's warm reception on the Continent, it is surprising that he completed very few commissions abroad, which may in part have been due to his heavy work commitments in Glasgow on Miss Cranston's tea rooms at around the same time. Before he ventured to Vienna as part of the Four, his work was known there only through the publication *The Studio* and the enthusiasm of his good friend Hermann Muthesius. Muthesius, an attaché at the German embassy in London and an important figure in architectural and cultural circles, put the German architect Alfred Grenander (1863–1931) in touch with Mackintosh. Through Grenander Mackintosh was commissioned by the industrial art company A. S. Ball to design a dining room for an interior design exhibition in Berlin. Mackintosh's simple geometric design for the wall displays a harmonious rhythmic asymmetry seen through the insertion of bright squares of blue panelling, suggestive of columns. The table design with its vertical detailing reinforces the pattern of the wall behind and the delicate suspended lighting arrangement further adds to the two-dimensional, vertical feel of the plan.

CREATED

Berlin

MEDIUM

Pencil and watercolour

SERIES/PERIOD/MOVEMENT

Continental designs

SIMILAR WORKS

The Scottish Section, wall treatment in a dining room exhibited at the 1900 Secessionist Exhibition, Vienna by Frances Macdonald MacNair and Herbert MacNair, *c.* 1900

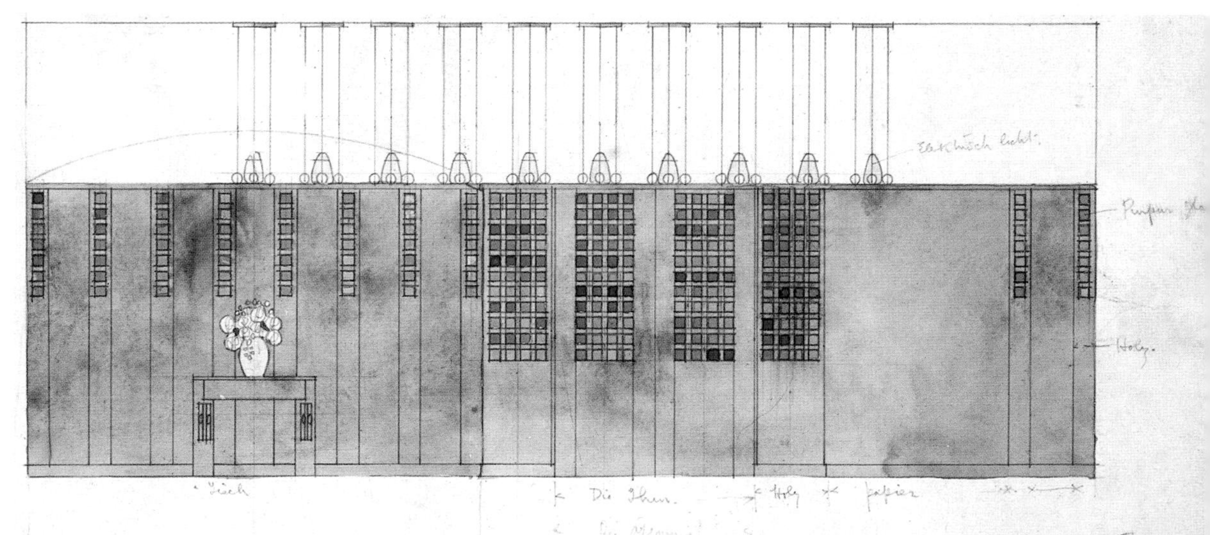
Elektrisch licht.
Holz.
Tisch
Die Thur.
Holz
papier
Chas: R. Mackintosh
120 Mains Street
Blythswood Square Glasgow

Masters of Interior Design, House for an Art Lover, title page of folio, 1902

In December 1900, at around the same time that the Mackintoshes were in Vienna for the Secessionist Exhibition, the publisher Alexander Koch announced a competition for *Haus Eines Kunstfreundes*, House for an Art Lover, in his journal, *Zeitschreift für Innendekoration*. The competition called for a house suitable for an art collector and built and furnished in an appropriately forward-thinking manner. Mackintosh did not win the competition, but the designs he submitted were significant because it was the first time that one of his complete architectural schemes had been seen on the Continent. His plans for the house were astonishingly innovative and modern in concept and had a profound effect on the subsequent development of architecture in Europe. They also established his reputation as a designer of interiors, furniture and architecture abroad.

The top three submissions, those by Mackintosh, the renowned English architect M. H. Baillie Scott (1865–1945) and Leopold Bauer (1873–1958), were published in portfolio form in 1902 by Alexander Koch. Mackintosh's title page featured his sinuous, elongated female figures and favoured rose motif, and was followed by an essay written by his friend Herman Muthesius discussing Mackintosh's 'art principles'.

PUBLISHED IN

Darmstadt

MEDIUM

Colour lithograph

SERIES/PERIOD/MOVEMENT

House for an Art Lover

SIMILAR WORKS

Tree of Knowledge, bookplate for John Turnbull Knox by Herbert MacNair, 1896

MEISTER DER
INNEN KUNST
II
CHARLES RENNIE
MACKINTOSH
GLASGOW
HAUS EINES
KUNSTFREUNDES
VERLAG
ALEX KOCH DARMSTADT
C.R.MACKINTOSH

House for an Art Lover competition entry: south elevation, *c.* 1901

The judges ruled that none of the competition entries truly fulfilled the brief and subsequently did not award a first prize. Baillie Scott was awarded second prize for his design, a well-conceived plan in the Romantic tradition with a symmetrical layout and a mixture of gables, turrets, half-timbering and mullioned windows. His interiors were richly ornate to the point of distraction, in total contrast to those of Mackintosh. Mackintosh's entry was actually disqualified for not having met the required number of designs, although he was awarded a 'purchase prize' of 600 marks. The designs that Mackintosh submitted were as unorthodox as Baillie Scott's were conventional. Mackintosh conceived the house from the inside out, the exterior arrangement reflecting those necessary features of the interior. As such his exterior plans were neither symmetrical nor traditional, but rather a combination of rugged monumentality evocative of ancient Scottish castles and modern functionalism. The plans for the south elevation demonstrate a balance and harmony achieved without the use of symmetry, and an aesthetic streamlined beauty created in the absence of adornment.

PUBLISHED IN

Darmstadt

MEDIUM

Black and green ink on paper

SERIES/PERIOD/MOVEMENT

House for an Art Lover

SIMILAR WORKS

Stenhouse, Edinburgh, typical seventeenth-century Scottish farmhouse

Pürkersdorf Sanitorium by Josef Hoffmann, 1904

IDEEN WETTBEWERB FÜR EIN HERRSCHAFTLICHES WOHNHAUS EINES KUNST=FREUNDES 4.

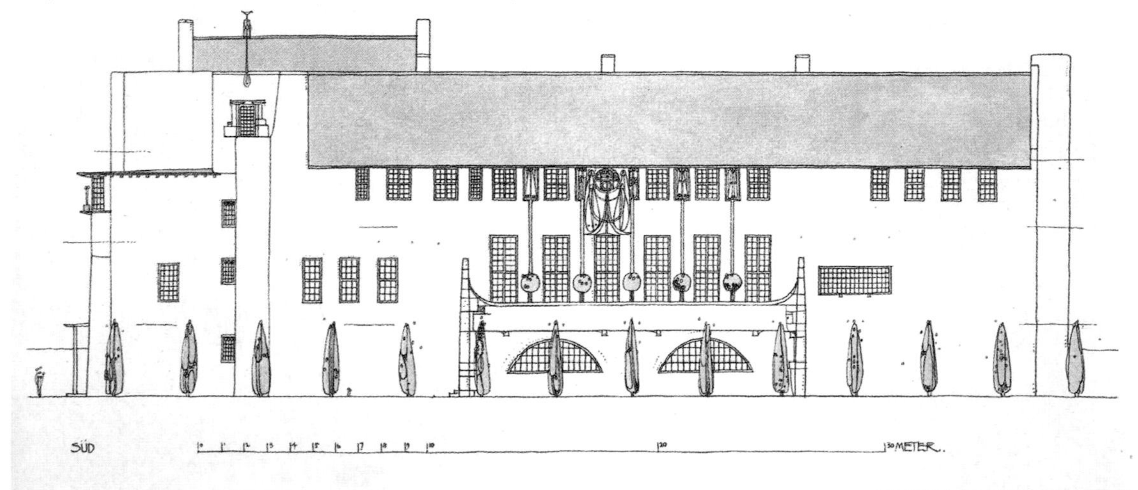

C. R. MACKINTOSH. GLASGOW. HAUS EINES KUNST-FREUNDES.
VERLAGS-ANSTALT: ALEXANDER KOCH-DARMSTADT. — TAFEL IX

House for an Art Lover competition entry: floor plans, 1902

In a similar way to the method with which Mackintosh manipulated interior space in the Glasgow School of Art, he again created stunning visual impact by the design of his floor plan. The porch and vestibule, the main entrance into the house, were extremely small. The porch being long and narrow, the vestibule tiny and square. Already he was contrasting his use of interior space. The vestibule opened into the hall, a suddenly huge and almost ethereal interior space, designed to make a monumental impact. He conceived the hall and adjoining dining room in rich, dark-wood panelling and to contrast with the bright whiteness of the reception room and music room. Each room within the house and the passage through it were designed to be visually stunning and emotive by the use of contrasting spaces and the treatment of the interiors. For the first time he was able truly to design the entire project, irrespective of financial restraints. It is tragic that his plans were not built at the time, although in spite of this they were significantly influential across Europe.

PUBLISHED IN

Darmstadt

MEDIUM

Pen and ink

SERIES/PERIOD/MOVEMENT

House for an Art Lover

SIMILAR WORKS

Floor plans for House for an Art Lover by M. H. Baillie Scott, 1902

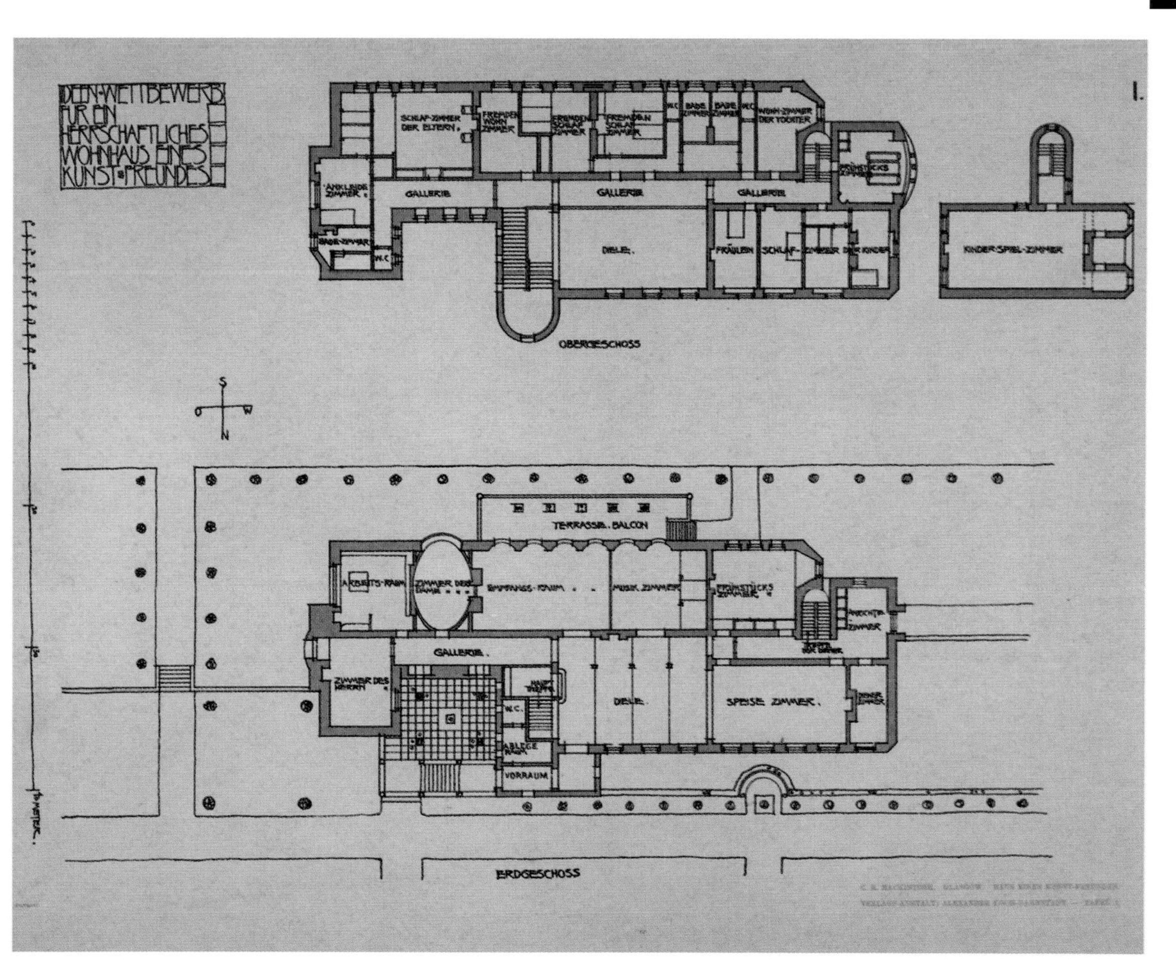
IDEEN-WETTBEWERB FÜR EIN HERRSCHAFTLICHES WOHNHAUS EINES KUNST-FREUNDES
I.
SCHLAF-ZIMMER DER ELTERN
FREMDEN WOHN ZIMMER
FREMDEN SCHLAF ZIMMER
FREMDEN SCHLAF ZIMMER
BADE ZIMMER
BADE ZIMMER
WOHN-ZIMMER DER TOCHTER
ANKLEIDE ZIMMER
GALLERIE
GALLERIE
GALLERIE
FRÜHSTÜCKS ZIMMER
BADE-ZIMMER
W.C
DIELE
FRÄULEIN
SCHLAF-ZIMMER DER KINDER
KINDER-SPIEL-ZIMMER
OBERGESCHOSS
S
O
W
N
TERRASSE, BALCON
ARBEITS-RAUM
ZIMMER DER DAME
EMPFANGS-RAUM
MUSIK-ZIMMER
FRÜHSTÜCKS ZIMMER
ZIMMER
GALLERIE
ZIMMER DES HERRN
HAUPT TREPPE
W.C.
DIELE
SPEISE ZIMMER
ABLEGE RAUM
VORRAUM
ERDGESCHOSS

House for an Art Lover competition entry: design for a dining room, 1901

Mackintosh's design for the dining room is clean and simple. He devised wood panelling for the walls and a plain curved white ceiling with suspended decorative coloured-glass lights. Art Nouveau style insets at the top of each wood panel and the repeated use of stylized design motifs through the walls, carpet and furniture added to the encompassing air of unity through the room. Mackintosh's treatment of the interiors was in direct contrast to Baillie Scott. Baillie Scott had an established reputation as one of the most progressive artist-architects within the Arts and Crafts movement in England and his work was growing increasingly popular in Europe. In 1898 he had been commissioned to furnish part of the new palace at Darmstadt by the Grand Duke of Hesse, a project that greatly enhanced his appeal on the Continent. Plans for his dining room show a mass of unrelated decorative detail that compete with the architectural schematics of the room. Nothing could have been further from Mackintosh's quiet unified space.

PUBLISHED IN

Darmstadt

MEDIUM

Colour lithograph

SERIES/PERIOD/MOVEMENT

House for an Art Lover

SIMILAR WORKS

Dining room, The Orchard, Chorley Wood by C. F. A. Voysey, 1900

WETTBEWERB FÜR EIN HERRSCHAFTLICHES WOHNHAUS EINES KUNST-FREUNDES
1
S SPEISE-ZIMMER

House for an Art Lover competition entry: dining room side table, 1902

Mackintosh's concern with the spatial effect of the House for an Art Lover was particularly evident in his design of the ground floor around the great hall. The dining room, which opened off the hall, was separated by a light moveable partition, which could be removed to create an enormous area. The use of partitions to engineer malleable space was not unlike traditional Oriental designs, something Mackintosh was well aware of. The music room and reception room were similarly partitioned and could, through the use of large double doors, be amalgamated into the hall and dining room space. The hall, as well as occupying a large planar space, also shot vertically upwards and rose two storeys high with a gallery; a similar arrangement to that seen in the Glasgow School of Art Library.

The furniture in the dining room was designed to be integral to the room itself. This is clearly seen in the side table, which seems to merge into and out of the panelled wall behind it. The piece, which was decorated with minimal geometric detailing, remained true to the fabric of its construction and perfectly complemented the aesthetic unity of the entire room.

PUBLISHED IN

Darmstadt

MEDIUM

Colour lithograph

SERIES/PERIOD/MOVEMENT

House for an Art Lover

SIMILAR WORKS

Buffet by Josef Hoffmann, 1911

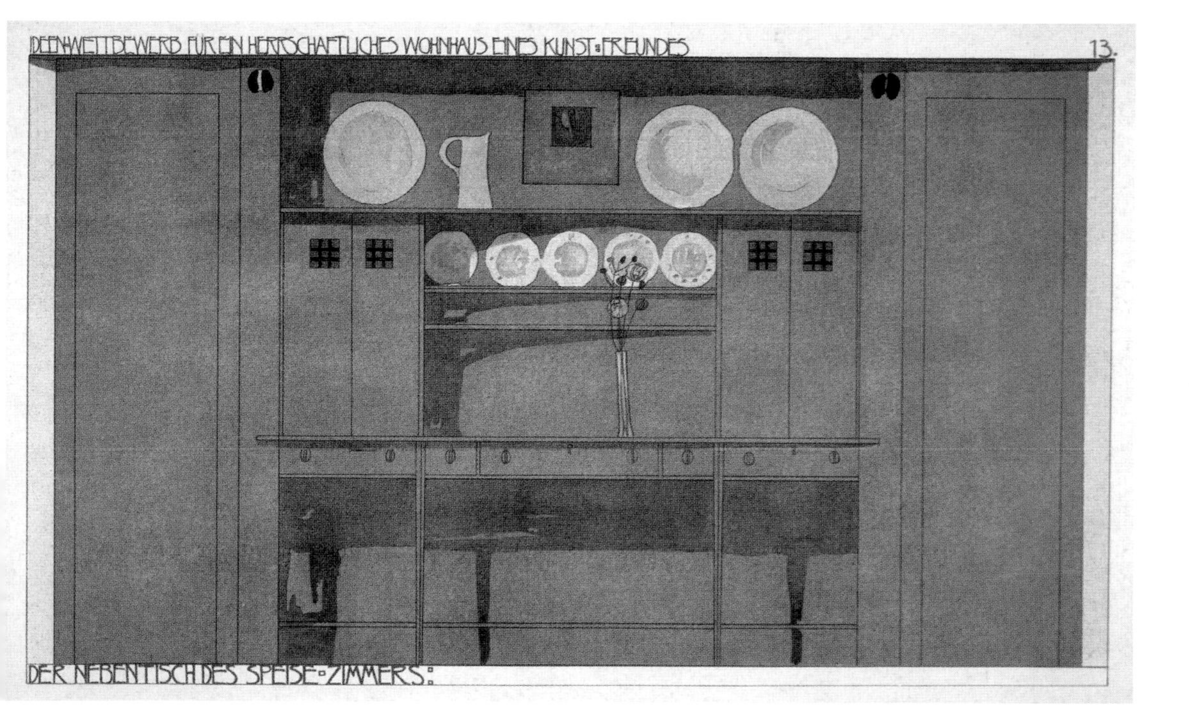
IDEEN-WETTBEWERB FÜR EIN HERRSCHAFTLICHES WOHNHAUS EINES KUNST-FREUNDES
13.
DER NEBENTISCH DES SPEISE-ZIMMERS.

House for an Art Lover competition entry: design for a music room with panels by Margaret Macdonald Mackintosh, 1901

Margaret and Charles collaborated on many commissions, Margaret often providing the detailing to fabrics and wall treatments within Charles's design concept. In the music-room plans the hand of Margaret is distinctive in her use of the unusual linen ladies panels and the elaborate and ornamental piano casing. The decorative nature of Margaret's input was a reflection of the Glasgow style, which the Glasgow School of Art became famous for nurturing. In spite of the excessively decorative nature of the room, the elegant physical proportions and the lofty sense of verticality preside. The pervading atmosphere is one of sophisticated entertainment, perfectly reflecting the function of the room. The fantastical piano design was based on an organ made for another project that Mackintosh was involved in at Craigie Hall, Glasgow. The music room attracted a great deal of attention and may have inspired the Wärndorfers to commission Mackintosh to design their music room, on which he worked at around the same time as the House for an Art Lover.

PUBLISHED IN

Darmstadt

MEDIUM

Colour lithograph

SERIES/PERIOD/MOVEMENT

House for an Art Lover

SIMILAR WORKS

Café Museum, Vienna by Adolf Loos, 1899

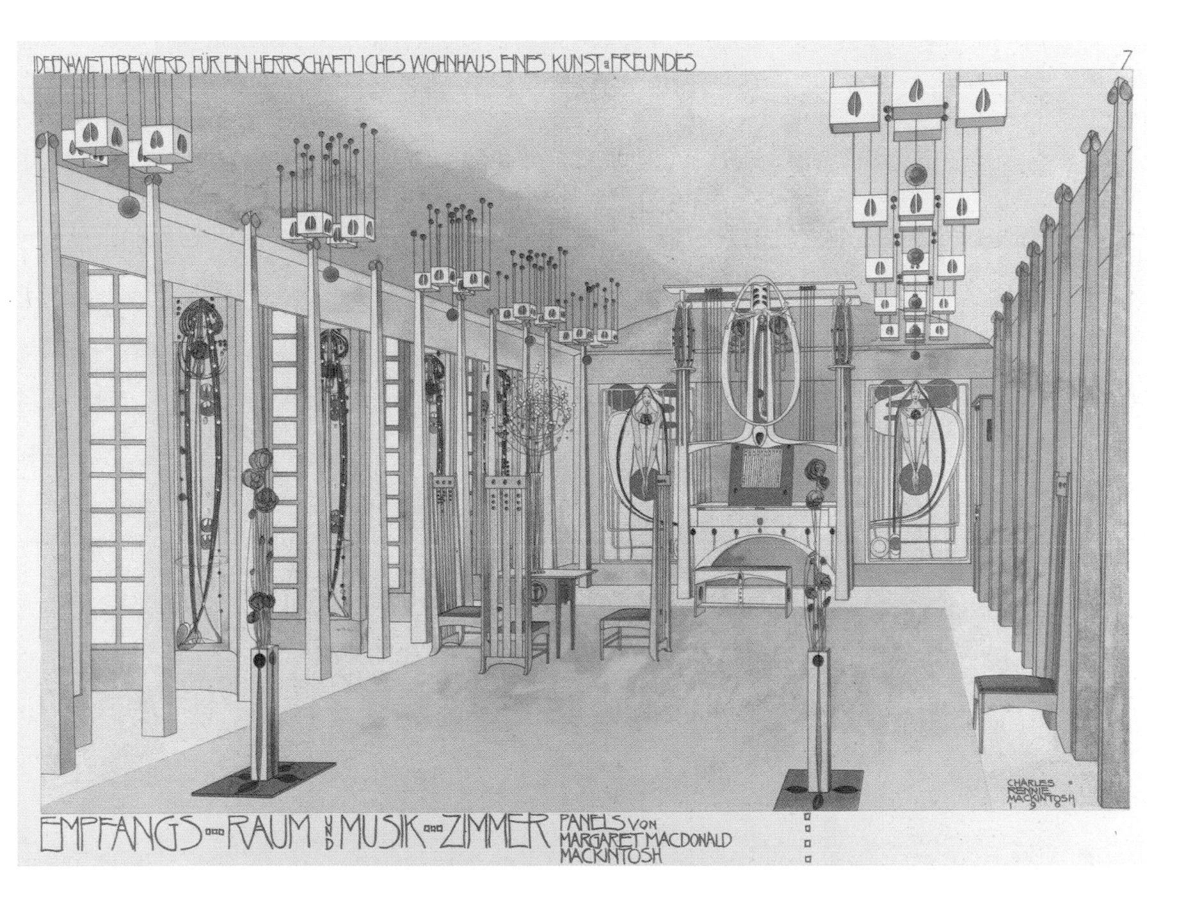
IDEEN-WETTBEWERB FÜR EIN HERRSCHAFTLICHES WOHNHAUS EINES KUNST-FREUNDES
7
EMPFANGS-RAUM UND MUSIK-ZIMMER PANELS VON MARGARET MACDONALD MACKINTOSH
CHARLES RENNIE MACKINTOSH 1901

House for an Art Lover competition entry: sides of the music room and reception room, 1902

Hermann Muthesius wrote in the preface to Mackintosh's competition portfolio, 'The exterior of the building ... exhibits an absolutely original character, unlike anything else known. In it we shall not find a trace of the conventional forms of architecture, to which the artist, so far as his present intentions were concerned, was quite indifferent.'

This can accurately be applied not just to the exterior but also to the strangely sensual and innovative interiors. The House for an Art Lover was designed and built in Bellahouston Park, Glasgow, 1989–96, to the original Mackintosh designs. Finally many years after his death the designs were realized and it is possible to see just how effective his spatial concept and interior arrangement was. Considering his designs for the Glasgow School of Art and his domestic commissions had not been seen on the Continent at the time of the competition, his plans must have appeared truly revolutionary. It is not insignificant that they were exhibited at the International Exhibition of Modern Decorative Art in Turin in 1902, where they would have been seen by the leading architects of the day from across Europe.

PUBLISHED IN

Darmstadt

MEDIUM

Colour lithograph

SERIES/PERIOD/MOVEMENT

House for an Art Lover

SIMILAR WORKS

Drawing room design by John Ednie, 1912

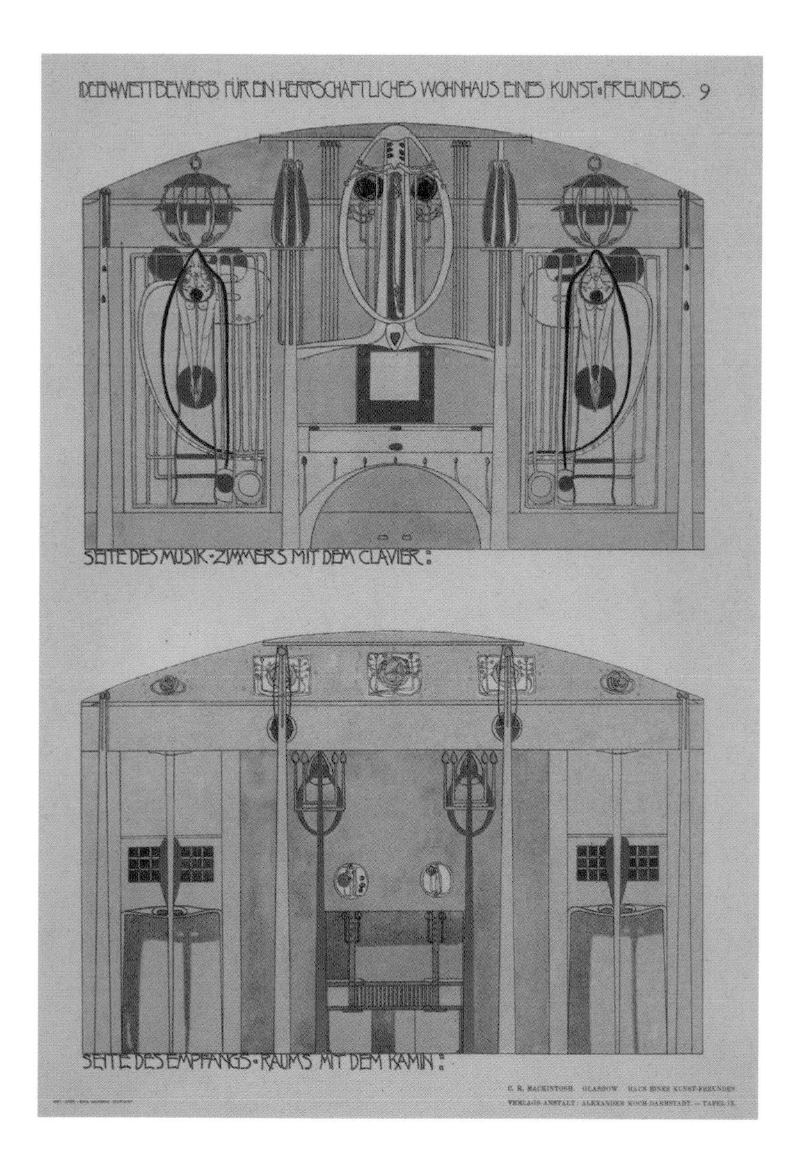
IDEENWETTBEWERB FÜR EIN HERRSCHAFTLICHES WOHNHAUS EINES KUNST-FREUNDES. 9
SEITE DES MUSIK-ZIMMERS MIT DEM CLAVIER:
SEITE DES EMPFANGS-RAUMS MIT DEM KAMIN:
C. R. MACKINTOSH. GLASGOW. HAUS EINES KUNST-FREUNDES
VERLAGS-ANSTALT: ALEXANDER KOCH-DARMSTADT. — TAFEL IX.

House for an Art Lover competition entry: the children's nursery room, 1902

Mackintosh's approach to design was one of total unity and in instances such as the House for an Art Lover, where he was in control of both the interior and exterior designs, he was most able to express himself. Sadly, many of his commissions were for interior decorations and to work within an existing structure, something that must have been immensely frustrating to the architect. As was fairly typical of his design practices, he paid great attention to the staircase in the House for an Art Lover. The stairs in his competition submission led to the first floor from the grand hall and were in the manner of the stairs he designed at both Windyhill and The Hill House. On the first floor the childrens' rooms are situated together, next to the nurse's quarters, with a large children's playroom up a separate staircase above the nursery wing. The nursery room was large and slightly cavernous with a gently curved ceiling and small windows along the horizontal edge. The interior scheme included unusual lights on poles, no doubt to appeal to children's fantastical imagination, and decorative panels in bright colours.

PUBLISHED IN

Darmstadt

MEDIUM

Watercolour

SERIES/PERIOD/MOVEMENT

House for an Art Lover

SIMILAR WORKS

Day and night nurseries by József Vágó, *c.* 1913

IDEEN-WETTBEWERB FÜR EIN HERRSCHAFTLICHES WOHNHAUS EINES KUNST-FREUNDES.
10.
CHARLES RENNIE MACKINTOSH 1901
DER SPIEL-RAUM DER KINDER
PANEL VON MARGARET MACDONALD MACKINTOSH

Mosside (later Cloak), Kilmalcolm: south elevation, c. 1906

Kilmalcolm was a beautiful area that Mackintosh was already well acquainted with by the time of the Mosside commission. In 1895 he had designed a few pieces of furniture for the Davidsons at their home, Gladsmuir, and then in 1899 was commissioned by them to design their new home, Windyhill. Mackintosh had also worked for Mr H. B. Collins in and around the area of Kilmalcolm, mostly in the form of decorating and small alterations to existing properties, as well as a gate lodge in 1901. Then around 1906 Mackintosh was commissioned by Mr Collins to build Mosside. The house is one of his less well-known commissions and is one of the most unusual houses in the context of his work, being in a style barely recognizable as his own. This was in great part due to a conflict of creative ideas between Mackintosh and Mr Collins. The rustic and slightly unwelcoming exterior with its coarse rubble texture and randomly scattered windows possessed none of the harmony or finesse most commonly associated with Mackintosh.

CREATED

Glasgow

MEDIUM

Pencil and wash on brown tracing paper

SERIES/PERIOD/MOVEMENT

Domestic commissions

SIMILAR WORKS

Villa Hermann Bahr by J. M. Olbrich, 1899

Cottages in Fortingall, Perthshire by James MacLaren, *c.* 1897

FLOOR.
FLOOR.
FLOOR.
FLOOR.
FLOOR.
FLOOR.
SOUTH ELEVATION.
10
5
0
10
20
30
40
50
60
FEET.

Roses on a chequered ground, textile design (detail), 1915–23

Walberswick is a tiny fishing village on the Suffolk coastline that has had a long tradition as an artists' retreat. Picturesque and invariably bathed with a soft, eerie luminescence associated with the surrounding area, Walberswick has provided an endless supply of inspiring scenery over a great many years to a succession of artists. Mackintosh first visited in happier times when he stayed at the holiday cottage of Francis and Jessie Newbery. After the dissolution of his partnership with the firm Honeyman and Keppie and his subsequent depression Charles and Margaret moved to the village and settled there for around 15 months. The extraordinarily delicate and vividly coloured watercolours that he produced during this short period belie his own personal unhappiness and subsequent turmoil surrounding the charges of espionage. This rose design is interesting because it is one of the first known designs that he made for textiles and is the only surviving design to include an inscription with a Walberswick address. However, it is possible that it was intended as a design for a wall decoration because it appears in a much larger scale than his later textile designs executed in Chelsea.

CREATED

Walberswick

MEDIUM

Pencil and watercolour

SERIES/PERIOD/MOVEMENT

Walberswick

SIMILAR WORKS

Antimacassar from The Hill House by Margaret Macdonald Mackintosh, *c.*1904

ROSE

Furnishing fabric designed for William Foxton, 1922

On moving to London the Mackintoshes were absorbed into the artistic scene and spent many enjoyable, long evenings at The Blue Cockatoo restaurant in Chelsea. Their time in the capital was nonetheless plagued with frustrations and bad luck. The First World War had taken a huge toll on society and the economy, and the number of architectural commissions had dropped dramatically. Mackintosh's vision of changing the pattern of architectural fashion through his own designs had failed to materialize in Glasgow and in London he was still relatively unknown. The admiration and recognition with which he had been received abroad was never reciprocated in his own country, a bitter pill to swallow for the man who was at heart fiercely nationalistic.

Charles and Margaret started to design textiles and worked for William Foxton of Foxton's Ltd for some years. The fabric pictured here is one of their later designs and is reminiscent of traditional Indonesian batik patterns. The craft of batik became popular during the 1920s through the work of Madame Pangon in Paris and Jessie M. King of the Glasgow School of Art.

CREATED

London

MEDIUM

Roller-printed cretonne

SERIES/PERIOD/MOVEMENT

Textile designs

SIMILAR WORKS

Mendip by Charles Grant, 1934

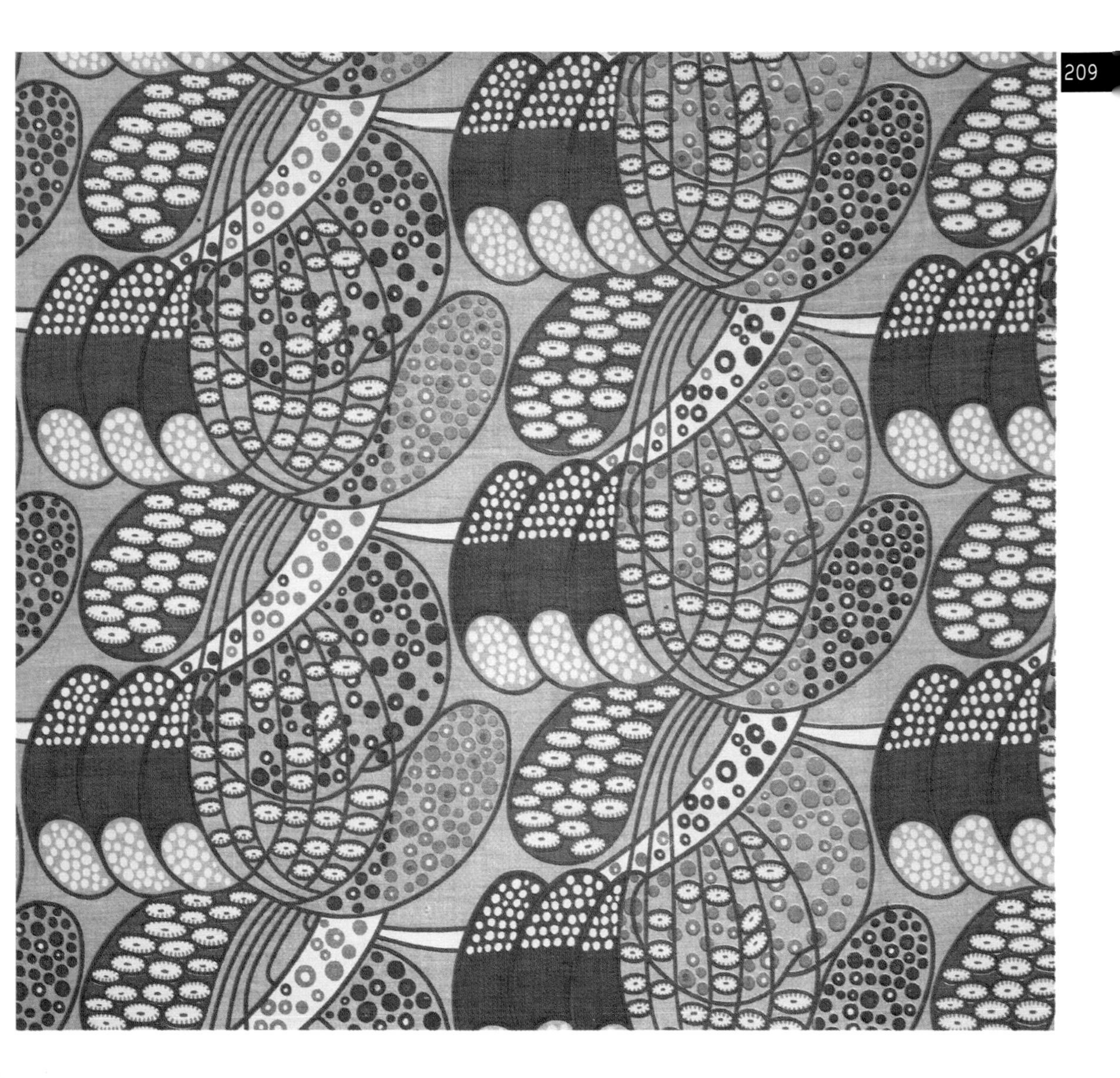

Furnishing fabric designed for William Foxton, 1918

With a minimal amount of architectural commissions, the Mackintoshes concentrated on their textile designs, primarily for Foxton's and Sefton's, while also becoming actively involved in the social life of their surrounding artistic community. Charles's designs had evolved from his former motifs of Art Nouveau style elongated figures and were now primarily geometric. He used distinctive strong, bold colours that were popular at this time and geometric shapes, both of which paved the way towards the emergence of Art Deco. The bright purple and green in the design, pictured, were typical of Mackintosh's colour scheme and were often seen in his various designs. Foxton's, which had been established in 1903 by William Foxton, produced some of the most innovative artist-designed textiles of the times and in this respect they were an ideal employer for the Mackintoshes. William Foxton also commissioned other notable artists such as Claude Lovat Fraser (1890–1921), F. Gregory Brown and Minnie McLeish (1876–1957) to produce Modernist designs for the company. In 1915 Foxton was instrumental in founding the Design and Industries Association in an effort to improve the standard of British industrial design.

CREATED

London

MEDIUM

Printed cotton

SERIES/PERIOD/MOVEMENT

Textile designs

SIMILAR WORKS

Ozon by Josef Hoffmann, 1923

Roundels by Minnie McLeish for William Foxton, 1921

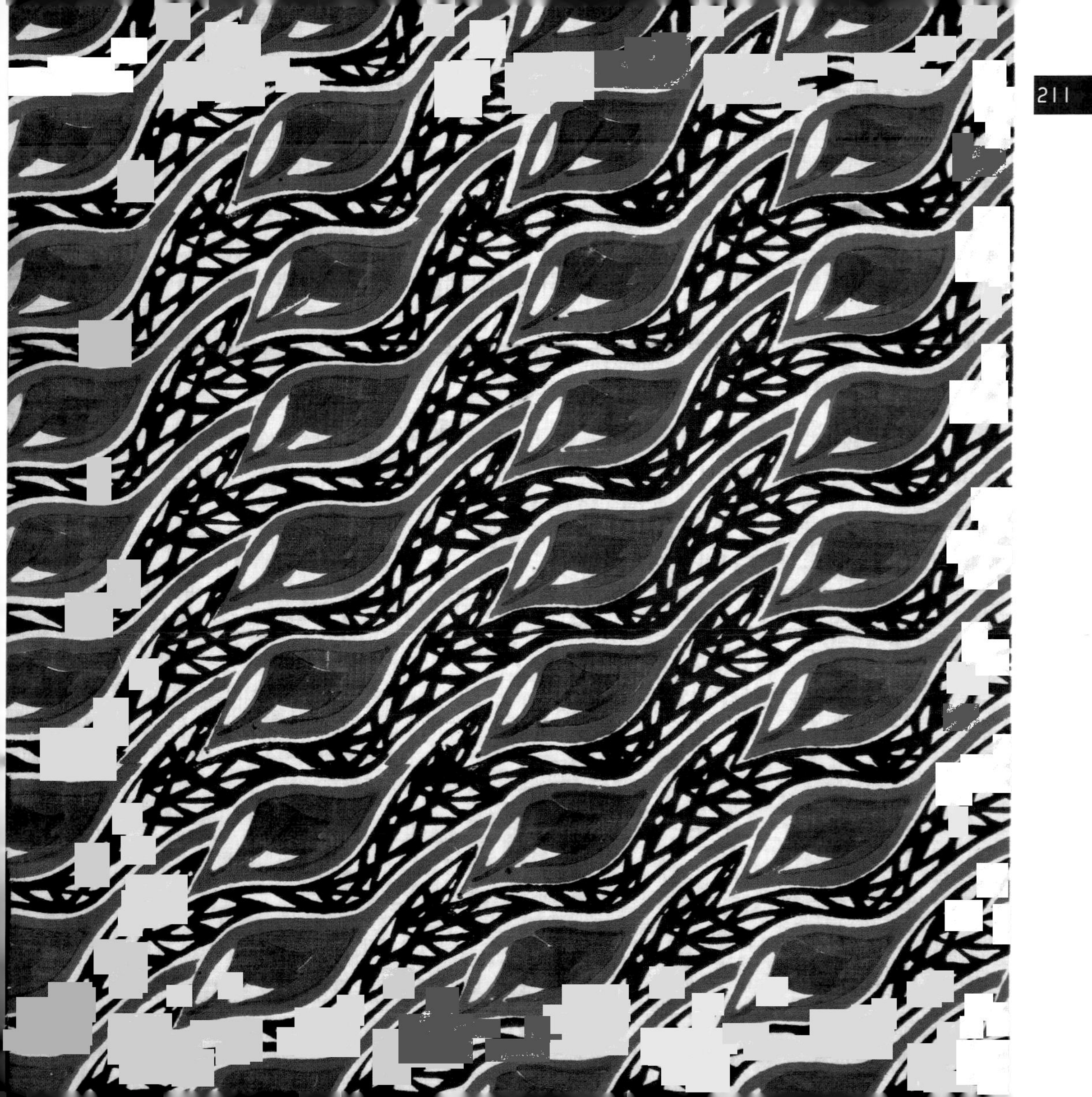

Yellow Tulips, c. 1922–23

Yellow Tulips is one of the few flower paintings with a discernible background and is interesting because it affords us a glimpse of the interior of the Mackintoshes' Chelsea flat. Apart from this painting there are sadly no surviving photographs or documentation describing the interior of their London home. The arrangement of the fireplace in the background with the adjacent curtain that can be seen behind the yellow tulips is similar to the interior organization of the second house they lived in in Glasgow, 78 Southpark Avenue. They moved there in 1906 from 120 Mains Street taking their furniture and decorative scheme with them.

There has been some debate over the dating of *Yellow Tulips*, but it is thought to have been painted in 1922, shortly before the Mackintoshes left London for the south of France. The style is very similar to Mackintosh's paintings done during the last years of his life living in Port Vendres.

CREATED

London

MEDIUM

Watercolour

SERIES/PERIOD/MOVEMENT

London

SIMILAR WORKS

Dead Spring by Paul Nash, 1928–29

The Lighthouse, 1927

For several years after his arrival in London from Walberswick Mackintosh concentrated his energies on his textile designs and several small architectural projects. He would not return to landscape painting until a visit to Dorset in 1920 with Margaret and some friends. The Dorset landscape appealed to him, especially the geometric effect created by the grid of stone walls and divided fields, sometimes with the sea barely glinting in the distance. The patterns that he saw in the natural scene around him and his distinctive stylized approach to landscape painting lent his pictures a surreal quality, which was again seen in the work he carried out in France. In 1923 Charles and Margaret moved to the Mediterranean coast on the advice of friends and remained there until 1927. The Scottish painter J. D. Fergusson (who was a neighbour to the Mackintoshes in Chelsea) made regular trips to see them throughout their time abroad. *The Lighthouse* was painted towards the end of Charles's life at a period when he was producing some of his most polished and interesting work.

CREATED

France

MEDIUM

Watercolour over pencil

SERIES/PERIOD/MOVEMENT

Late period landscapes

SIMILAR WORKS

The Red Bathhouse by Max Pechstein, 1910

A Southern Town, c. 1923–27

Letters from Charles and Margaret to J. D. Fergusson and to their old friend Francis Newbery indicate that the couple moved around while in France, tending to spend the summer months in Mont Louis and returning to Port Vendres in the winter. Mackintosh was attracted to the rural villages nestling in the hillsides of southern France, drawn by the organic way in which the towns sprang from their surrounding landscape. The simple geometric shapes of the houses provided a patterned landscape ideally suited to the stylized manner in which Mackintosh interpreted the scene around him. This painting of *A Southern Town* reflects the strong Mediterranean sunlight, throwing dark long shadows and illuminating the brilliant white of the buildings. Mackintosh was unusual in his approach to painting by treating the entire canvas in the same detailed manner. A strange but effective dynamic is created in his use of strong, bold perspective.

CREATED

France

MEDIUM

Pencil and watercolour

SERIES/PERIOD/MOVEMENT

Late period landscapes

SIMILAR WORKS

Le Marche aux Pommes by Raoul Dufy, 1904

The Road Through the Rocks, c. 1926–27

Mackintosh was especially drawn to the simple, squat forts that lined the coast and the border with Spain. The great forms that rose out of the equally hulking rocks provided him with the design element and organic unity that he sought. Letters recall how Charles and Margaret would make trips out from their home at Port Vendres often walking along the coastline with sketchbooks in hand. During their settlement in France they also travelled to Italy and crossed the border to Spain where Mackintosh executed two paintings, *Fetges* and a *Spanish Farm*.

The forts dotted through their surrounding countryside became the subject of several watercolour studies. The slab-sided monumentality of man-made structures growing from the landscape and the contrast of the texture of rocks to fields to distant sea became a great source of inspiration to the artist. Charles worked slowly on his paintings, sometimes taking weeks to finish a single canvas, and preferred to work outside. It is interesting that while Margaret and Charles often collaborated on projects through the years, there are no surviving paintings that indicate Margaret's involvement.

CREATED

France

MEDIUM

Watercolour

SERIES/PERIOD/MOVEMENT

Late period landscapes

SIMILAR WORKS

Melting Snow by Pal Szinyei Merse, 1884–95

The Rocks, 1927

Mackintosh, though much happier, still struggled with self-confidence issues and his laboriously slow working process was in part a reflection of this. He would continually return to a canvas over a period of time and wrote to Margaret in 1927, 'I find that each of my drawings has something in them, but none of them have everything'.

He was, however, pleased with the finished canvas *The Rocks*, a startling composition combining whimsical natural formations contrasted against the rhythmic regularity of man-made structures. He worked on the picture for a long time, over a month, before being satisfied with it. Correspondence with Margaret affords us a glimpse of his interesting working process, 'I have an insane aptitude for seeing green and putting it down here, there and everywhere the very first thing – this habit complicates every colour scheme... *The Rocks* has some green, and now I see that instead of painting this first I should have painted the grey rock first then I probably would have no real green. But that's one of my minor curses – green-green-green...'.

CREATED

France

MEDIUM

Pencil and watercolour

SERIES/PERIOD/MOVEMENT

Late period landscapes

SIMILAR WORKS

We are Making a New World by Paul Nash, 1918

Collioure, c. 1923–24

Charles and Margaret first moved to Collioure from London and spent some time here before settling in Port Vendres. Only two paintings of Collioure exist, this one and *Collioure, Pyrénées-Orientales – Summer Palace of the Queens of Aragon*. It is likely that Charles spent much of his time here painting scenes from the landscape surrounding the small town. Port Vendres itself was only a short walk away and the hillsides provided many of the scenic forts that he favoured. This depiction of Collioure was probably painted shortly after their arrival in France and it is interesting to note the similarities between his treatment of the reflections in the water and some of his late textile designs. One of the most distinctive qualities about Mackintosh's landscapes was his lack of concern with depicting movement. His main aesthetic quest was for pattern and the correlation of organic and inorganic forms. The design quality to his pictures is further clarified through his handling of colour to evoke the brilliance of the Mediterranean sun and the contrast of sun and shadow.

CREATED

France

MEDIUM

Watercolour

SERIES/PERIOD/MOVEMENT

Late period landscapes

SIMILAR WORKS

Etude – Anvers by Othon Friesz, 1906

THE W
Mackintosh
GREAT

Influences

White oval side table

To appreciate Mackintosh's development fully, as one of the most innovative design talents of his time, although perhaps the least recognized, it is important to view the climate of artistic change preceding and during his evolution as an artist. In Scotland there was a resurgence of national pride, fuelled by a Celtic Revival and kept alive through the writings of Patrick Geddes and his followers during the 1890s. The Glasgow style was taking shape and quickly became synonymous with the Glasgow School of Art. In England the Arts and Crafts movement was firmly established with the influence of William Morris (1834–96) extending across to the Continent. There, Art Nouveau had emerged as a conscious style in Brussels and spread through France and Germany, and in Vienna the Secessionists were challenging the conservative Viennese Academy of Arts.

Since the 1860s there had been an increasing influx of Oriental decoration and art that played a significant part in the development of artistic trends. The simple clean lines of this oval white-painted table and minimal decorative features display an appreciation of Japanese furniture design combined with Art Nouveau elements.

CREATED

Glasgow

MEDIUM

Painted wood

SERIES/PERIOD/MOVEMENT

Furniture designs

SIMILAR WORKS

Mahogany occasional table by M. H. Baillie Scott, *c.* 1906

Charles Rennie Mackintosh *Born* 1868 Glasgow, Scotland

Died 1928

78 Derngate, Northampton: design for the staircase screen in the hall, 1916

The commission to redecorate and design Derngate for Mr Bassett-Lowke was one of the few architectural projects that Mackintosh received while living in London. His treatment of the difficult and cramped interior space was startlingly modern in concept and has been compared to the French architect, Auguste Perret's (1874–1954) work in reinforced concrete on the apartment at No. 25 Rue Franklin in Paris, 1903. Whether Perret's work was known to Mackintosh is a point for conjecture, but worth considering. Peter Behrens (1868–1940) later designed New Ways, for the Bassett-Lowkes in 1925. This building has been claimed as the first true example of modern architecture in domestic buildings in England, although it seems reflective of Mackintosh's progressive design concept. The strongly geometric patterning of the screen and the bold colours anticipate the later development of Art Deco in the 1920s and 1930s. His use of triangular motifs is similar to the work of the Viennese artist Josef Urban (1872–1933), whose designs Mackintosh would have been familiar with. The decorative elements of Mackintosh's early career had by this point largely evolved into a more direct and sturdy functionalism, especially evident in his furniture designs at Derngate.

CREATED

Northampton

MEDIUM

Pencil and watercolour on wove paper

SERIES/PERIOD/MOVEMENT

Derngate

SIMILAR WORKS

Screen with geometric design by Eileen Gray, *c.*1928

Design for a room, 1885

The Arts and Crafts movement that developed through the latter years of the nineteenth century was significantly influential in changing the tide of design from Victorian extravaganza to something altogether more morally appeasing. It was Ruskin's words that laid the foundations for the principles of the Arts and Crafts movement, whose reality was formalized chiefly through the unstinting doctrines of the socialist William Morris. Mackintosh greatly admired John Ruskin, and his book *Stones of Venice* accompanied Mackintosh on his Italian tour. W. R. Lethaby who trained as an architect in the offices of Norman Shaw (1831–1912) and circulated within the Arts and Crafts circle, published his book, *Architecture, Mysticism and Myth*, in 1892. This was to prove so impressive to the young Mackintosh, that he based his 1893 lecture on Lethaby's text. Lethaby was a great proponent of learning from ancient building techniques and materials in order to revive vernacular forms of architecture.

This unusual design for a room is indicative of Lethaby's aim for a modern vision through the use of historic features, although lacks a cohesiveness. The drawing was probably exhibited at the first Arts and Crafts Society Exhibition in 1888.

CREATED

London

MEDIUM

Pen and brown ink, watercolour and coloured chalks, heightened with white

SERIES/PERIOD/MOVEMENT

Arts and Crafts

SIMILAR WORKS

Upper Landing at Red House, Kent by Philip Webb, 1859

William Richard Lethaby *Born* 1857 Barnstaple, Devon

Died 1931

Table with carved and chamfered decoration, 1852

Augustus Pugin, the intellectual and architect, was a revolutionary designer and a key figure in the Gothic Revival. His theories rested on the concept of form for function, that the external appearance of the building should be reflective of its internal organization and that architecture should be imbued with a moral dimension. This sparked great debate, fuelling rivalry between the Gothic Revivalists and the Classicists of Victorian England. His ideas were further propagated through the Ecclesiological Society, formed in 1839. William Butterfield and G. E. Street, both members of the society, promoted the case for Gothic architecture within 'modern' society through their innovative architectural designs. At the core of Mackintosh's design beliefs also lay the 'form for function' premise, his asymmetrical façades and unusual designs symptomatic of his internal spatial arrangement, although one was never at the expense of the other.

The table pictured here was made to Pugin's designs by J. G. Crace and demonstrates the simple construction and pure lines typical of Gothic Revival furniture.

CREATED

Sussex

MEDIUM

Oak

SERIES/PERIOD/MOVEMENT

Gothic Revival

SIMILAR WORKS

Trestle table by Philip Webb

Augustus Welby Northmore Pugin *Born* 1812 London, England

Died 1852

Stylized Rose

Mackintosh had loved nature since he was a small boy. This passion was at first generated by time spent gardening with his father in the family's garden and later through long walks in the country, prescribed by his doctor on medical grounds. Nature would prove to be one of the greatest and most long-lived sources of inspiration to the artist, culminating in his eventual career as a landscape and still-life painter. The rose motif, along with the tulip, was one of his favourites and he would return to it again and again in varying form. It was adopted by the Glasgow Four, whose distinctive style quickly provoked considerable interest. The Glasgow Four evolved their own artistic language from the decorative Glasgow style of the late 1880s, seen in the work of George Henry (1858–1943) and E. A. Hornel (1864–1933). The Glasgow style and the Glasgow School of Art became synonymous, flowering under the auspicious leadership of Francis Newbery who was elected Director of the School in 1885. Newbery, who moved to Glasgow from England, encouraged his students to look beyond Scotland and to study artistic trends from England and abroad.

CREATED

Glasgow

MEDIUM

Watercolour

SERIES/PERIOD/MOVEMENT

Decorative

SIMILAR WORKS

Fire screen panel by Johnann McCrae

Rose Motif, The Hill House, Helensburgh, *c.* 1902–03

The evolution of the Glasgow style and that of the Glasgow Four was symptomatic of a widespread rejection of conventional art in favour of a new direction. The exuberance of Art Nouveau, which was so popular on the Continent, had largely been ridiculed in England, a fact that made the style all the more readily accepted into the vocabulary of the forward-thinking young Scots. The simple stylized imagery and use of motifs seen in the increasingly popular Oriental art was also influential in the development of the Glasgow style, which took these elements and translated them into a Scottish idiom. Art was flourishing in Glasgow and not just in painterly circles. There was a huge interest in the decorative arts, metalwork, glasswork and textiles, with much of the renewed enthusiasm attributed to the direction of Francis Newbery.

The Hill House was commissioned by Walter Blackie in 1902 and is considered to be one of the most successful domestic buildings that Mackintosh completed. In contrast to the Scottish vernacular treatment of the exterior, the interior is evocative of Oriental influence and has a continuing theme of the rose motif.

CREATED

Glasgow

MEDIUM

Stained glass

SERIES/PERIOD/MOVEMENT

Hill House

SIMILAR WORKS

Leather tooled book cover with rose motif, artist unknown

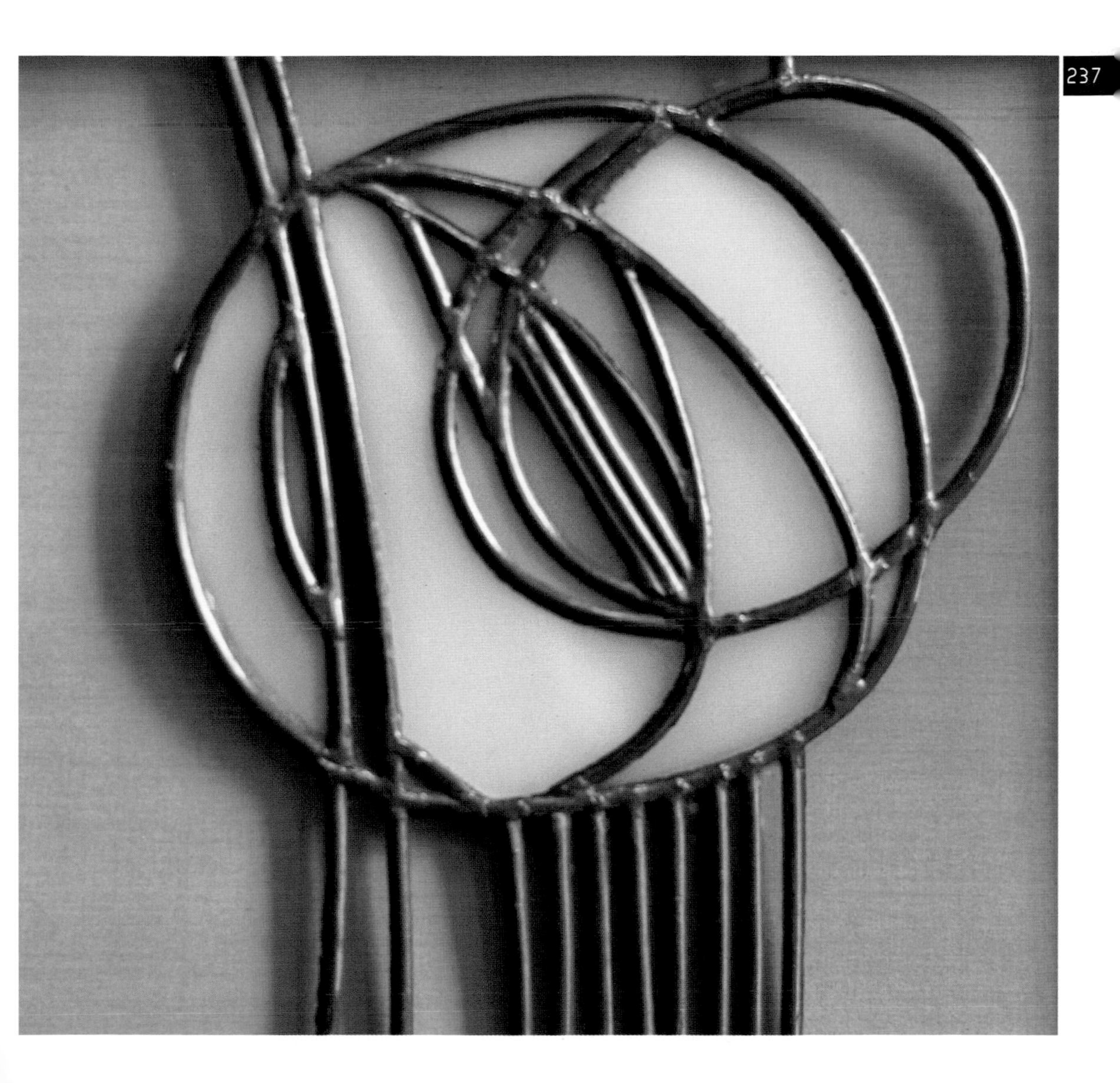

Detail of a design for a printed textile

The influence on Mackintosh of the Arts and Crafts movement, spearheaded by William Morris, was significant, especially through the ideas of W. R. Lethaby. Although the Glasgow Four moved away from the Arts and Crafts movement in spirit, the two groups shared a common preoccupation with organic forms and nature as a source for inspiration. The Four were invited to exhibit at the London Arts and Crafts Society Exhibition in 1896 although it proved to be a disaster for them.

The rose motif was one that Mackintosh continued to use through his career, from the early days of the Glasgow Four to the later London years when he made frequent use of the stylized flower form in his textile designs. The design pictured here could have been intended for use as a handkerchief border and demonstrates his synthesis of organic form into a geometric context, a method of designing that he finally evolved through his landscape paintings of southern France. His textile designs with their vibrant colours and strong linear boldness anticipated the emergence of Art Deco, the style of the 1920s and 1930s.

CREATED

Glasgow

MEDIUM

Watercolour

SERIES/PERIOD/MOVEMENT

Textile designs

SIMILAR WORKS

Rose embroidered cushion cover by Jessie Newbery, *c.* 1900

Detail from a display cabinet made for 14 Kingsborough Gardens, Glasgow, 1902

The pieces that the Four chose to exhibit at the Arts and Crafts Exhibition in 1896 were severely criticized and ridiculed. The group were unkindly labelled the 'Spook School' and the mystical, ethereal nature of their elongated female forms misinterpreted. The exhibition marked a parting of ways between the Arts and Crafts proponents and the style of the Four. The only good to come from their disastrous 1896 exhibition was that Gleeson White of *The Studio* magazine spotted and liked their work. *The Studio* would go on to be virtually the only publication to give them any positive publicity.

The influence of Oriental imagery can be seen in the detail pictured. The elegantly stylized figure is also reflective of the work of the Symbolists and Aesthetes and the Viennese Secessionists. Mackintosh exhibited in Vienna in 1900 and in Turin in 1902. His influence, and that of the Four, was later seen in the work of the Secessionists, especially in Gustav Klimt's (1862–1918) *Beethoven Frieze* (1902) exhibited at the Fourteenth Exhibition of the Vienna Secession.

CREATED

Glasgow

MEDIUM

Painted oak

SERIES/PERIOD/MOVEMENT

Furniture designs

SIMILAR WORKS

The White Rose and the Red Rose by Margaret Macdonald Mackintosh, *c.* 1902

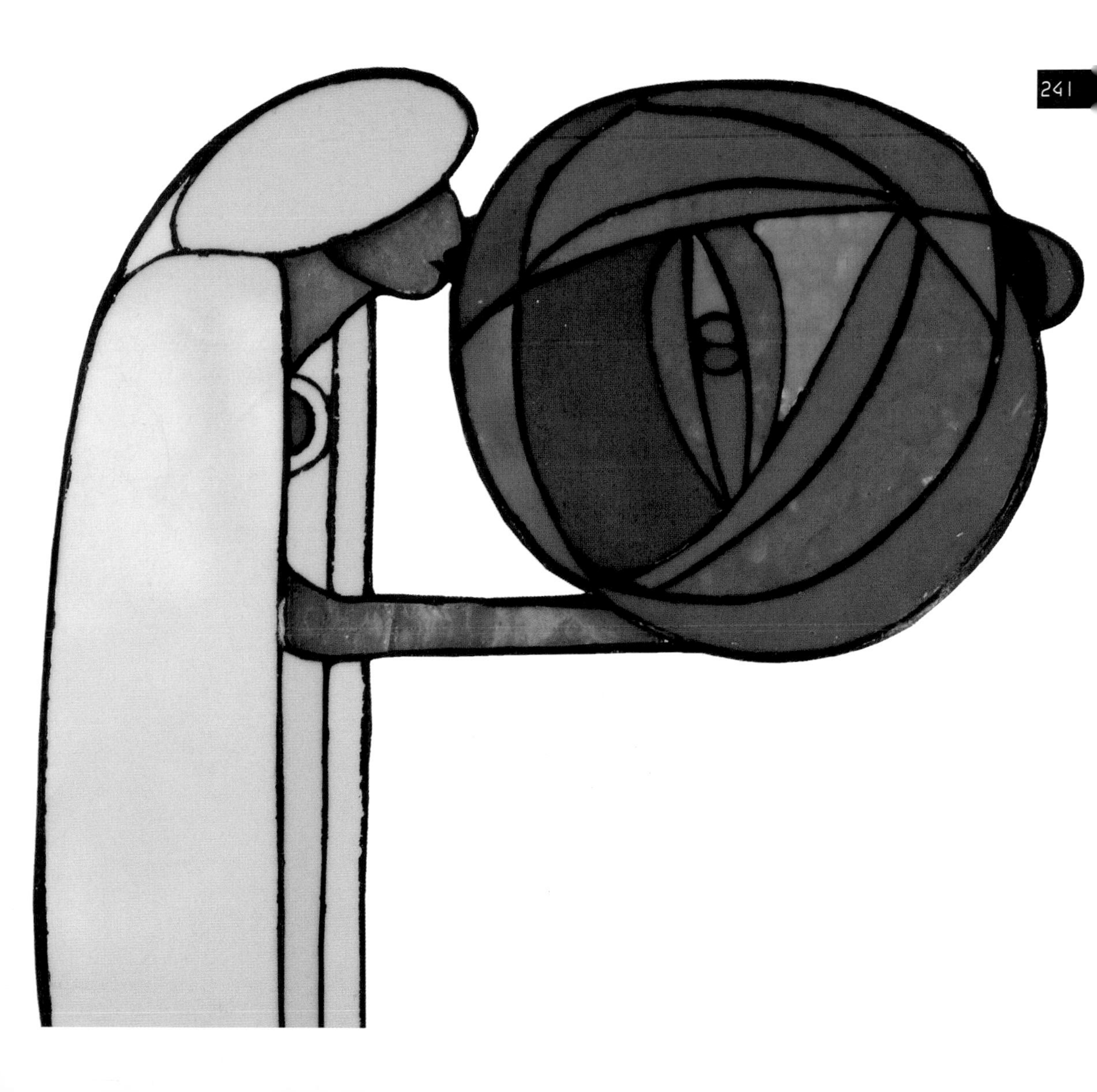

Metal and leaded-glass hanging shade, *c.* 1900

Part of Mackintosh's brilliance lay in his astonishing ability to encompass all the arts. He was the consummate designer, from planning buildings to designing furniture, light fittings, cutlery, fabrics and painting. His designs for hanging lampshades and lights were among the most innovative of his time and drew heavily on inspiration from nature and natural forms. The blue petal motif seen on this glass shade was one that he used frequently and was seen again in many of his textile designs. It was an organic shape that was favoured by Mackintosh and his contemporaries and can be seen in the painting *Emile Flüge* by Gustav Klimt. The Pre-Raphaelites, and most especially the work of Dante Gabriel Rossetti (1828–82), were also influential on the style of the Four, who adopted their jewel-like colours and love of natural forms. Many of Mackintosh's light fittings were designed to hang, appearing to float in the room. He would often group several shades together such as those clustered over the central table in the School of Art Library, which would take on an organic mantle, part flower, part foliage, part tree top, part sunlight.

CREATED

Glasgow

MEDIUM

Metal and leaded glass

SERIES/PERIOD/MOVEMENT

Fixture and fitting designs

SIMILAR WORKS

Stained-glass flower motif in window at Blackwell by M. H. Baillie Scott, *c.* 1898–1900

Yellow Clover, 1901

Mackintosh was highly skilled as a draughtsman and had sketched and drawn quite independently from his lessons at the Glasgow School of Art. After meeting Herbert MacNair through the offices of Honeyman and Keppie, the two would go off on sketching trips into the surrounding countryside. Drawing at first from nature the two friends gradually developed a new graphic style of their own; part nature, part stylized. In 1901 Mackintosh travelled to Holy Island in Northumberland on holiday, making sketches of the flowers that he saw there. The Holy Island sketches hold a significant place within his oeuvre because they show him in a transitional stage. He was beginning to add colour to his studies, but still tentatively. By the time he painted *Yellow Tulips* around 1922 he had found a definitive method of expression.

In his lecture 'Seemliness' Mackintosh urged, 'Art is the flower – life the green leaf. Let every artist strive to make his flower a beautiful living thing, something that will convince the world that there may be; that there are things more precious, more beautiful, more lasting than life'.

CREATED

Holy Island, Northumberland

MEDIUM

Pencil and watercolour

SERIES/PERIOD/MOVEMENT

Flower studies

SIMILAR WORKS

Sketch from Nature by Jessie Keppie, 1895

YELLOW CLOVER,
HOLY ISLAND
JULY 1901

The Garden at The Hill House, Helensburgh, by Jane Younger

Walter Blackie commissioned Mackintosh to design The Hill House in 1902, on the advice of Talwin Morris. Morris was Art Director at Blackie's publishing firm and was a keen collector of the Fours' work. The Hill House is now widely regarded as Mackintosh's most successful and cohesive domestic building, with Windyhill a close second. Typical of Mackintosh's meticulous attention to detail, it is thought that he spent some time staying with the Blackie family in order to evaluate their lifestyle and domestic requirements. In this way he was able to design a home that would fully encompass all of their needs. Part of the success of the house was based on the ideal building site that Blackie had acquired, a hillside site overlooking the Clyde Estuary. Mackintosh was especially sensitive to location and integrated the house within its surroundings to its best advantage. As was customary of his visionary design technique he took traditional Scottish vernacular architecture as his point of departure and made it into an entirely modern statement. This unusual painting of the garden by Jane Younger reflects both Oriental and Symbolist influences, both of which could be discerned in Mackintosh's treatment of the interiors.

CREATED

Glasgow

MEDIUM

Watercolour

SERIES/PERIOD/MOVEMENT

The Hill House

SIMILAR WORKS

Pandora by Odilon Redon, *c.* 1910

Blackthorn, 1910

After Charles's marriage to Margaret Macdonald in 1900, there was a change in his pattern of sketching. He executed more sketches with a greater degree of finish from one location, with the addition of colour washes and his distinctive signature box. Roger Billcliffe makes the valid point in his book *Mackintosh Watercolours* (1992) that this was due to the addition of a wife. Mackintosh's holidays were now spent in one place for a longer period of time, rather than the pit-stop sketching trips of his bachelor days. On his trip to Chiddingstone, Kent, in 1910 Mackintosh made a number of exquisite watercolour studies of flowers that reflect his interest in Oriental art, especially seen in his painting of *Japonica*, 1910. His inclusion of a signature box, generally providing the date of the picture, the location, title and his initials, is also interesting. Invariably the initials of Margaret, Herbert MacNair and others would appear alongside his own. Rather than this being an indication of other people contributing to his work, it is thought to represent the people who were present with him while he was sketching.

CREATED

Chiddingstone, Kent

MEDIUM

Pencil and watercolour

SERIES/PERIOD/MOVEMENT

Flower studies

SIMILAR WORKS

April by Katharine Cameron

BLACKTHORN
CHIDDINGSTONE
1910 KENT
CRM MMM

Butterfly Flower, 1912

By 1912 Mackintosh's career had started its inevitably tragic decline. The glory years faded with the completion of the West Wing of the Glasgow School of Art in 1909 and from that point on his commissions began to dry up. The relationship between Mackintosh and John Keppie had started to deteriorate, a process that resulted in the dissolution of their partnership in 1913. Mackintosh became increasingly depressed, difficult to work with and for, and erratic in his behaviour. His vision of leading the arts forward in a new direction had failed. Where he had hoped for recognition and appreciation for a style born from the Scottish tradition and matured into the realization of modernity, he found criticism, ridicule and total incomprehension.

He continued to work for Miss Cranston, an enlightened and sympathetic patron. In 1912 he designed the White Cockade exhibition café for her and the same year travelled to Bowling, Dumbartonshire, where he made a number of flower studies. The combination of pattern and colour within an organic context seen in his *Butterfly Flower* looks back to the tradition of William Morris and anticipates the bold textile patterns that Mackintosh would design in London.

CREATED

Bowling, Dumbartonshire

MEDIUM

Watercolour

SERIES/PERIOD/MOVEMENT

Flower studies

SIMILAR WORKS

Daisy 2 wallpaper design by William Morris, 1864

BUTTERFLY FLOWER
BOWLING 1912
CRM — MMM

Fritillaria, 1915

After resigning from Honeyman and Keppie in 1913 Mackintosh continued to try and practise from home. It proved fruitless and finally in despair Charles and Margaret left Glasgow and moved to Walberswick on the east coast, before settling in London. Parallels are drawn between the working life of Mackintosh and that of the innovative American architect, Frank Lloyd Wright (1867–1959). Like Mackintosh, Wright initially worked for a firm of architects, Adler and Sullivan, but found the working practice of the formalized office environment claustrophobic and frustrating. When Wright resigned and set up on his own he did so within a more liberally minded and progressive climate, making an initially successful foray into private practice. Mackintosh was not so fortunate.

The flower studies made at Walberswick are among the most finely drawn in his work, combining a high degree of botanical correctness within a stylized context – a distinctly Mackintosh language of expression. The chequerboard pattern on the petals of *Fritillaria* was a motif that he favoured and had used extensively in the Willow Tea Rooms scheme. In this painting he extends the geometric pattern into his signature box, further exemplifying his penchant for unity in his designs.

CREATED

Walberswick

MEDIUM

Pencil and watercolour

SERIES/PERIOD/MOVEMENT

Flower studies

SIMILAR WORKS

L'Agonie des Fleurs by Theodore Roussel, 1911–12

FRITILLARIA
WALBERSWICK
1 9 1 5
CRM
MMM

Floral and checked fabric design, *c.* 1916

Mackintosh's vision had developed from the 'white interior' period of his early designs in Glasgow to a modern concept of design articulated through his bold patterns and bright colours. The fine decorative detailing born from the Scottish equivalent of Art Nouveau and the Four's ethereal mysticism was now replaced with a startlingly vivid new language. Here he combines a stylized organic motif with a strong geometric chequerboard pattern, a contrasting method of expression that he utilized frequently. His use of distorted perspective creates the illusion of an undulating motion through the centre of his design. This further contrasts with the flowers, the organic element, that are totally flat and stylized; as such he inverts the rationale of organic to geometric. As is the case with innovators of style, Mackintosh's textile designs preceded that which was to come. By the time the bold colours and designs of Art Deco were seen at the Exposition des Arts Décoratifs in Paris in 1925, Mackintosh had turned his back on architecture and designing and was pursuing a career as a watercolourist.

CREATED

London

MEDIUM

Pencil and body colour on tracing paper

SERIES/PERIOD/MOVEMENT

Textile design

SIMILAR WORKS

Ameise by Eduard J. Wimmer-Wisgrill, 1910–11

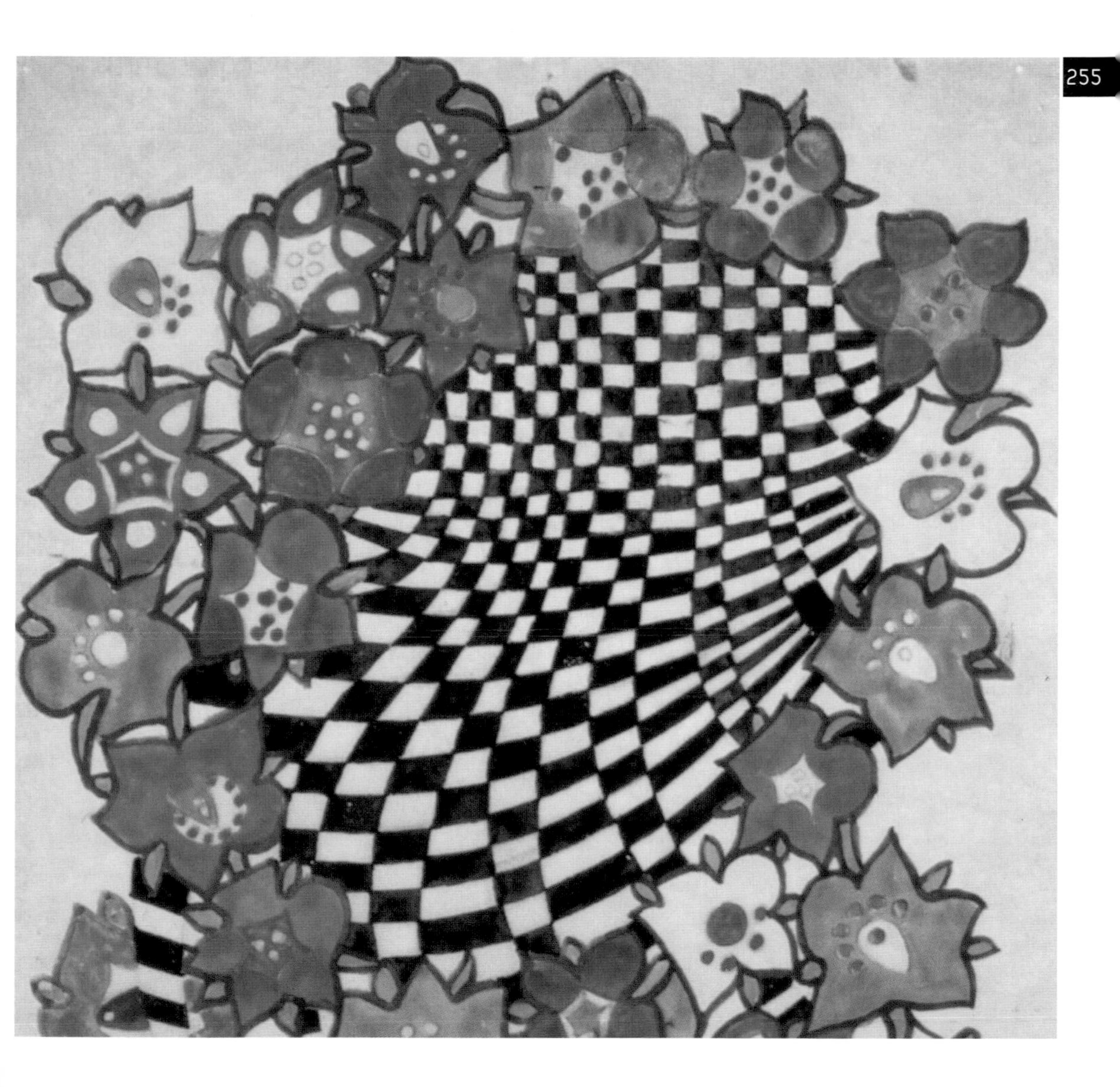

Still Life of Anemones, c. 1915

In his 1902 lecture, 'Seemliness', Mackintosh likened art to a flower and rallied his audience to draw from, 'flowers that grow from but above the green leaf – flowers that are not dead – are not dying – not artificial – real flowers springing from your own soul – not even cut flowers ...'. The message of truth to oneself, to cultivate an artistic expression born from within in honesty sits beside the obvious literal interpretation of his words. Through his early career he did draw directly from nature. By the time of *Anemones*, he had turned to the depiction of cut flowers. The greater symbolic meaning provides significant content for debate. Did Mackintosh now feel that his artistic expression was something entirely different? That he no longer could draw from within his soul? Or perhaps the fallen petals of the *Anemones* painting suggest the realization that his artistic vision would not be fulfiled?

This was one of his earliest pictures of cut flowers and was probably painted shortly after his arrival in London. Visible in the painting behind the flowers is a swatch of one of his fabric designs.

CREATED

London

MEDIUM

Watercolour, pencil and gouache

SERIES/PERIOD/MOVEMENT

Still life

SIMILAR WORKS

St Pancras Lilies by Paul Nash, 1927

Mont Louis Flower Study (detail), 1925

Mont Louis in the Pyrenees was one of the places that the Mackintoshes stayed at before finally settling in Port Vendres. When Charles and Margaret left London in 1923 Mackintosh closed yet another door in his life, turning his back on designing and architecture and taking up landscape painting instead. The influence of other artists and architects on Mackintosh, varied during his career. During early days of the Four in Glasgow clear links to the work of other artists could be discerned through their evolving style. Mackintosh alienated himself from his contemporaries during his architectural endeavours and was not able to spearhead the 'new movement' that he so wanted to. The move to London was a bold one, the Mackintoshes' work was little known in England and what was known had been poorly received. Their final move, to France, isolated the couple still further both culturally and geographically from the artistic climate of their contemporaries. His flower studies in France were the summation of a career experimenting with colour, form and pattern, a brilliant display of botanical awareness shot through with the irrepressible eye of a modern master.

CREATED

Mont Louis, France

MEDIUM

Pencil and watercolour

SERIES/PERIOD/MOVEMENT

Flower study, late period

SIMILAR WORKS

Title page of *The Craftsman's Plant Book*, artist unknown, 1909

Pine Cones, 1925

After moving to France Mackintosh concentrated primarily on landscape painting, his work developing in an entirely original manner, as one would expect. His strongly linear style, broad bold colours and play on two-dimensional and three-dimensional effects were not to be seen in the work of his contemporaries, with the possible exception of Paul Nash (1889–1946). Before devoting himself to landscapes he completed a small number of flower studies, done at Mont Louis in the Pyrenees. These reflect his earlier studies made at Walberswick in spirit, but were more vivid and jewel-like with a greater stylization. *Pine Cones*, with its brilliant greens and reds, almost takes on the appearance of enamel, which then contrasts with the delicate fronds behind. Another study, *Mixed Flowers, Mont Louis*, 1925, again positively zings with vibrant colour and includes the metamorphosis of stylized bird heads from the petals. These paintings were the last of his botanical works and represent his enduring embracement of nature. In letters to Margaret written in 1927 he wrote of his delight at the spring time 'fairyland' of flowers.

CREATED

Mont Louis, France

MEDIUM

Pencil and watercolour

SERIES/PERIOD/MOVEMENT

Flower study, late period

SIMILAR WORKS

Iris Iberica by F. H. Round, 1913

MONT
LOUIS
1925

Design with stylized bird motif

Mackintosh often returned to the same motifs in his textile designs, most commonly employing stylized flowers, birds and a widespread use of strong geometric patterns. The bird motif was one that sprang from the decorative Oriental works that were in wide circulation at this time. James Abbott McNeill Whistler (1834–1903), who had lived in Chelsea before Mackintosh had settled there, had been strongly influenced by Oriental design and design practices, the Peacock Room that he devised for F. R. Leyland being a case in point. Aubrey Beardsley (1872–98) whose distinctive sinuous illustrations had been influential on the style of the Four in the Glasgow days was also an avid collector of Oriental art.

Here the vibrant blue and green is evocative of the eye of the peacock feather, with the flowing organic lines strongly contrasting against the rhythmic triangular pattern. The bold overlaid lines and distortion of perspective through the chequerboards is suggestive of early Cubist works, a movement that had surfaced around 1909 in the work of Pablo Picasso (1881–1973) and Georges Bracques (1882–1963). Mackintosh executed a similar design to this, Tendrils, Squares and Triangles, that again combines organic lines against a wall of repeated triangles.

CREATED

London

MEDIUM

Pencil and watercolour

SERIES/PERIOD/MOVEMENT

London designs

SIMILAR WORKS

Landscape with House, Dog and Cow by Franz Marc, 1914

Stylized floral design on trellis background, *c.* 1918

The numerous surviving sketches that Mackintosh made for designs are interesting because they afford us a glimpse at the process with which he built up his finished piece. In many cases he first drew a pencil grid on his paper and then worked his design up from the grid base, such as in *Flowering Bulb*. In this pattern with the stylized flowers on a trellis he actually incorporated his grid lines into the design to form his trellis. The trellis motif with flowers has Oriental associations, but is more obviously an example of Mackintosh's continued method of contrasting organic forms with geometric shapes. His art and architecture were grounded in the use of opposites. To Mackintosh the play of light in his interiors was singularly important to him and he manipulated his rooms accordingly, moving from a light and airy drawing room into a sombre darker dining room, a formula that he used throughout his career. His approach to design was similarly based on contrast and surprise.

CREATED

London

MEDIUM

Pencil and watercolour

SERIES/PERIOD/MOVEMENT

London designs

SIMILAR WORKS

Designs for printed cretonnes by Jessie M. King, 1917

Interior view of Queen's Cross Church, Glasgow, 1897

Queen's Cross Church, which was turned into the headquarters for the Charles Rennie Mackintosh Society in 1977, is one of the earliest examples of the architect truly synthesizing traditional and modern elements to produce a cohesive expression of his innovative vision. The exterior of the church is at once recognizable by the tower, which is similar to the tower of the Merriot Church in Somerset that Mackintosh had visited and sketched two years previously. The façade looks to the Gothic tradition, especially in the window treatments, but has been expressed with Mackintosh's own language of organic detailing. On the interior, the lofty barrel-vaulted ceiling has been compared by the C. R. Mackintosh Society to that of the Basilica of Vicenza that Mackintosh would have studied during his Italian tour of 1891 and clearly draws on the influence of Norman Shaw's Harrow Mission Church, Holy Trinity, 1887, situated on the Latimer Road, London. One of the most striking aspects of Queen's Cross is the contrast between the busy exterior of Gothic extraction with the eternally restful and spacious interior presided over by the fantastically unexpected barrel-vaulted roof.

CREATED

Glasgow

MEDIUM

Interior design

SERIES/PERIOD/MOVEMENT

Early architectural designs

SIMILAR WORKS

Holy Trinity Church by Norman Shaw, 1887

EXIT
EXIT

Detail of a beam above the altar at Queen's Cross Church, 1897

Through the treatment of the interior of Queen's Cross Mackintosh made bold use of the structural elements, leaving the steel crossbeams exposed. In this way, and typical of Mackintosh's holistic approach to his designing, the very structure of the building fills both fundamental and decorative functions. He used ironwork through the whole scheme from the crossbeams to the iron railings, contrasting the natural wood elements with industrial steel. The decorative detailing used is reminiscent of Celtic imagery, something that Mackintosh frequently drew on for inspiration, as seen here, and organic motifs associated with the style of the Four. The tree design carved on the outside of the pulpit was a motif with decorative and symbolic functions for Mackintosh who returned to it again and again through his architectural designs and decorative work. His use of traditional building elements with industrial materials was another working practice that typifies his modern approach to architecture. By the time he began work on Queen's Cross he had completed the drawings for the Glasgow School of Art, where his audacious mix of traditional and modern was realized in perfect harmony.

CREATED

Glasgow

MEDIUM

Interior design

SERIES/PERIOD/MOVEMENT

Early architectural designs

SIMILAR WORKS

Window latch from Blackwell by M. H. Baillie Scott, *c.* 1898–1900

Brass alms tray with enamel insets by Mary Gilmour, 1901

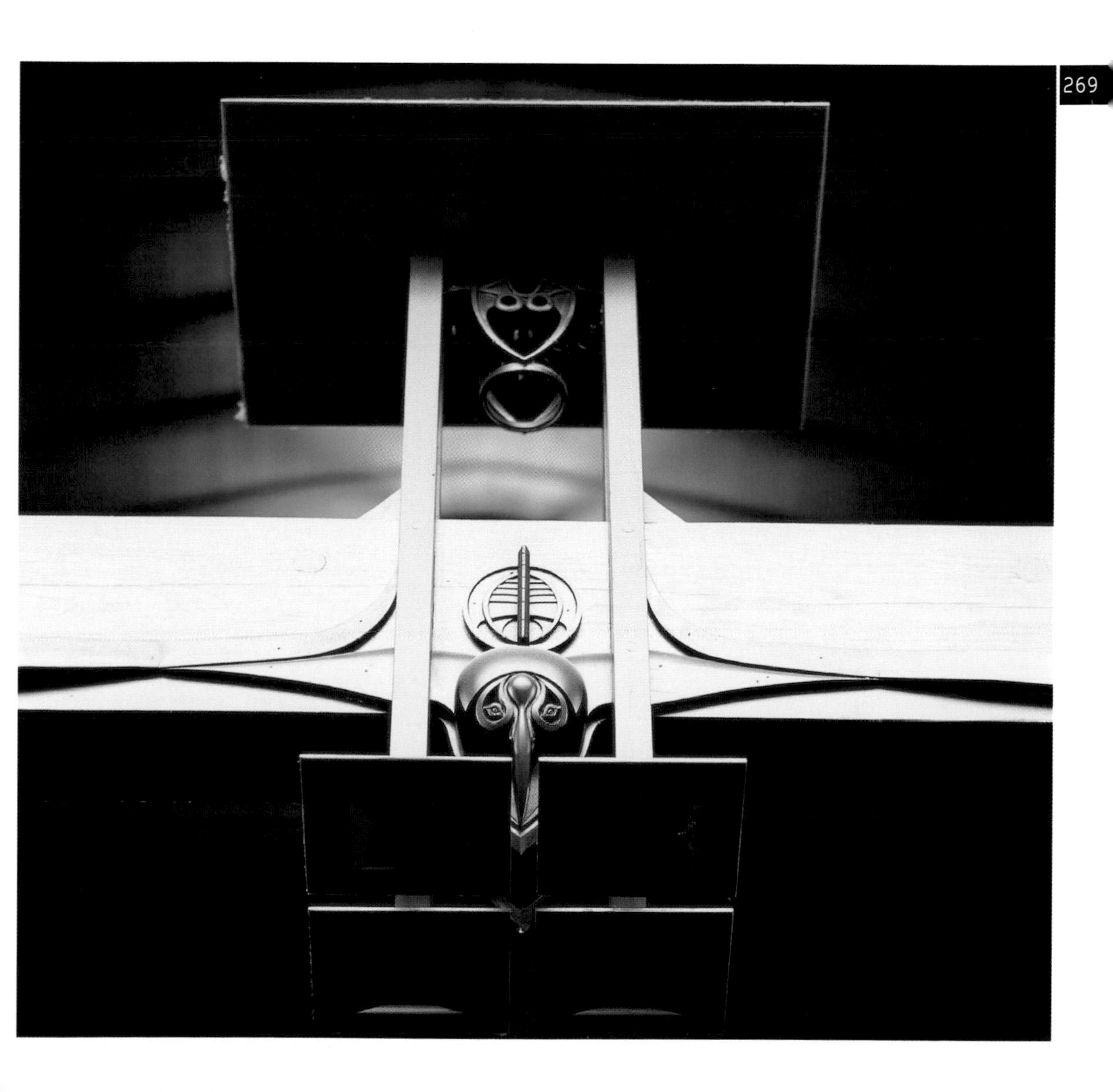

Lornes cabinet with painted panels by Margaret Macdonald Mackintosh

Although Mackintosh was one of the members of the Four in Glasgow during the last years of the nineteenth century, his work gradually developed in a new direction from their particular style. He remains the best known of the four young artists, but his work was the least representative of their aims. The evolution of the Four's particularly distinctive style came about through a number of early influences. The elaborately decorative works employing Celtic imagery and vibrant colours by George Henry and E. A. Hornel were undoubtedly significant examples to the Four. The Pre-Raphaelites under the leadership of Dante Gabriel Rossetti, too, provided inspiration, as did the Aesthetic movement. Margaret, whose work is so often overshadowed by Charles, was an accomplished and visionary artist in her own right. The panels are strongly evocative and a new twist on the Byzantine icon tradition. The elongated figures recall the work of Edvard Munch (1863–1944) and Gustav Klimt, the colours and inlaid gold, that of Henry and Hornel in *The Druids*, 1889. Her use of Celtic detailing on the frame reflects the interest in the Celtic Revival.

CREATED

Glasgow

MEDIUM

Ebonized and painted wood

SERIES/PERIOD/MOVEMENT

Work of the Four

SIMILAR WORKS

Beethoven Frieze, The Hostile Powers by Gustav Klimt, 1902

Four Painted Panels by William Morris, Dante Gabriel Rossetti and Edward Burne-Jones, *c.* 1857

Opera of the Seas, 1903

This decorative gesso panel by Margaret is typical of the eerily symbolic and mystical works of the Four, especially seen in the work of Margaret and Frances Macdonald. Aubrey Beardsley's powerfully sinister graphic works, most notably his illustrations for *The Yellow Book* first published in 1894 and for Oscar Wilde's *Salome*, were of some consequence in the development of Margaret's style. Beardsley was a keen collector of Japanese art and artefacts as were Whistler and Rossetti. In *Opera of the Seas* the idiom of Japanese art can clearly be felt and the rhythmic repetition of line and form suggests Beardsley. Symbolism was a movement that was becoming increasingly popular through Europe at this time and the symbolic content of Margaret's work is significant. The Dutch artist Jan Toorop (1858–1928) was also influential on Margaret's style with his particular brand of Art Nouveau and Symbolism. However, as much as the young artists drew from the examples of those around them, they also evolved a unique tradition of their own. *Opera of the Seas* is the dreamy, lyrical, melancholic manifestation of Margaret's early work as a designer.

CREATED

Glasgow

MEDIUM

Gesso panel

SERIES/PERIOD/MOVEMENT

Work of the Four

SIMILAR WORKS

The Three Brides by Jan Toorop, 1893

When Iceflakes Fell by Frances Macdonald MacNair, *c.* 1900

Margaret Macdonald Mackintosh *Born* 1864 Tipton, Wolverhampton

Died 1933

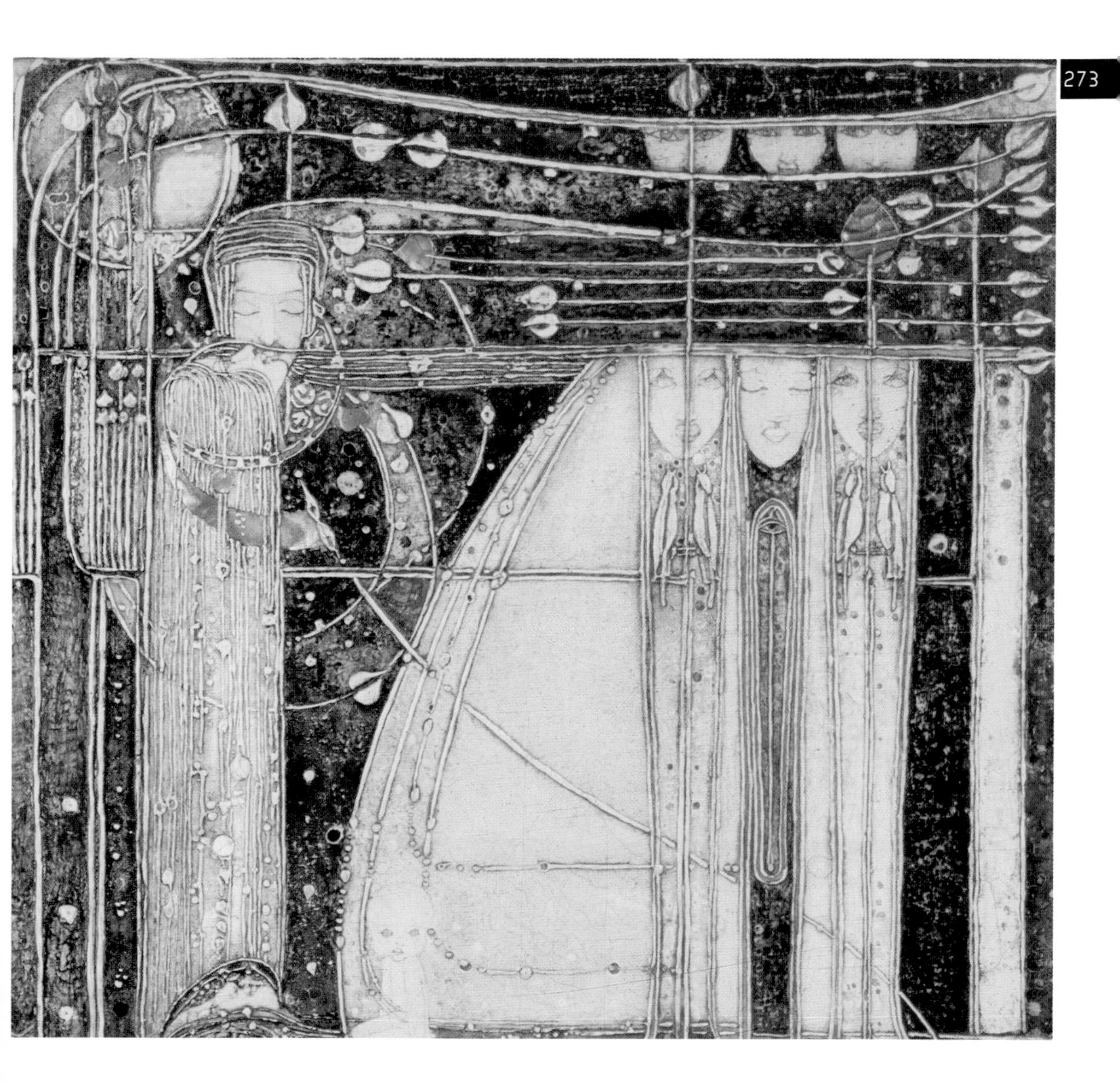

Blue and pink tobacco flower design

Mackintosh produced a series of designs incorporating the tobacco flower, the majority of which were executed in zinging colours: blues, reds, pinks and greens contrasting with bold geometric black and white. His tobacco flower designs were inspired by the decorative detail on Margaret's gesso panel, *Opera of the Seas*. Her original gesso panel done in 1903 was conceived as a decorative panel for the Wärndorfer Music Room in Vienna designed by Mackintosh. A later work with the same title was then painted by Margaret and Charles and formed part of a group of seven gesso panels that were exhibited in 1916 under the group title, *Voices in the Woods*. The blue and pink tobacco flower design was taken from the flowers in the hair of one of the figures, and a surviving tracing directly from the painting shows Mackintosh in the early stages of developing his flower designs. His working process experimenting with different colour combinations and graphic interpretations can be seen through the repeated adjacent patterns. This is a technique he often used, seen, for example, in his working drawings entitled *Stylized Foliage and Flowers*.

CREATED

London

MEDIUM

Pencil, watercolour and gouache

SERIES/PERIOD/MOVEMENT

London designs

SIMILAR WORKS

Dynamics of Colour by Alexandra Exter, *c.* 1916–18

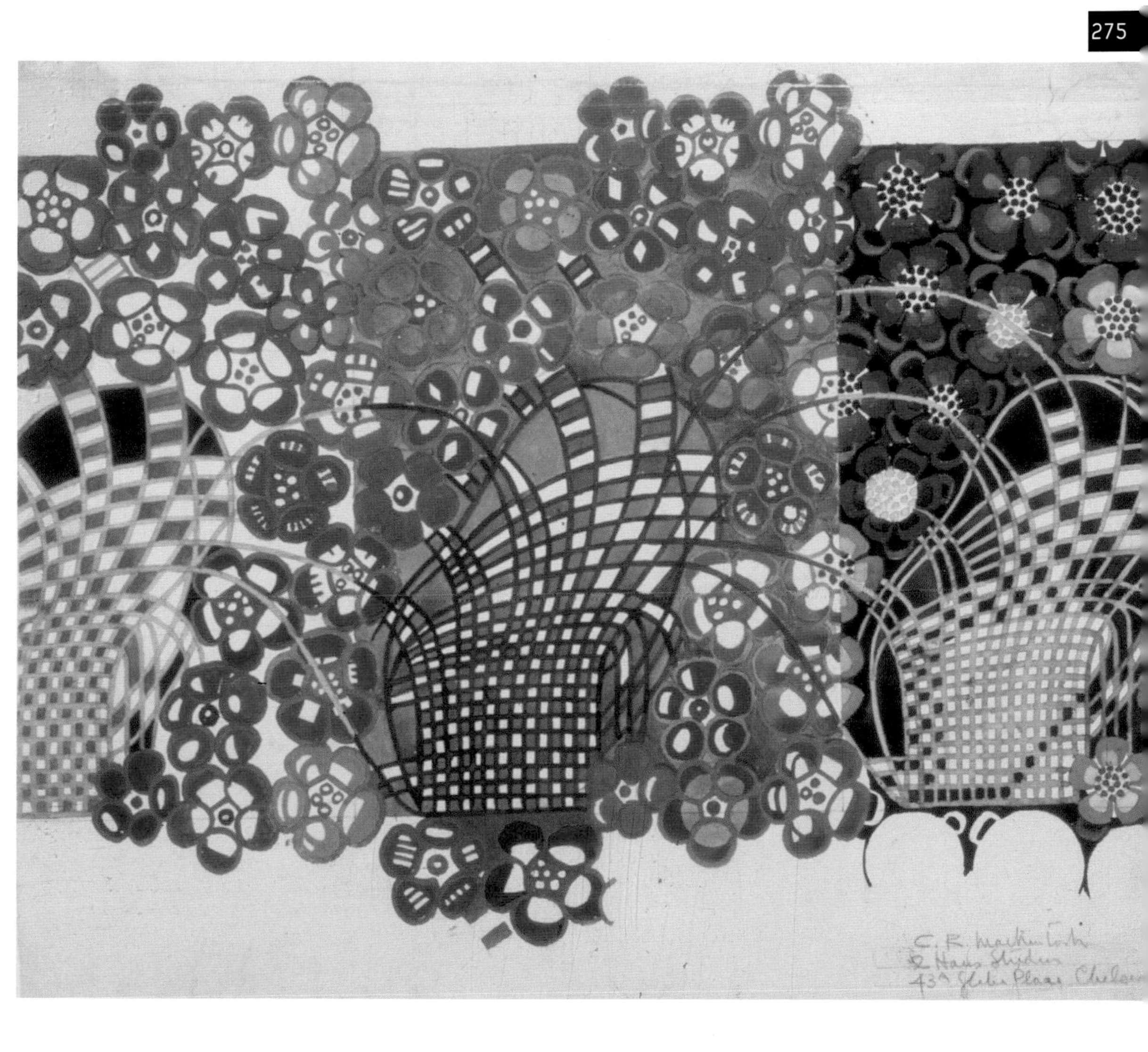
C. R. Mackintosh

Poster for an Exhibition at the Glasgow Institute of Fine Arts, *c.* 1896

During the early 1890s the Four collaborated on a series of poster designs. At this time in Glasgow commercial advertising was still very much in its infancy and the stunningly original designs of the Four were shocking and controversial to the conservative public. The poster, by Mackintosh and MacNair, for the Fine Arts Institute was over two metres (seven feet) tall, making it hard to miss and unlikely to shrink into the background of complacency. Their posters were invariably tall and narrow, similar in proportion to the sinuous figures and elongated motifs that they favoured. The organic motifs of roses and doves and the figures with flowing hair and cupped hands were typical of their style at this time. These were all favoured motifs amongst the Pre-Raphaelites and Rossetti, although the Four stamped them with their innovative hand. Gleeson White, editor of *The Studio*, was quick to defend the boldness of their poster designs, 'it must never be forgotten that the purpose of a poster is to attract notice, and the mildest of eccentricity would not be out of place provided it aroused curiosity and so riveted the attention of passers-by'.

CREATED

Glasgow

MEDIUM

Colour lithograph

SERIES/PERIOD/MOVEMENT

Work of the Four

SIMILAR WORKS

Poster for Fifth Secession Exhibition by Koloman Moser, 1899

Herbert MacNair *Born* 1868 Glasgow, Scotland

Died 1955

THE GLASGOW
INSTITVTE
OF THE FINE ARTS
OPEN FEBRVARY TILL MAY

Ysighlu, from *The Yellow Book*

Continental Symbolism and *Jugendstil*, the German and Austrian evocation of Art Nouveau, particularly influenced the Four. *The Studio* magazine that was first published in 1893 was also to prove highly influential, both in introducing the Four to the works of other artists and in turn propagating their own work. The first issue of the magazine included works by Beardsley and Jan Toorop, whose particular brand of ethereal Symbolism the young artists greatly admired. The following year *The Yellow Book* was launched, with Beardsley as art editor and contributor. The magazine aimed to publicize new movements in art and literature and received heavy criticism from the conservative ranks. Herbert MacNair's disturbing and eerie painting *Ysighlu*, which was published in *The Yellow Book*, is strikingly similar to the haunting style of Frances Macdonald, who later became his wife. The picture was accompanied by the text, 'The very shadows of the cave worshipped her, the little waves threw themselves at her feet and kissed them'. MacNair and Mackintosh would often sketch together in the countryside and evolved an emotive and innovative manner of expression peculiarly their own.

CREATED

Glasgow

MEDIUM

Watercolour

SERIES/PERIOD/MOVEMENT

Work of the Four

SIMILAR WORKS

Ill Omen by Frances Macdonald MacNair, 1893

Herbert MacNair *Born* 1868 Glasgow, Scotland

Died 1955

Sconce, *c.* 1896

During the Mackintoshes' years in Glasgow there was a resounding resurrection of the decorative arts, primarily fuelled by the enthusiastic directorship of Francis Newbery at the Glasgow School of Art. Margaret and Frances Macdonald, who were both accomplished designers in metalwork, would undoubtedly have also influenced the subsequent interest in this medium. Peter Wylie Davidson, head of the metalwork department at the art school, also played a significant role in the increase of independent artists working with metal. He worked within an Arts and Crafts tradition and frequently used Celtic motifs in his decorative detailing. This sconce, designed to reflect and magnify the light from a candle, illustrates Margaret combining Celtic imagery with the delicate curvilinear detailing of an Art Nouveau nature. Talwin Morris, the Art Director for Blackie's publishing company collected many of Margaret's and Frances's metalwork pieces and was a talented metalworker in his own right. He became great friends with the Four, supporting their innovative design concept, and was later a key figure in gaining Mackintosh the commission for The Hill House from Walter Blackie.

CREATED

Glasgow

MEDIUM

Copper, hand-beaten, embossed and chased

SERIES/PERIOD/MOVEMENT

Margaret Macdonald, metalwork

SIMILAR WORKS

Crescent moon sconce by Agnes Bankier Harvey

Margaret Macdonald Mackintosh *Born* 1864 Tipton, Wolverhampton

Died 1933

Reflections (detail), 1898

The disquieting shimmering transparency of *Reflections* provokes a note of mystical aestheticism. The strangely tangible head hovering above a phantasmagorial body imbues Mackintosh's painting with all the elements that the style of the Four embodied. The work of Dante Gabriel Rossetti and that of Edward Burne-Jones (1833–98) is called to mind. Mackintosh is known to have had works by the Pre-Raphaelites hanging in his first studio and greatly admired their style. These artists strove to resurrect the inherent goodness of medievalism, which they portrayed through the use of jewel-like colours, exacting decorative detail and natural forms. Their use of symbolism, imagination and romantic subject matters were all appealing to Mackintosh and the other members of the Four. The illustrations of Carlos Schwabe (1866–1926) were also influential on the young Scottish artists, who would have seen them in Newbery's copy of *Le Rêve* by Zola. In 1893 the first issue of *The Magazine* came out. This handwritten quarterly periodical was produced by the students at the Art School and contained their illustrations. Works of the Four were included in virtually all the editions, leading to their ideas and influence being circulated amongst their contemporaries.

CREATED

Glasgow

MEDIUM

Watercolour, pencil and silver paint on brown tracing paper, laid on board

SERIES/PERIOD/MOVEMENT

Early watercolours

SIMILAR WORKS

Adele Bloch-Bauer I by Gustav Klimt, 1907

The Maids of Elfenmere by Dante Gabriel Rossetti, 1855

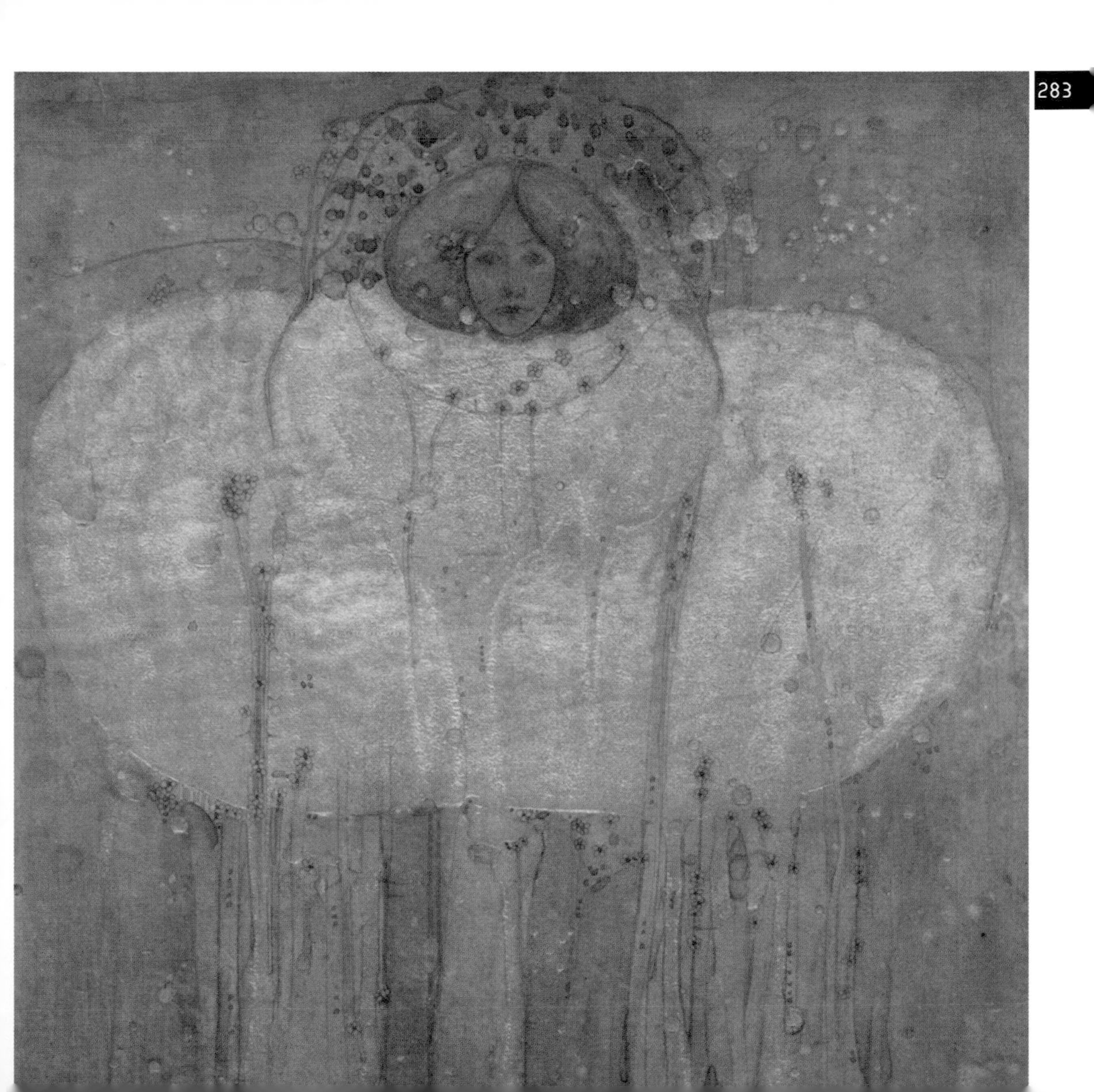

Diploma of Honour designed for the Glasgow School of Art Club, 1894–95

Thomas Howarth has made the interesting identification in his book on *Mackintosh and the Modern Movement*, of a *Conversazione Programme*, dated 1894, as being one of the first examples of Mackintosh using purely symbolic imagery. The comparison between this graphic work and the diploma is significant in that it shows the enormous advancement in this style within a relatively short period of time. The *Conversazione* is decorative, but is also awkward and lacking true rhythm, even the lettering appears hesitant and somewhat childlike. The diploma, however, is supremely rhythmic with symmetrically arranged elegant female forms. Mackintosh has created great contrast between the curvilinear lines of their hair and the angular pattern of verticals and horizontals, a use of contrasting line and form that he would use throughout his career. His female figures and elements of the composition in the diploma echo those seen in Frances Macdonald's frontispiece for *The Magazine*, done in 1893, and an invitation designed by Margaret in the same year. This highlights the close working practice and swapping of creative ideas that the four artists experienced.

CREATED

Glasgow

MEDIUM

Offset lithograph on board

SERIES/PERIOD/MOVEMENT

Early illustrative work

SIMILAR WORKS

Frontispiece for *The Magazine* by Frances Macdonald MacNair, 1893

Glasgow School of Art Club 'At Home' Invitation by Margaret Macdonald Mackintosh, 1893

THE GLASGOW SCHOOL OF ART CLUB DIPLOMA OF HONOUR
AWARDED TO
JUDGES
CHAS R MACKINTOSH

Design for a bookplate, 1896

Margaret's design for a bookplate recalls again the earlier examples of her sister Frances's graphic designs and Mackintosh's Diploma of Honour. During these years the Four drew heavily on each other and in some instances the authorship of their work is hard to differentiate. The bulb or tulip-head motif that encompasses the central imagery was a feature that they all employed often, looking continually for inspiration from organic sources. The delicate linear quality of the design is reminiscent of Beardsley's work and especially the florally inspired illustrations of Carlos Schwabe. Margaret has employed her own version of Art Nouveau decorative emblems in the stylized tree and has imbued it with a nostalgic Celtic accent.

Towards the end of the 1890s Charles Mackintosh's graphic style began to move away from the overtly mystical and Symbolist paintings of the other members of the Four as he became more involved in his architectural commissions. In 1898 Herbert MacNair was appointed Instructor of Design at Liverpool University, a move that marked the beginning of the end of the halcyon days of the Four.

CREATED

Glasgow

MEDIUM

Pencil on paper

SERIES/PERIOD/MOVEMENT

Early illustrative work

SIMILAR WORKS

Illustration for Samain's *Au Jardin de L'Enfant* by Carlos Schwabe, 1908

Margaret Macdonald Mackintosh *Born* 1864 Tipton, Wolverhampton

Died 1933

OMNE · BONVM · DEI · DONVM ·
BY · THE · TREE · OF · KNOWLEDGE · DWELLS · WISDOM ·
WITH · HER · CHILDREN · WHICH · ARE · PLEASANT · THOVGHTS.
JOHN EDWARDS.

Decorative panel of beaten metal, 1898–99

Margaret and Frances Macdonald spent the latter years of their childhood living at the impressive stately home, Chesterton Hall, in Staffordshire. The hall was situated in an area of wild beauty on the site of an ancient Celtic stone circle. The romantic wilderness must have greatly appealed to the two young girls, who would spend their lives drawing on natural inspiration and using the Celtic history associated with their upbringing in their imagery. Their interest in symbolism, fairy stories, mysticism and romantic subjects could have been fuelled by barefoot days of imagined adventures in the capacious surroundings of their youth. Margaret's treatment of this decorative panel displays the organic design features and delicate curvilinear pattern typical of her work at this time. She was as adept at designing for illustrations as she was for metal, gesso panels and textiles.

The particular brand of mystical beauty seen in the work of the Four would earn them the derogatory label of the Spook School, after they exhibited at the 1896 Arts and Crafts Exhibition in London, one that they would not shake off.

CREATED

Glasgow

MEDIUM

Beaten metal

SERIES/PERIOD/MOVEMENT

Metal work

SIMILAR WORKS

Night, repoussé brass wall sconce by Marian Henderson Wilson

Margaret Macdonald Mackintosh *Born* 1864 Tipton, Wolverhampton

Died 1933

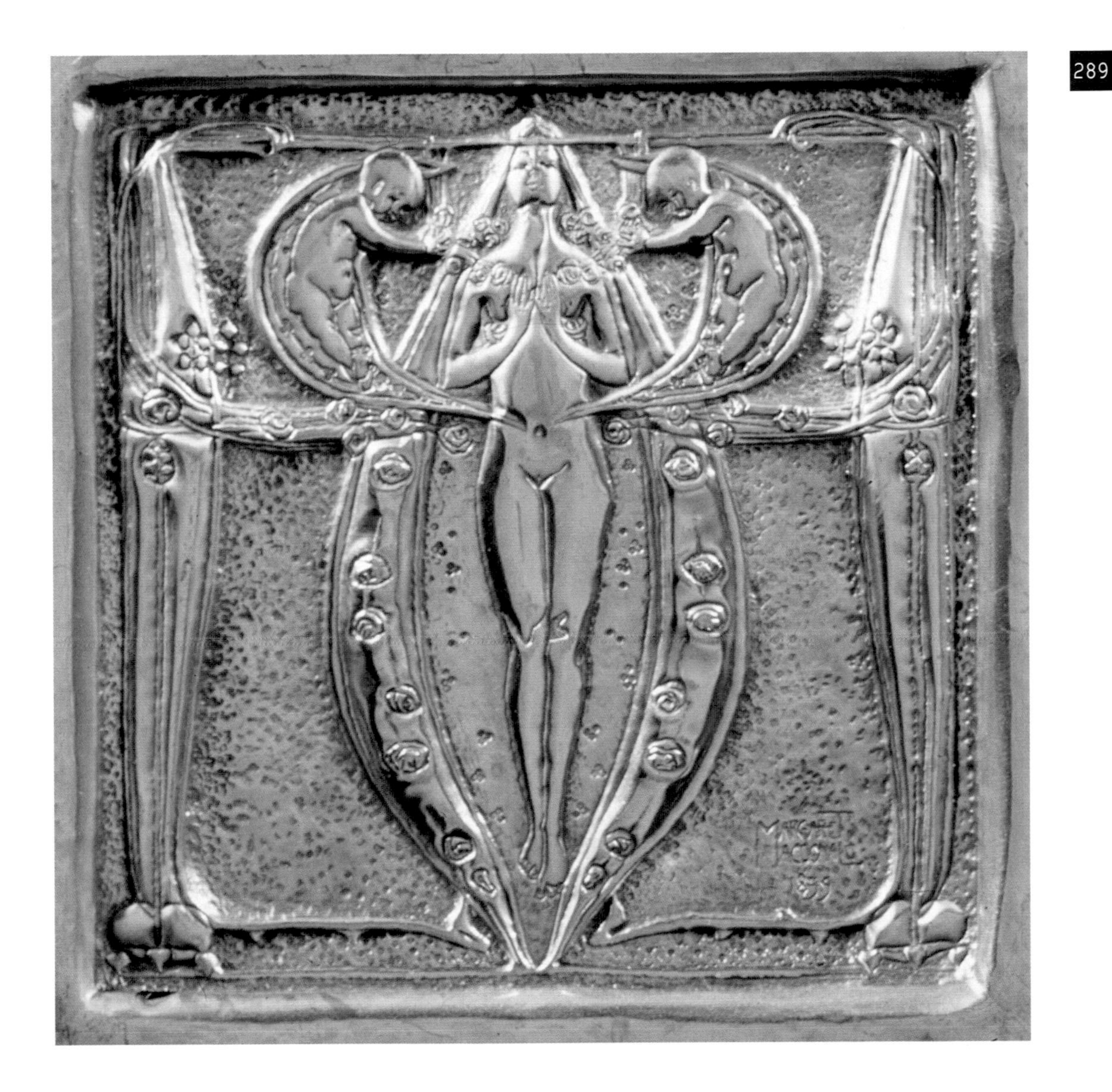

The May Queen, 1900

Margaret produced *The May Queen* gesso panel to hang in Miss Cranston's Ingram Street Tea Room, opposite a panel by Charles, *The Wassail*. The two panels hung in the White Dining Room in which Charles had created one of his stunning white themes that was evocative of pure light and air. The two panels have strong parallels and were executed in a similar style. Margaret has often been blamed for influencing Mackintosh too much, by her romantic vision and overtly Symbolist expression. Clearly being in such a symbiotic and close relationship the two would doubtlessly have communicated their individual styles to one another. Their initial individual outlooks could not, however, have been more diverse; Charles a man of line and function and Margaret the consummate romantic. It is testament to their relationship that they complemented each other's differences.

Both *The May Queen* and *The Wassail* were strongly three-dimensional in application. The pictures were worked up from a plaster base on coarse canvas and thick string was used to form the outline of the figures. Both pictures had decorative inlaid beads, coloured glass and pieces of metal.

CREATED

Glasgow

MEDIUM

Pencil, watercolour and body colour, heightened with silver on oiled tracing paper

SERIES/PERIOD/MOVEMENT

Gesso panels

SIMILAR WORKS

Beethoven Frieze by Gustav Klimt, 1902

Margaret Macdonald Mackintosh *Born* 1864 Tipton, Wolverhampton

Died 1933

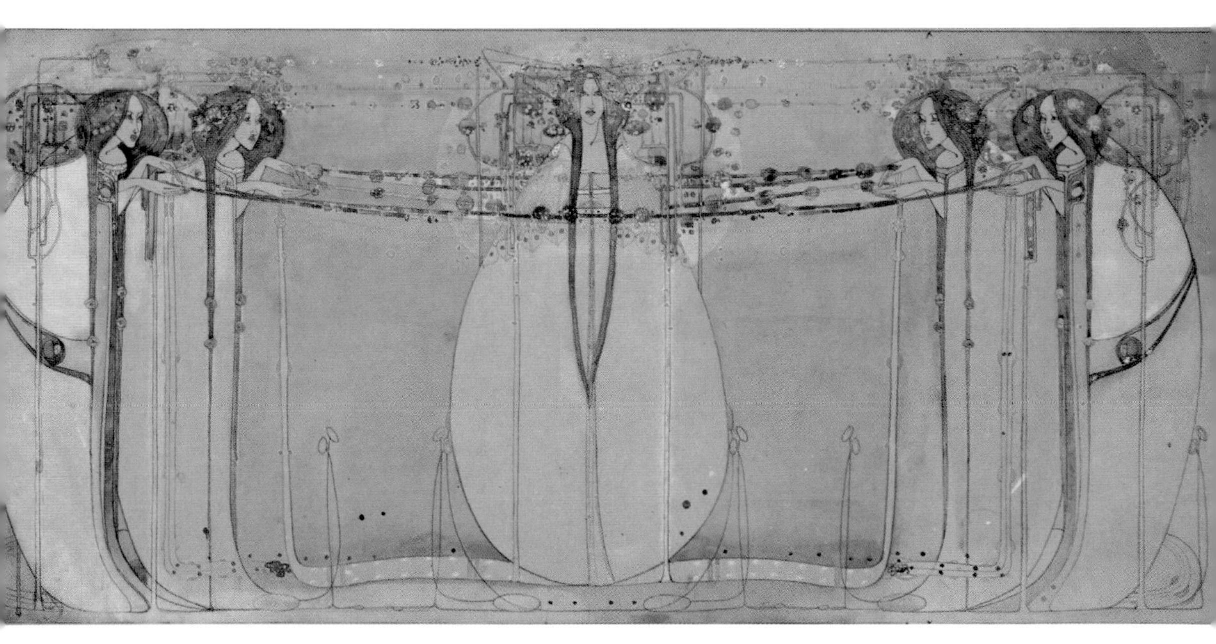

The Wassail (detail), 1900

In 1900 the Glasgow Four were invited to exhibit at the Eighth Secessionist Exhibition in Vienna, their reputation preceding them on the Continent due to Gleeson White's coverage of their work in *The Studio*. *The Wassail* and *The May Queen* were exhibited in the Scottish Room, facing each other from opposite walls. The room also included furniture from the Mackintoshes' home on Mains Street and a number of watercolours, illustrations and custom-designed furniture. *The Wassail* and *The May Queen* were greatly influential on the Viennese Secessionists, whose work in turn influenced Charles and Margaret. It was an extraordinary phenomenon that two such similar concepts of style had developed independently of each other in two different countries. Gustav Klimt was especially drawn to the Four's style and his *Beethoven Frieze* of 1902 shows clear parallels to the work of Margaret in particular. Josef Hoffman, a founding member of the Secessionists and organizer of the exhibition became a great supporter of Mackintosh and visited him in Glasgow. The Four's work was criticized by some at the Vienna exhibition, but on the whole, they were received with much more understanding and comprehension than they had been anywhere else.

CREATED

Glasgow

MEDIUM

Watercolour and pencil

SERIES/PERIOD/MOVEMENT

Gesso panels

SIMILAR WORKS

Beethoven Frieze by Gustav Klimt, 1902

The Tower of Brass by Edward Burne-Jones, 1888

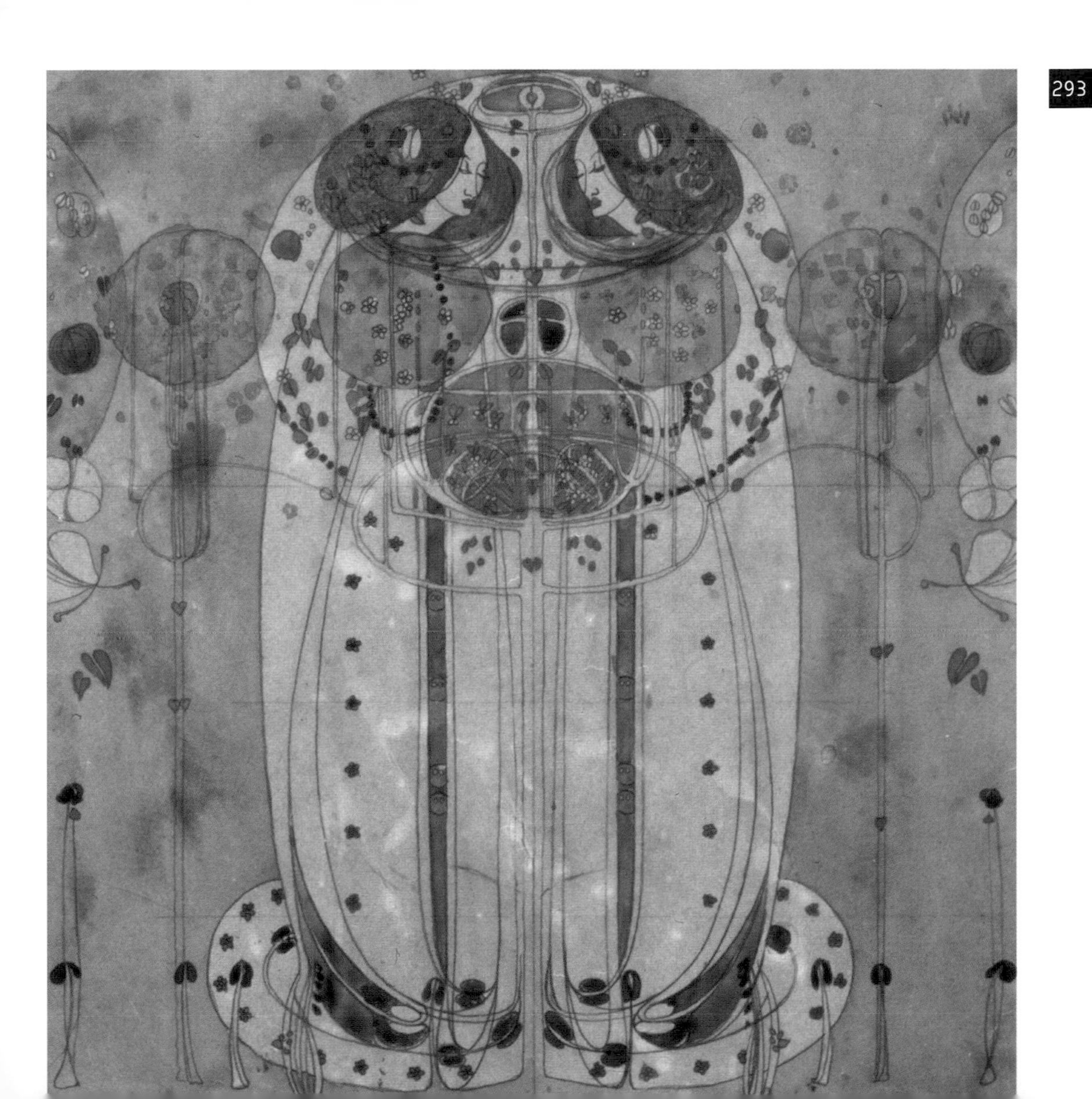

Design for a decorative frieze, 1895–97

The enigmatic frieze design completed by Frances may have been hung at Dunglass Castle, her family's home from 1899. Frances was 10 years junior to her sister Margaret, but was equally artistically prodigious and was accepted as a contemporary by the other three members of the Four. Margaret and Frances set up a studio in 1894 and worked closely together devoting themselves to the applied arts. Their work developed in a similar style, although Frances's figures tended to be more melancholy and despairing and Margaret's more romantic. *The Frieze* draws on the tree of knowledge motif that was used by all members of the group. The stylized rhythmic pattern demonstrates her synthesis of elements from Art Nouveau, Celtic decorative detail and Symbolist imagery. Her work has been cited as reflecting the influence of Egyptian art, which could be applied to this particular frieze. However, after visiting the Four in 1897 Gleeson White wrote in *The Studio*, 'those sons and daughters of Scotland who appear to be most strongly influenced by Egypt affect to be surprised at the bare suggestion of such influence and disclaim any intentional reference...'.

CREATED

Glasgow

MEDIUM

Watercolour

SERIES/PERIOD/MOVEMENT

Work of the Four

SIMILAR WORKS

Poster for *Jung Wiener Theater Zum Lieben Augustin* by Koloman Moser, 1901

Frances Macdonald MacNair *Born* 1834 Glasgow, Scotland

Died 1921

Panel from a lampshade, *c.* 1903

Margaret and Charles worked in close collaboration on commissions for interior schemes, with Margaret tending to deal with fabrics and window dressings as well as other decorative details. How much specific input she had on the design concepts is not known, and whether or not she worked to Charles's specifications or on her own is a matter for conjecture. Bearing in mind the strength and closeness of their relationship a collaboration of ideas would seem realistic. Later in life Charles would glowingly rate his wife's contributions to their interiors and cite her as a chief and constant source of inspiration to him. She was undoubtedly his rock and steered him through passages of depression and lack of self-confidence with a steadfast devotion.

The rose motif that appears on her lampshade was one that the pair used frequently in their interiors. The decorative scheme at The Hill House was one that incorporated the stylized rose and trellis or chequerboard pattern to great effect. Margaret's lampshade design also features the pine-cone shape, another of their well-used forms, here suggested with an outline of ribbon.

CREATED

Glasgow

MEDIUM

Embroidered cream silk with ribbons and braids

SERIES/PERIOD/MOVEMENT

Margaret Macdonald

SIMILAR WORKS

Waist buckle with stylized birds and roses by Jessie M. King, *c.* 1902

Margaret Macdonald Mackintosh *Born* 1864 Tipton, Wolverhampton

Died 1933

O Ye, All Ye That Walk in Willow Wood, 1903

Margaret's beautifully melancholy gesso panel was designed for the Salon De Luxe in the Willow Tea Rooms, the only tea-room commission for which Mackintosh had control over both the exterior and interior renovations. The Salon De Luxe was its sparkling luxurious heart, brilliant with mirrored leaves and coloured glass, the room emanated light and colour from a hundred different reflections. The entire building was designed to echo the willow tree, a natural and symbolic point of reference for the Mackintoshes. Margaret's panel was the focal point of the room, hanging on the wall opposite the fireplace. This haunting and mystical piece takes its title from a sonnet by Dante Gabriel Rossetti, who was influential on the early development of the style of the Four. The sonnet describes the grief of widowhood, the sadness being so great that, 'who so in vain invite your lips to that their unforgotten food ere ye, ere ye again shall see the light'.

The outline of pattern on the panel was created using string and the design embellished with beads and fragments of shell.

CREATED

Glasgow

MEDIUM

Painted gesso with twine and coloured beads

SERIES/PERIOD/MOVEMENT

Gesso panels

SIMILAR WORKS

Grief by Carlos Schwabe, 1893

Margaret Macdonald Mackintosh *Born* 1864 Tipton, Wolverhampton

Died 1933

Here's a Kiss to the Whole World!, detail of the *Beethoven Frieze*, 1902

Gustav Klimt was one of the leaders of the Viennese Secessionists, a group of artists and architects who had broken ranks from the conservative Academy of Art in Vienna. They established an Austrian form of Art Nouveau, which looked back to the tradition of William Morris and the Arts and Crafts movement and forward to a modern interpretation of these ideals. Mackintosh and the style of the Glasgow Four had a significant effect on the work of the Viennese Secessionists and vice versa. Klimt produced his *Beethoven Frieze* for the Fourteenth Exhibition of the Association of Fine Artists of Austria Secession, which took place in the spring of 1902. The theme of the frieze was based on Wagner's interpretation of Beethoven's Ninth Symphony and is regarded as the start of Klimt's 'golden period'. This section of the frieze is reminiscent of the Symbolist, ethereal works of the Four, especially those by Margaret and Frances Macdonald. He used applied gold leaf, semi-precious stones and mother-of-pearl, building the surface of his canvas up in a manner similar to the Macdonald sisters.

CREATED

Vienna

MEDIUM

Casein, gold leaf, semi-precious stones, mother-of-pearl, gypsum, charcoal, pastel and pencil on stucco

SERIES/PERIOD/MOVEMENT

Vienna Secessionist

SIMILAR WORKS

The Opera of the Sea by Margaret Macdonald Mackintosh, *c.* 1915–21

Gustav Klimt *Born* 1862 Baumgarten, Austria

Died 1918

Part Seen, Imagined Part, 1896

It has been suggested that the small original picture of *Part Seen, Imagined Part* was painted by Charles as a gift for Margaret. The painting was then used as a basis for the much larger figures in the frieze of the decorative scheme at the Buchanan Street Tea Rooms, 1896–97. These were the first tea rooms that Mackintosh worked on for Miss Cranston and in this instance he worked in conjunction with the architect George Walton. The female figure in *Part Seen, Imagined Part* grows from a substantial trunk, tendrils of plants and organic foliage snaking from the figure in a sinuous cylindrical upward motion. The figure is similar to those seen in his poster designs, but has more volume and mass. His use of organic forms springing from and around the human figure was one adopted by the Four and can be seen again in *In Fairyland* (1897). Interestingly Talwin Morris, Art Director of Blackie's publishing and friend of the Four, created the frame for the small *Part Seen, Imagined Part*. Morris was an artist in his own right and was a keen collector of Margaret's and Frances's metalwork.

CREATED

Glasgow

MEDIUM

Pencil and watercolour on tracing paper

SERIES/PERIOD/MOVEMENT

Early decorative

SIMILAR WORKS

The Ugly Sisters by Annie French, *c.* 1900

The Dew by Margaret Macdonald Mackintosh, 1901

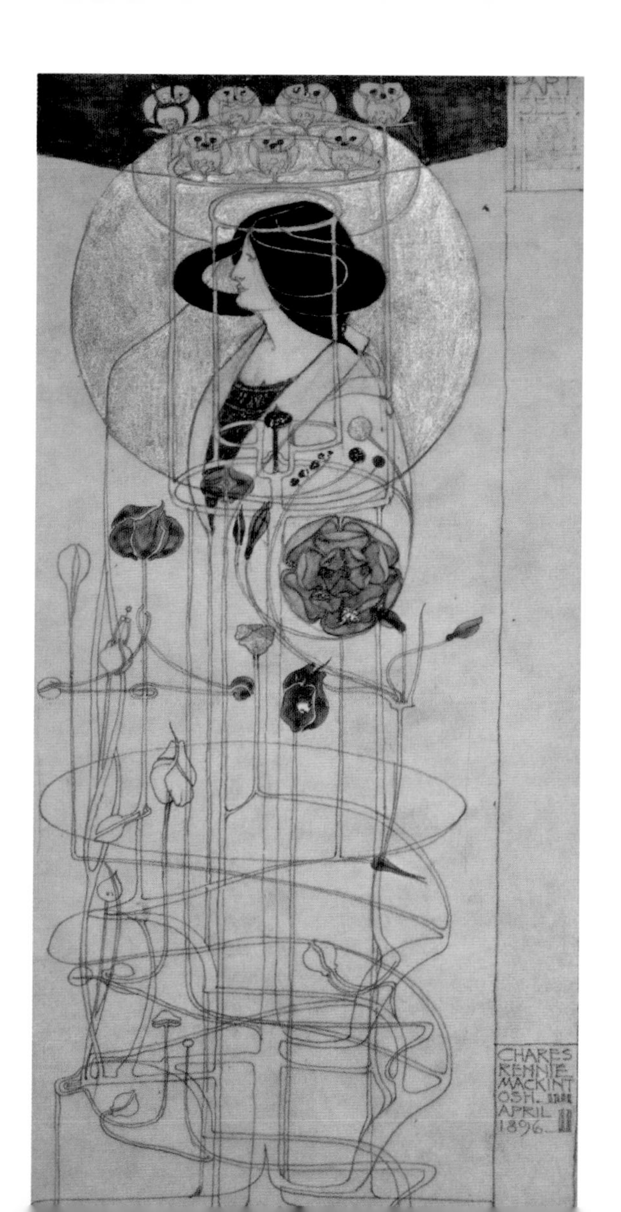
CHARES
RENNIE
MACKINT
OSH.
APRIL
1896.

Titania, 1909

From out of the Viennese Secessionists grew the *Wiener Werkstätte*, Viennese Workshop, developed by Josef Hoffman and Koloman Moser (1868–1918) and funded by Fritz Wärndorfer. The workshops placed great emphasis on the applied arts and operated with the aim of making all facets of the human life into one unified work of art. The initial three-room workshop grew into a much larger concern, providing facilities for a group of forward-thinking and artistically progressive individuals. Wärndorfer commissioned the redecoration of his music room by Mackintosh, a scheme that would be well received amongst the Secessionist followers. Margaret produced a series of gesso panels for the room, based on Maurice Maeterlinck's play *The Seven Princesses*. The panels are currently in an art gallery in Vienna, but two paintings of a similar theme, *The Mysterious Garden*, provide an interesting comparison with *Titania*. The paintings all exude a hauntingly sad and ethereal presence and were realized using similar imagery. Their ghostly melancholy and Symbolist allusions were reflected in the works of the Mackintoshes' Viennese contemporaries.

CREATED

Glasgow

MEDIUM

Watercolour

SERIES/PERIOD/MOVEMENT

Margaret, late period

SIMILAR WORKS

Fatalisme by Jan Toorop, 1893

Margaret Macdonald Mackintosh *Born* 1864 Tipton, Wolverhampton

Died 1933

The Spirit of the Rose, c. 1900

In 1898 Herbert MacNair was appointed Instructor of Design at Liverpool University and the following year he married Frances Macdonald and moved her back to Liverpool with him. MacNair and Frances were both talented artists who were considerably influential on the development of the Glasgow style. Their story is, however, one beset with tragedy, not dissimilar to the path the Mackintoshes trod. The move to Liverpool effectively brought about the end of the Four and it has been suggested that Herbert was inspired to take the position to escape growing unfavourable comparisons with the more accomplished Charles Mackintosh. Certainly it marked a distinct downward spiral in their fortunes. Beset with problems the couple struggled, until Frances's early death in 1921. Herbert was devastated and tragically destroyed the majority of his and her works.

The Spirit of the Rose is a highly stylized design with a striking Minimalist appeal. The rose is typical of her vocabulary, but the pattern is unusually geometric for her work. The chubby figure of the spirit is again a departure from her normal elongated form.

CREATED

Liverpool

MEDIUM

Embroidery

SERIES/PERIOD/MOVEMENT

Frances Macdonald MacNair

SIMILAR WORKS

Glasgow Rose cushion cover by Jessie Newbery, *c.* 1900

Frances Macdonald MacNair *Born* 1834 Glasgow, Scotland

Died 1921

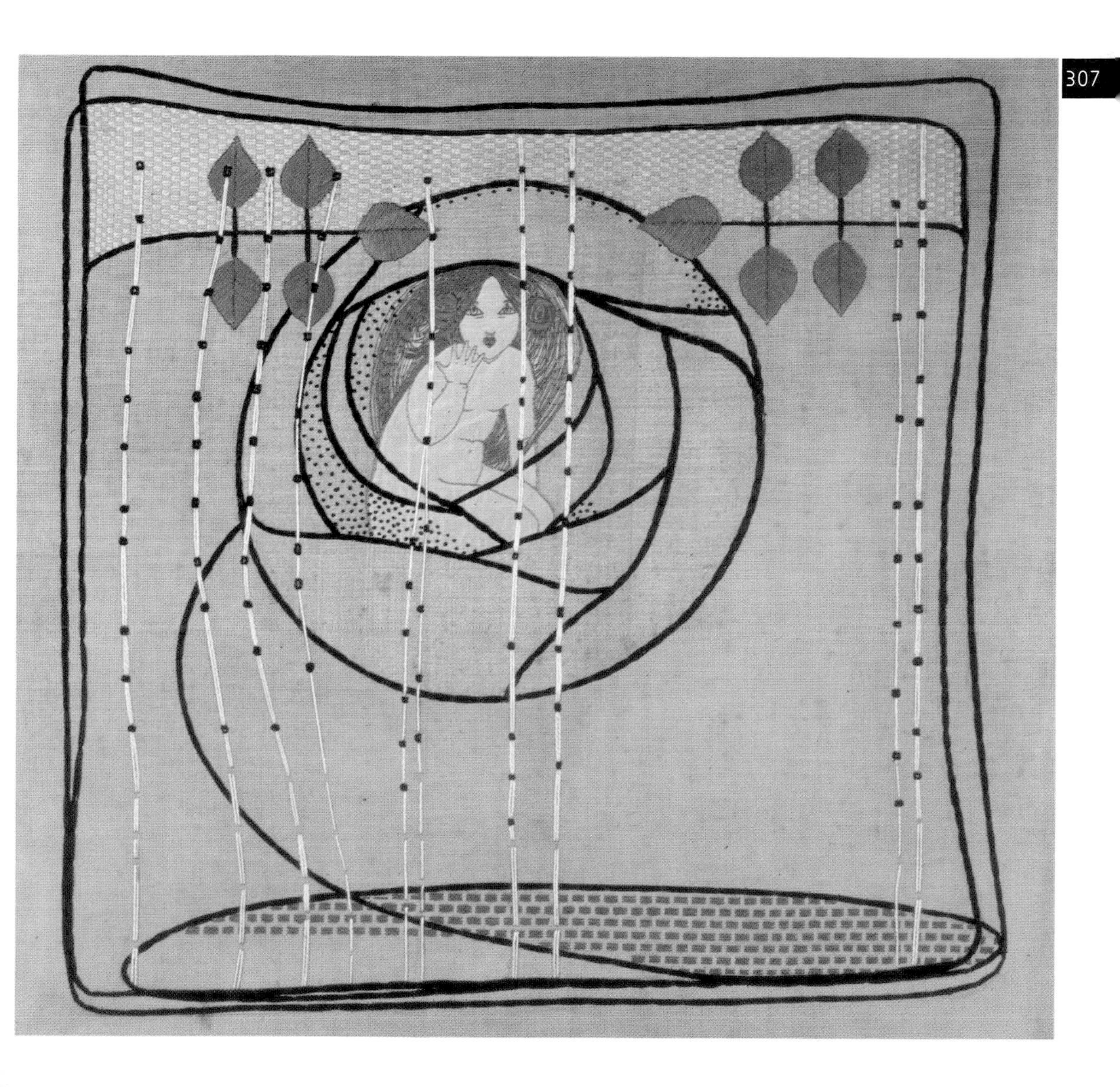

The Spirit of the Rose, 1903

This later version of *The Spirit of The Rose* is totally different in feel, being more reminiscent of an earlier painting, *Ophelia*, 1898. The fluidity of line and circular structure is seen in both these paintings, although *Ophelia* is less stylized. The delicate linear quality to *The Spirit of the Rose* is reminiscent of Mackintosh's *The Wassail*, 1900, and in both paintings the female figures have similar stylized faces. Frances's picture, however, is shot through with movement, defined by the elegant organic swirling line and tendrils of flowing hair that sweep across the canvas.

Frances and Herbert moved back to Glasgow in 1908 and lived for a short time with Charles and Margaret at their 78 Southpark Avenue home. From this period Frances's paintings became increasingly despairing, surely a reflection of her own personal turmoil. *The Choice*, *c.* 1909, has none of the decorative beauty of *The Spirit of the Rose*, but is haunting and mysterious. She has still retained the symbolic motif of the rose, but here her figures have more in common with those of Edvard Munch.

CREATED

Liverpool

MEDIUM

Watercolour

SERIES/PERIOD/MOVEMENT

Frances Macdonald MacNair

SIMILAR WORKS

The Heart of the Rose by Margaret Macdonald Mackintosh, *c.* 1902–03

Frances Macdonald MacNair *Born* 1834 Glasgow, Scotland

Died 1921

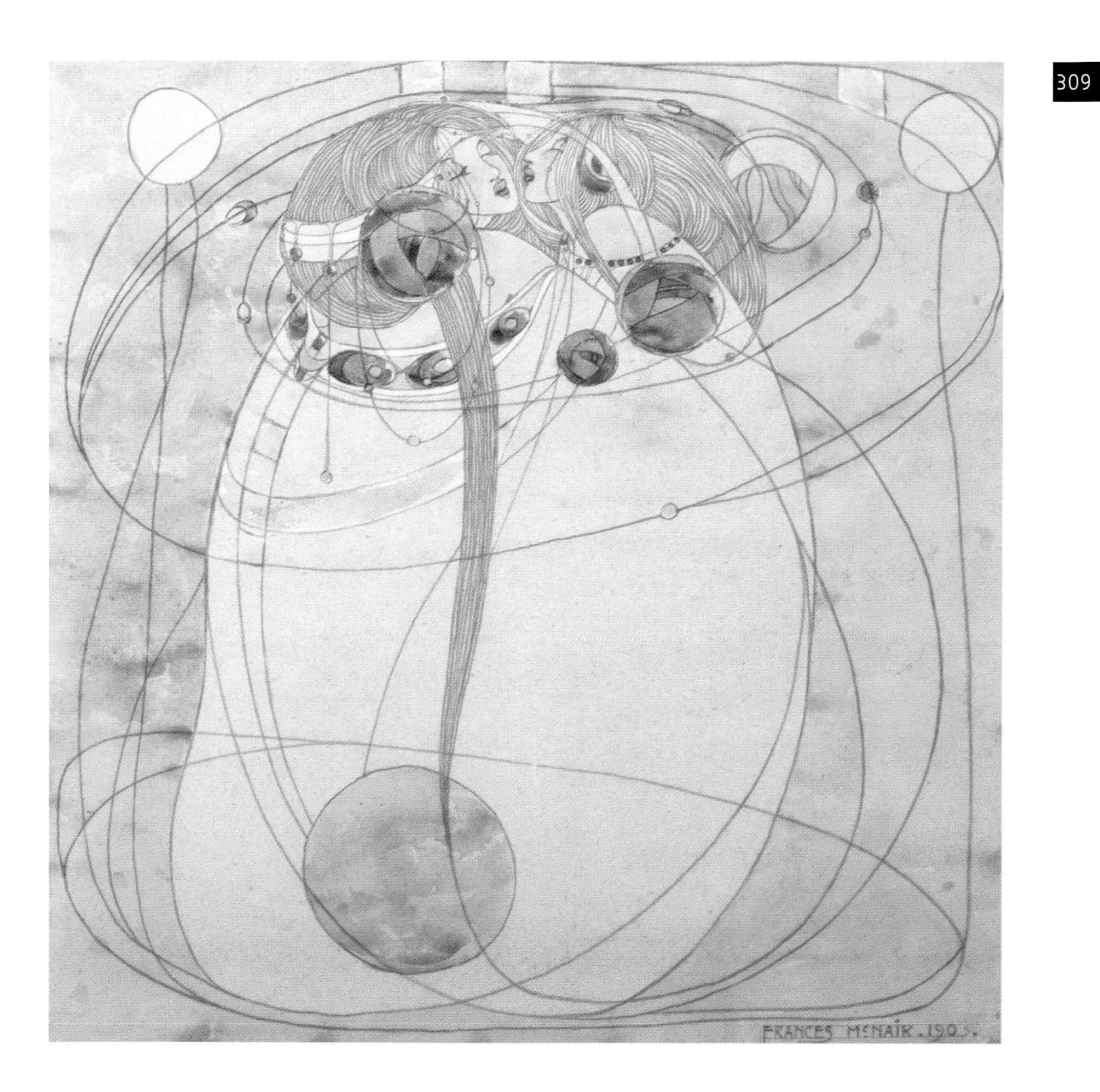
FRANCES McNAIR .190

Mackintosh

Styles & Techniques

Glasgow School of Art: detail of iron-work on the north façade, 1897–99

Mackintosh was devoted to the principle of form for function and it is this premise that lends his architectural style the asymmetrical harmony typical of his buildings. The interior function is reflected in the position of both windows and stone on the façade, and never the other, and more conventional, way around. The Art School's north façade was no exception. Built in Giffnock and Whitespot sandstone in a mixture of ashlar and squared, sneck rubble, its imposing simplicity is relieved through the use of ironwork in an ornamental and functional capacity. Mackintosh used decorative constructive ironwork frequently through his architectural career and this in part reflects Glasgow's burgeoning iron technology. The first-floor window brackets pictured here are in the form of flower heads, pinned back towards the wall. To the east of the main entrance these brackets show an emerging seed from stamen to pod in the centre of the flowers. To the west of the main entrance the flower heads do not exhibit the same conceptual format.

CREATED

Glasgow

MEDIUM

Architecture and ironwork

SERIES/PERIOD/MOVEMENT

Glasgow School of Art

SIMILAR WORKS

Argyle Arcade by John Baird, 1827

Charles Rennie Mackintosh *Born* 1868 Glasgow, Scotland

Died 1928

Railing from the Willow Tea Rooms, Glasgow, *c.* 1901–04

The scheme for the Willow Tea Rooms was the only one for which Mackintosh had total control over both the exterior and interior. He designed the entire building based on a tree-and-leaf motif, of which the latter can clearly be seen in the green glass insets in the wrought-iron railing. The distinctive narrow elegant form of the willow leaf was one that particularly appealed to Mackintosh and here he includes this organic shape within the solid geometric restrictions of the iron surround. Light was especially important to Mackintosh, who made artistic and dramatic use of light sources. His coloured glass insets, seen best in his windows, would bathe his interiors in pools of reflected light, an effect that was systemically created through his absorbing attention to detail. Metal was one of his favourite media, due to its versatility for decorative and structural detail, and he frequently used stained glass and metal together. Glasgow was one of the most progressive cities at this time in the iron industry and as a result iron became a popular medium for architects and designers.

CREATED

Glasgow

MEDIUM

Wrought iron and leaded glass

SERIES/PERIOD/MOVEMENT

Glasgow

SIMILAR WORKS

Leaded glass in the *Tree of Life* door by Frank Lloyd Wright, 1904

Gate by Hans Eduard Von Berlepsch, *c.* 1900

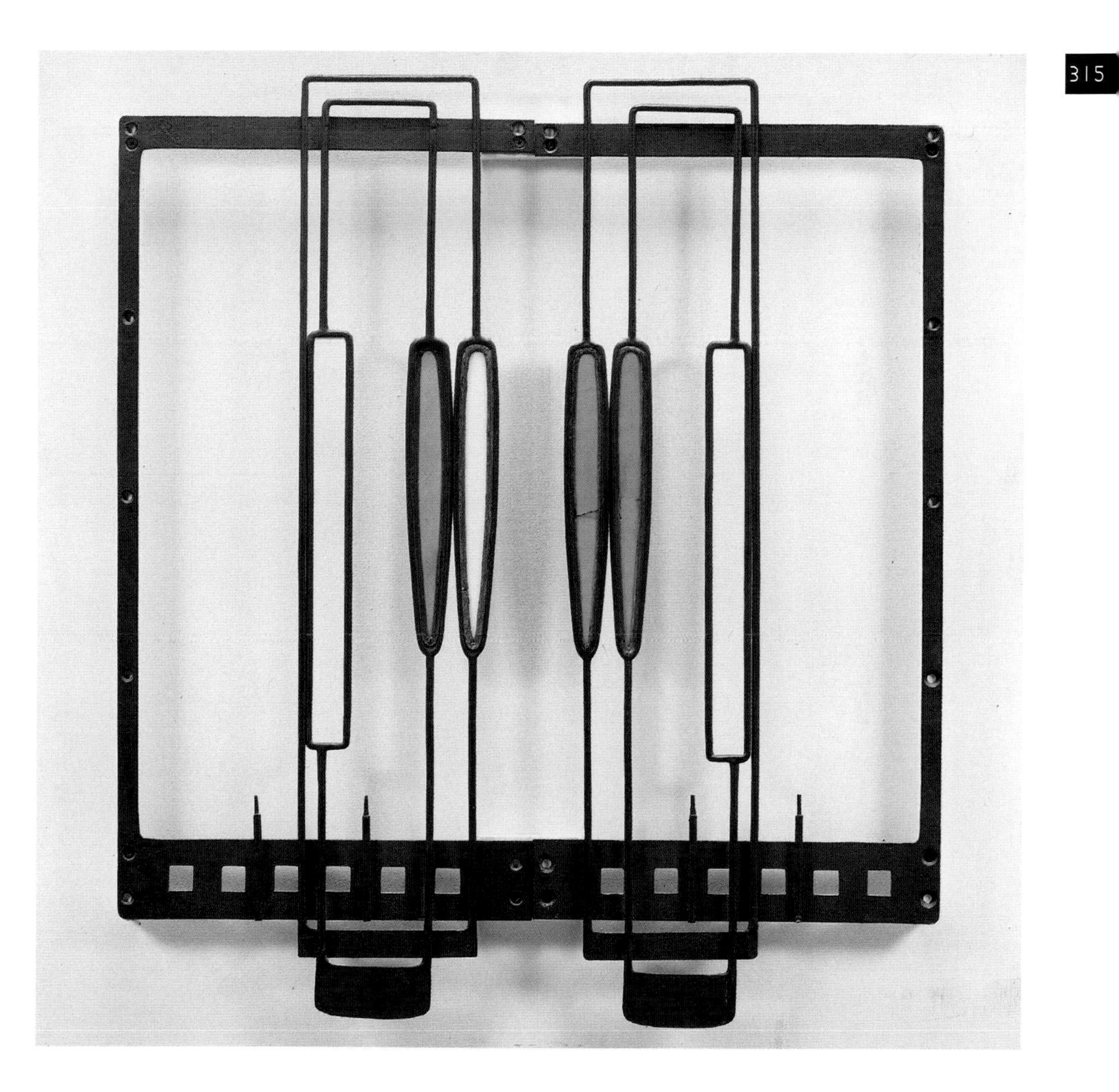

Casket, 1909

Mackintosh designed this exquisite casket for Sir James Fleming, Chairman of the Board of Governors of the Glasgow School of Art on completion of the final building work to the west wing. This was a design that was popular at the time and was traditionally used for holding presentation scrolls of address. The clean simple lines of the casket were in keeping with Mackintosh's approach to architecture and design. The only ornamentation was the applied semi-precious stones and narrow band of decorative detail, used sparingly, but to great aesthetic effect. The hallmarks relay the date of 1909 and also the maker's mark, WAD. This belonged to William Armstrong Davidson who had established a metalwork studio during the 1890s with his brother Peter Wylie Davidson. Peter was also the head of the metalwork department at the Glasgow School of Art and was widely credited with being a superb craftsman. It is interesting to compare the polished maturity of this casket with the jewellery box that Mackintosh designed around 1895 for Jessie Keppie.

CREATED

Glasgow

MEDIUM

Silver set with lapis lazuli and varieties of chalcedony

SERIES/PERIOD/MOVEMENT

Glasgow

SIMILAR WORKS

Jewellery tray by Rhoda Wager, *c.* 1900

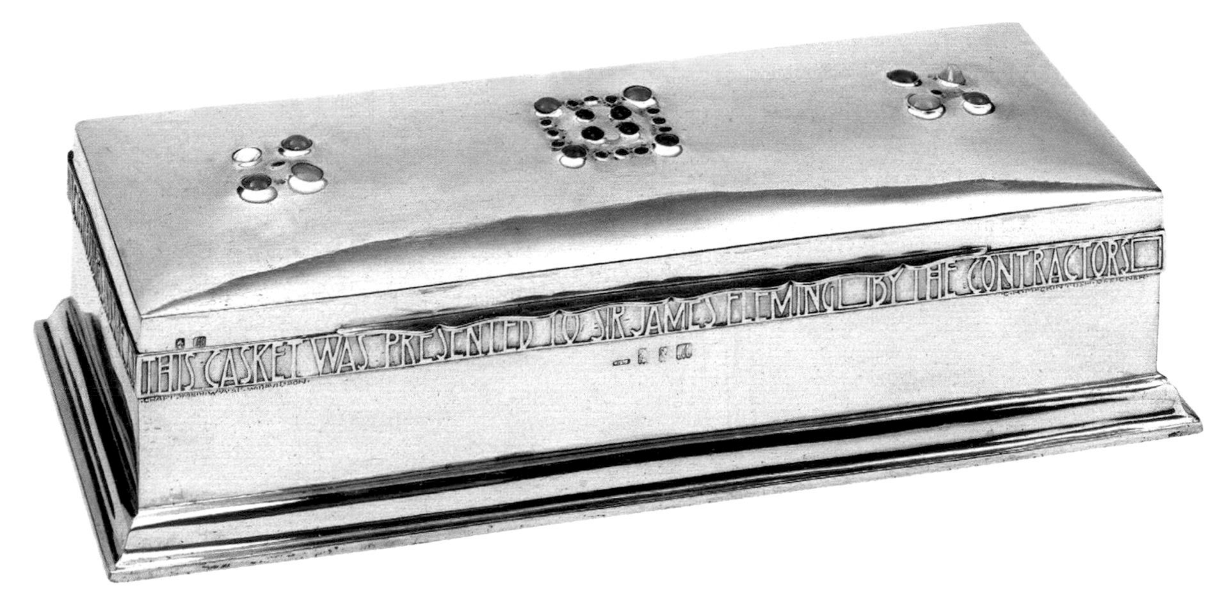
THIS CASKET WAS PRESENTED TO SIR JAMES FLEMING BY THE CONTRACTORS

Table service designed for E. Bingham and Co., *c.* 1906

Mackintosh's approach to design was typified by an encompassing attention to detail, no matter how small. This holistic approach to his interiors ensured that a completely unified air prevailed. The work that he executed for Miss Cranston on her four different tea rooms was amongst the most complete of his design schemes and covered for the most part everything from the interior structures to the wall treatments, plates, cutlery and fabrics and furnishings. He was particularly fortunate that Miss Cranston had such a progressive attitude and allowed him virtually a free hand in his designing. He produced several different cutlery sets for her, of which the Willow Tea Rooms set is one of the most elegant. Some years later he produced a set for E. Bingham & Co. of an entirely different nature. His Bingham cutlery has clear Celtic reference in its motifs and is robust and somewhat utilitarian. By contrast his Willow Tea Rooms cutlery employs the chequerboard motif seen on the exterior of the building and is elegantly modern in its simple, clean lines.

CREATED

Glasgow

MEDIUM

Electroplated metal

SERIES/PERIOD/MOVEMENT

Cutlery

SIMILAR WORKS

Tableware by C. F. A. Voysey, *c.* 1908

E. BINGHAM & Co
SHEFFIELD
SECURE
HANDLE

Armchair, *c.* 1897

In a short working life of just 25 years, Mackintosh produced over 400 pieces of furniture; a staggering amount considering that the majority of these were from intense periods of work during 1897 to 1905 and 1916 to 1918. Another factor to consider when evaluating his furniture is that for the most part he utilized local craftsmen to produce his designs, in many cases employing the services of carpenters and joiners who worked in the shipping industries situated up and down the Clyde. The significance of this is that they were not specialized in the art of furniture making.

This short-backed chair is one of a pair from the Glasgow School of Art. The squat form of the chair makes it sturdy and utilitarian, while the small cut-out detail in the arms and the fine chair rails prevent it from becoming overly bulky in design. Mackintosh has employed an Arts and Crafts style approach seen in his use of large areas of natural wood and the rush seat.

CREATED

Glasgow

MEDIUM

Oak and rush

SERIES/PERIOD/MOVEMENT

Chairs

SIMILAR WORKS

Egyptian chair by Ford Maddox Brown, 1857–58

High-backed chair, *c.* 1898–99

Of all his chair designs the high-backed chair remains one of Mackintosh's most famous and most popular. He first developed the design through his chairs for the Argyle Street Tea Room and was experimenting with the chair in terms of spatial division. The high back naturally forms a room divider in place of structural walls or screens. He was also interested in the symbolic allusion of the chair back resonating the tree from which it was crafted. True to Mackintosh's style he formulated a chair that was both functional and comfortable with a greater symbolic reference. The high-back chair design was one that he would use in modified form through his career and is one of the styles of chair that has enjoyed a recent enormous revival. His Argyle Street high-backed chairs were decorative in form alone, their elegant shape being as suitably refined as the art of drinking tea. Added ornament was either in the form of carving on the oval back panel, his first successful use of carving, or through stylized cut-out shapes in the form of a flying bird.

CREATED

Glasgow

MEDIUM

Oak

SERIES/PERIOD/MOVEMENT

Chairs

SIMILAR WORKS

Oak chair by F. C. Nielsen, *c.* 1908

Armchair designed for the billiards and smoking room at Miss Cranston's Tea Rooms, 1898–99

The famous tea rooms of Glasgow were much more than a humble café and the larger ones offered restaurants, smoking rooms, billiard rooms and libraries. They were establishments that ladies could go to unaccompanied without fear of dishonourable recourse and also where gentlemen could congregate in the male-only smoking and billiard areas. Mackintosh, who was keenly aware of female and male elements in his designs, treated his interiors accordingly. Typically the male areas would invariably be darker and stouter in atmosphere. His armchair is a classic example of this approach. In contrast to the fine and elegant high-backed chairs used in the dining area, his short-backed chair here has a distinctly masculine attitude. The design is sturdy, yet refined and is extraordinarily modern in its geometric form. Mackintosh designed a chair for his own house along similar lines, but with the added feature of small knobs on the rear posts. The Argyle Street commission was independent from Honeyman and Keppie and shows Mackintosh designing without the influence of his employers.

CREATED

Glasgow

MEDIUM

Dark stained oak

SERIES/PERIOD/MOVEMENT

Chairs

SIMILAR WORKS

Mayor's chair, Northampton Hall by E. W. Godwin, 1865

Ladder-back chairs designed for the Willow Tea Rooms, *c.* 1903

The Willow Tea Rooms are amongst the most elegant and unusual of Mackintosh's tea room schemes. The entire interior arrangement and decoration is designed to echo the building's namesake – the willow tree. The ladder-back chair, pictured, is a variation of his high-backed chairs and is one of the most widely recognized chair forms today. He used this design frequently, part of its success resting on the combination of comfort, durability and stylishness. These chairs were used in the front saloon of the Willow Tea Rooms, a room that was basically white in colour scheme. The ladder backs of the dark stained chairs stood out from the white surround, emphasizing their height and tree-like attributions. The black-and-white scheme and the design of the ladder back was also evocative of Oriental influence. This room was in sharp contrast to the interior he designed for the Salon De Luxe, also in the Willow Tea Rooms. The solid naturalness of the utilitarian ladder-back chairs in the front saloon was the antithesis of the silver-painted elongated version of the high-backed chair in the Salon De Luxe.

CREATED

Glasgow

MEDIUM

Stained oak

SERIES/PERIOD/MOVEMENT

Chairs

SIMILAR WORKS

High-backed chair by Percy A. Wells, *c.* 1919

Windyhill, Kilmalcolm: plan of the ground floor, 1900

Mackintosh received the commission for Windyhill in 1899 from William Davidson. Davidson was a successful local businessman and a significant collector of art, especially that of the Glasgow Boys. He was particularly open minded and creative in spirit, providing an almost ideal patron for Mackintosh. Windyhill was Mackintosh's first major independent commission and was also the first opportunity he had to design an entire domestic arrangement, both inside and out. He drew on a mix of traditional Scottish vernacular architecture and reinterpreted it in a modern manner. As can be seen from the ground-floor plan, he used a traditional L-shape layout, with the principal rooms running east to west and the service areas running at right angles. This floor plan afforded him one long roofline on the main elevation, which added to the robust and massive feel to the exterior. Sitting within the angle of the L on the exterior he designed a square-shaped pool that echoed the squares in the windows. Mackintosh always went to great lengths to fit his houses into the landscape of their surroundings.

CREATED

Glasgow

MEDIUM

Pencil and wash on Whatman paper

SERIES/PERIOD/MOVEMENT

Domestic architecture

SIMILAR WORKS

Blackwell at Windermere, Cumbria by M. H. Baillie Scott, 1898

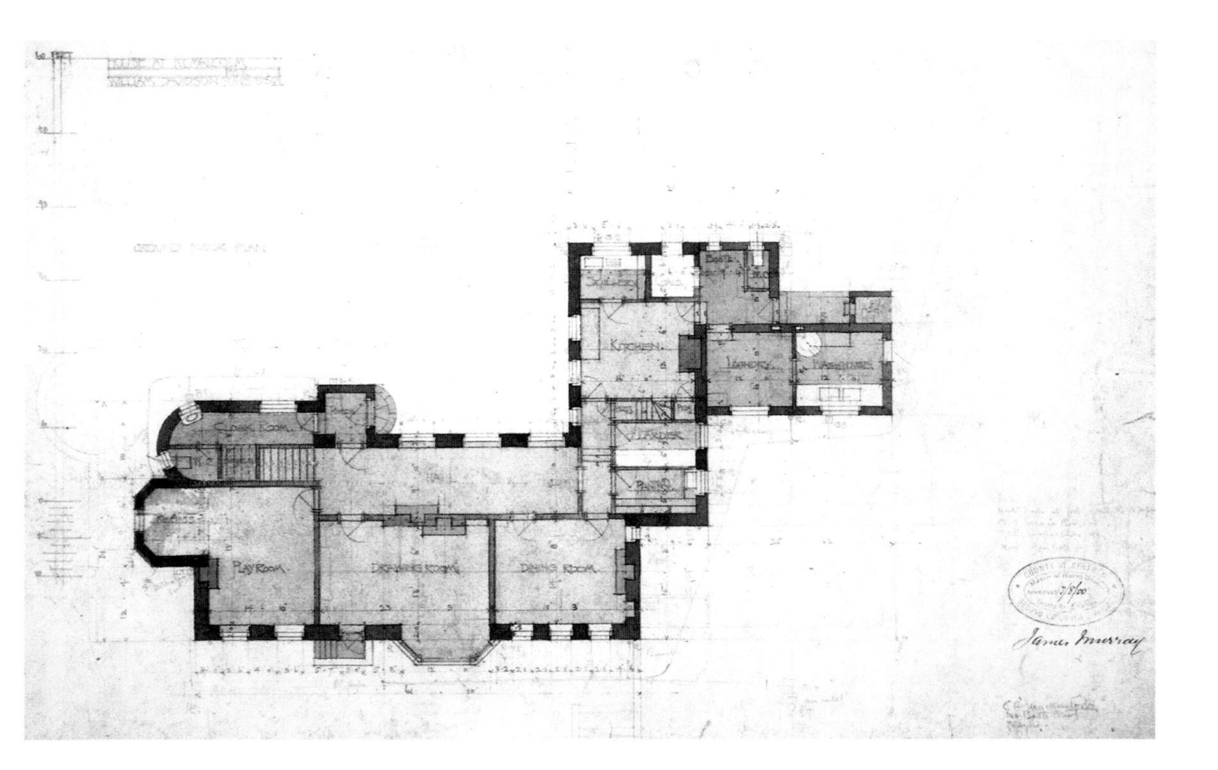

Windyhill, Kilmalcolm: design for a hall chair, 1901

Mackintosh designed the hall at Windyhill, and his other more successful domestic commission The Hill House, along similar lines. Both rooms are long, running almost the entire length of the east-west axis and have the staircase opening off them directly. Staircases were always of particular importance within Mackintosh's designs, although in this instance the integration of stairwell to hallway is more articulate in The Hill House. He designed the halls so that they could double as dining rooms and were able to seat a large number of people. The chair pictured here was one of his most unusual chair designs and was used in the hall at Windyhill. The high tapering back of the chair was a reinterpretation of his high-backed chair, but the shape lent it an appealing modern idiom. It shows him employing one of his most used techniques; that of the effectiveness of contrast. The striking straightness of the chair back sets off the gentle and unexpected curve of the arms, while the rustic nature of the natural wood and rush is at once at odds with the uniquely Modernist concept of its shape.

CREATED

Glasgow

MEDIUM

Pencil and watercolour on wove paper

SERIES/PERIOD/MOVEMENT

Chairs

SIMILAR WORKS

Oak Shakespeare chair by E. W. Godwin, *c.* 1881

Oak chair, Oak Park, Illinois by Frank Lloyd Wright, 1904

Exterior of Windyhill, Kilmalcolm, 1901

The exterior of Windyhill demonstrates Mackintosh drawing on the tradition of Scottish vernacular, but translating it into a modern context. He finished the house in a silver-grey rough cast, or harling, which was a traditional method of weatherproofing used since the fifteenth century. The house evokes the spirit of a Scottish farmhouse with the steeply pitched roof and stout chimneys, but the distribution of the windows, reflective of the internal arrangement, was inspiringly modern. The tall and narrow stairwell windows were particularly unusual in domestic architecture at this time and would not become popular for another 20 years or so. The remaining windows are small and irregularly placed with the grey harling extending right into the window openings. In traditional houses of this size and stature the windows would have been dressed with stone sills, lintels and reveals. The unremitting grey of the façade and its monumentality was criticized by local residents who referred to the house as a 'barracks'. In view of this the Davidsons later added shutters to relieve the oppressiveness of the external features.

CREATED

Glasgow

MEDIUM

Architecture

SERIES/PERIOD/MOVEMENT

Domestic architecture

SIMILAR WORKS

14 South Parade, Bedford Park, London by C. F. A. Voysey, 1891

Pen box for the White Bedroom, Hous'Hill, *c.* 1904–09

Mackintosh was commissioned by Major John Cochrane and his wife Catherine Cranston to work on their home, Hous'Hill in 1903. He was asked to redecorate the interior and design a substantial amount of furniture for the seventeenth-century mansion and so had to work within the restraints of an existing shell. The designs that Mackintosh produced for Hous'Hill are particularly interesting because they show a marked change in direction for the artist. The interiors were more stark and Minimalist in feel than anything he had designed to date and show a predominance of geometric motifs replacing his natural, organic patterns. The White Bedroom at Hous'Hill was also one of the last instances of his use of the 'white room' technique. Although he used some organic decoration on the wall lamps and bedspread, the overriding style was geometric with simple, square and oblong furniture designs. The pen box reflects the simplicity of the furniture design and was decorated with the small square motif that he continued through the house. A further unifying technique he employed was his use of mother-of-pearl inlay. This can be seen as a decorative detail on the pen box and was also used in the bedside tables in the White Bedroom.

CREATED

Glasgow

MEDIUM

Ebonized wood inlaid with mother-of-pearl and walnut

SERIES/PERIOD/MOVEMENT

Domestic interiors

SIMILAR WORKS

Jewellery casket in ebony and mother-of-pearl by Alfred Attherr, 1911

Desk for the Blue Bedroom at Hous'Hill, 1904

The Blue Bedroom was the first occasion on which Mackintosh did not use a white scheme in a bedroom. The room still retained white walls and ceiling, but all the furniture was either stained dark or was ebonized. Similar to the White Bedroom he used a predominantly geometric style, with all the furniture being designed around basic, square or rectangular forms. His main use of alleviating decorative detail was in stained-glass inlays, such as the stylized organic panel in the desk pictured. This desk is interesting because he designed a very similar one for the White Bedroom, although in that instance he painted the wood with his characteristic white enamel paint. This was one of the last instances that he painted his furniture in this way. In the Blue Bedroom he concentrated on the beauty of the wood itself, paying great attention to the fine grain and using this as a decorative feature. Little remains of the furniture that he designed for Hous'Hill and the house was later destroyed by a fire, before being pulled down by the Glasgow Corporation to make room for a housing estate.

CREATED

Glasgow

MEDIUM

Wood with glass and metal inlay

SERIES/PERIOD/MOVEMENT

Domestic interiors

SIMILAR WORKS

Bookcase by Koloman Moser, 1904–05

Chair in the drawing room, Hous'Hill, 1904

The physical restrictions of working within an existing frame coaxed from Mackintosh some of his most imaginative examples of manipulation of space. In the drawing room he used a technique that he had employed frequently in past schemes, that of subtly dividing rooms by differing ceiling heights. Mackintosh was always concerned with retaining a sense of unity through his rooms, but also focused on treating spaces to reflect their individual function. He divided the drawing room into an area for music and an area for seating, using an elegant screen that kept the overall continuation of detail and space throughout the room. One window of the room gently curved out and he made use of this slight curve as a unifying decorative detail. The dark stained chair reflects the curve feature, while also being strongly geometric in shape. This is one of three chairs of the same design, with a matching fourth armchair. They were crafted from fine-grained sycamore or beech and had the addition of a coloured-glass inset in the back.

CREATED

Glasgow

MEDIUM

Wood stained dark and inlaid with coloured glass

SERIES/PERIOD/MOVEMENT

Chairs

SIMILAR WORKS

Beechwood lacquered chair from Pürkersdorf Sanitorium by Josef Hoffmann, 1903

Armchair for the Blue Bedroom, Hous'Hill, 1905

Mackintosh kept the scheme and arrangement of furniture in the Blue Bedroom very simple and placed all of the furniture around the walls with the exception of a small square table. This technique gave the room a very uncluttered and modern feeling, in keeping with the clean and simple lines of his furniture. The chair pictured here was one of a pair that he designed to sit in front of the fireplace in the Blue Bedroom. They are highly unusual in design and beautifully plain in concept. Their semicircular shape slopes gently backwards through the elevation of the chair back, a style that reflects the slope to the sides of the room's washstand and dressing table. Each individual oak-stained plank is visible with the grain of the wood becoming as much a detail as the small inlaid squares of mother-of-pearl. Typical of his attention to detail, the back of the chairs are as attractive as the front. In this case the back of the chairs would have been seen first, as the chairs sat facing the fire.

CREATED

Glasgow

MEDIUM

Stained oak with mother-of-pearl inlay

SERIES/PERIOD/MOVEMENT

Chairs

SIMILAR WORKS

Oak chair by Gustav Stickley, *c.* 1905

Barrel chair at Martin House, Buffalo, New York by Frank Lloyd Wright, 1904

Design for the north wall of the main bedroom of The Hill House, *c.* 1903

The Hill House commissioned by Walter Blackie is considered one of the most successful examples of Mackintosh's domestic architecture. Mackintosh drew on his work at Windyhill House and his designs for the House for an Art Lover Competition as precedents for the development of The Hill House. As was often the case he was impeded by some degree of financial restraint and so was not able to realize the completely unified scheme that he had envisaged. Blackie had purchased an excellent plot of land with fantastic views across the Clyde estuary and commissioned Mackintosh to build him a family home. According to some sources, Mackintosh spent a weekend staying with the Blackie family to determine their particular domestic requirements. He then submitted the plans, having based the exterior on the interior arrangement of rooms, a technique of planning that he favoured.

The design for the north wall of the master bedroom demonstrates Mackintosh building his decorative scheme around the primary feature of the fireplace. He used a combination of small square motifs with stylized organic designs and kept a soft colour palette of pale green, silver, lilac and pink.

CREATED

Glasgow

MEDIUM

Pencil and watercolour

SERIES/PERIOD/MOVEMENT

Domestic interiors

SIMILAR WORKS

Ver Sacrum room, First Secession Exhibition, Vienna by Josef Hoffman, 1898

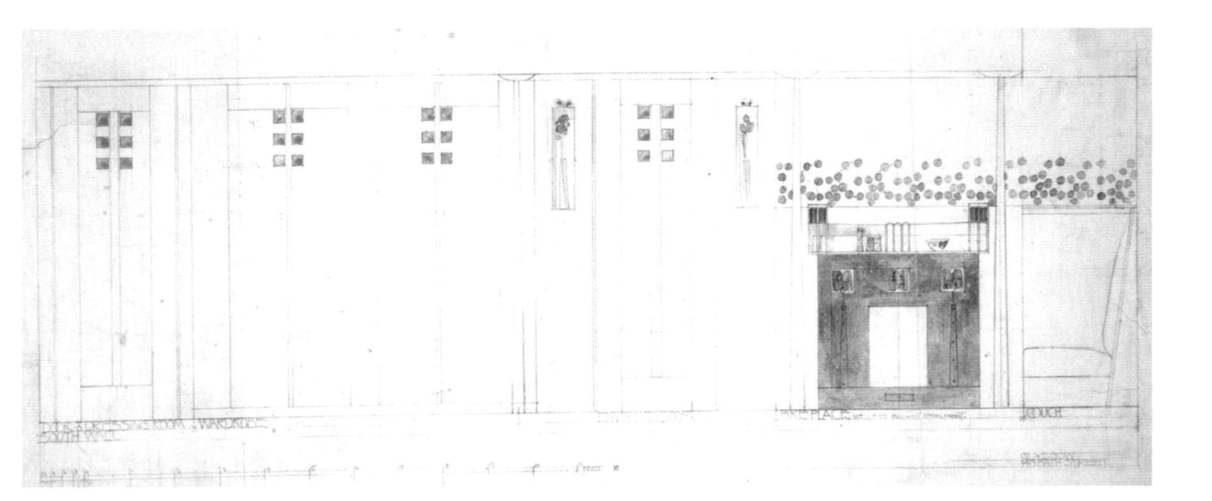
SOUTH WALL
FIREPLACE
COUCH

Detail of a wardrobe at The Hill House, *c.* 1903–04

Mackintosh's furniture designs were costly and consequently Blackie could not afford to commission all of his furniture from the artist. In order to maintain as much unity through his design as possible, Mackintosh concentrated the furniture that he did design together. The main bedroom at The Hill House is a good example of this and was exclusively furnished by Mackintosh designs. The detail, pictured, comes from one of the fitted wardrobes in the main bedroom. Mackintosh customarily included wardrobes in his bedroom schemes and in this instance made two ranges of wardrobes, running along the east and north walls of the room. The detail demonstrates his style of using pared-down organic motifs within a geometric frame and his use of colour to highlight decorative details. This pattern of basic ovals and squares was repeated throughout the bedroom, especially evident in the washstand. The pink in the wardrobe detail was one of the colours that Mackintosh used through the whole interior scheme of the house, along with pale green, silver and lilac.

CREATED

Glasgow

MEDIUM

Painted wood

SERIES/PERIOD/MOVEMENT

Domestic interiors

SIMILAR WORKS

Cabinet, exhibited at the 1900 Secessionist Exhibition, Vienna by Josef Hoffmann, *c.* 1900

Fireplace in the drawing room at The Hill House, *c.* 1903–04

The drawing room at The Hill House was a large room that Mackintosh divided into specific areas for certain functions. This was a technique that he used continually when designing interior arrangements. The fireplace occupied one end of the room, which served as the 'winter' end. He successfully combined motifs from other fireplace designs, most notably from Windyhill, the Willow Tea Rooms and 120 Mains Street into the The Hill House design. Mackintosh always paid great attention to the treatment of his fireplaces and they came to hold a significant place within his rooms. The striking mosaic surround and coloured-glass decorative motifs emphasized and complemented Margaret's gesso panel hanging directly above. Margaret and Charles collaborated extensively in the interior schemes for The Hill House, with Margaret being responsible for the fabrics, soft furnishings and some decorative details. Mackintosh used white-painted pine for the surround of the fireplace and continued this through the fireplace cabinet adjacent to the fire. The cabinet design is evocative of his favourite tree of life motif seen through the slender, decorative treatment of the shelves.

CREATED

Glasgow

MEDIUM

Interior design

SERIES/PERIOD/MOVEMENT

Domestic interiors

SIMILAR WORKS

Lounge Hall, The Orchard, Chorley Wood by C. F. A. Voysey, 1900

Writing desk for The Hill House, *c.* 1902

Mackintosh submitted several designs for this writing desk to Blackie before the final version was decided on. It is one of the most elegant of Mackintosh's designs and combines his unique stylistic vision with an unprecedented attention to detail. Mackintosh himself was very pleased with the finished piece, so much so that he made an almost identical desk for his own house. Mackintosh firmly believed in form for function, but the artist in him addressed every form with an aesthetic approach. This desk is the epitome of a functional, but beautiful work of art. The desk with its doors open conjures up the shape of a kimono and further Oriental influences are seen in the simple geometric detailing of inlaid mother-of-pearl. Mackintosh typically used the technique of applying coloured glass, metal, or semi-precious materials to his furniture and this instantly brought to life his larger, more solid pieces. A true reflection of the extent to which Mackintosh has enjoyed a recent revival is the £800,000 that was paid at auction for this writing desk.

CREATED

Glasgow

MEDIUM

Ebonized wood with inlaid mother-of-pearl, metal and glass

SERIES/PERIOD/MOVEMENT

Domestic interiors

SIMILAR WORKS

Bookcase for Mautner Markhot by Koloman Moser, 1910

Master bedroom at The Hill House, *c.* 1903–04

The master bedroom and the hall were the only two rooms at The Hill House that were furnished exclusively by Mackintosh. In this respect they offer the most unified interior schemes. The master bedroom again demonstrates Mackintosh's technique of delineating separate areas of a room. Here he has created a shallow barrel-vaulted effect in the ceiling that denotes the bed and sleeping area. The curve of the ceiling is reiterated in the curve at the foot of the bed. Mackintosh was always intensely concerned with the manipulation of light and the effect of light on his interiors. Here the small windows allow a soft illumination beyond the level of the sleeping area, while artificial lighting throws a decorative pattern on the walls to the side of the bed. The decorative wall stencilling, which was later covered over, was applied through the room and is contrasted by the dark geometric ladder-back chairs. The overall colour scheme with pastel-pink tones again unifies the room and continues through the rest of the house. In comparison to his later bedroom schemes this one remains feminine in its delicate handling and pale palette.

CREATED

Glasgow

MEDIUM

Interior design

SERIES/PERIOD/MOVEMENT

Domestic interiors

SIMILAR WORKS

The Scottish section of the dining room at the International Exhibition of Modern Decorative Art, Turin by Frances Macdonald MacNair and Herbert MacNair, 1902

Design for a Rose Boudoir by George Logan, 1903

Drawing room at The Hill House, c. 1903–04

The drawing room at The Hill House was another one of Mackintosh's 'white rooms'. In his early domestic commissions he followed a pattern of using predominantly white in bedrooms and drawing rooms, and treating dining rooms, libraries and billiard rooms with a darker colour scheme. The drawing room at The Hill House was a particularly fine example of his white rooms and was divided into a summer and winter end. The summer end, pictured, was denoted by a lower ceiling than the rest of the room and comprised a light-filled space surrounding a long horizontal bank of windows. A long window seat with adjacent magazine racks ran the length of the windows and had built-in heating under the seat to ward off the all-pervasive Scottish chill. From the inside looking out there was a spectacular view down to the Clyde, from the exterior the little bay was presented as a glazed projection from the main elevation of the house. The curtains would have been designed by Margaret and echoed the shapes of the window panes and the geometric motifs on the wall stencilling.

CREATED

Glasgow

MEDIUM

Interior design

SERIES/PERIOD/MOVEMENT

Domestic interiors

SIMILAR WORKS

Drawing room, Middleton, Lancashire by Edgar Wood, 1891

Exterior view of The Hill House, *c.* 1903–04

Mackintosh's L-shape floor plan allowed the living quarters to sit on one axis, while the service areas were kept separate on their own axis. At The Hill House the join between them is marked by an unusual, round, stairwell encased within a turret. This design was unusual in domestic architecture at this time and was further emphasized by the smaller turreted tool shed sitting below it. The exterior looks to the tradition of Baronial Scottish architecture in spirit and rendering with the time-worn use of harling on the outside walls. The surprising Mackintosh twist, however, is displayed through his use of highly varied window shapes. His exacting approach to detail was demonstrated in his use of the dark grey roofing tiles. During building, a strike at the quarry severely delayed the delivery of the tiles and it was suggested that he look for a different material. None other would do; Mackintosh remained firm and eventually he got his required tiles! Blackie later said of the architect, 'Every detail inside, as well as outside, received his careful, I might say loving, attention'.

CREATED

Glasgow

MEDIUM

Architecture

SERIES/PERIOD/MOVEMENT

Domestic interiors

SIMILAR WORKS

Blackwell, Cumbria by M. H. Baillie Scott, 1898–1900

Extension to Stirling High School by James MacLaren, 1888

Detail of a wall stencil for The Hill House, *c.* 1903–04

The technique of stencilling was one that Charles and Margaret both used extensively, primarily for wall decorations, but also on furnishing fabrics and curtains. This design that was used in the drawing room at The Hill House is characteristic of Mackintosh, combining his favourite organic motif of the rose, within a geometric form. Mackintosh had the seemingly divergent interests in organic and geometric visualizations but brought the two together in a totally harmonious manner. The black and white chequerboard pattern was one that he employed frequently in his designs and his use of squares as decorative details became increasingly prevalent. The soft pink and green contrasted with the black and white was typical of this period of Mackintosh's designs. After moving to London in 1915 his colours became bolder and more vibrant, with his designs evolving ever more geometrically.

This particular design was used to create a panelling effect on the walls in the The Hill House drawing room and echoed the design of the central light fitting and the squares in the carpet. The hanging light fitting was later replaced by wall lights and the ceiling was then painted a dark plum colour.

CREATED

Glasgow

MEDIUM

Green, pink, silver and black-painted wall stencil

SERIES/PERIOD/MOVEMENT

Domestic interiors

SIMILAR WORKS

The Enchanted Farm by Jessie M. King, 1904

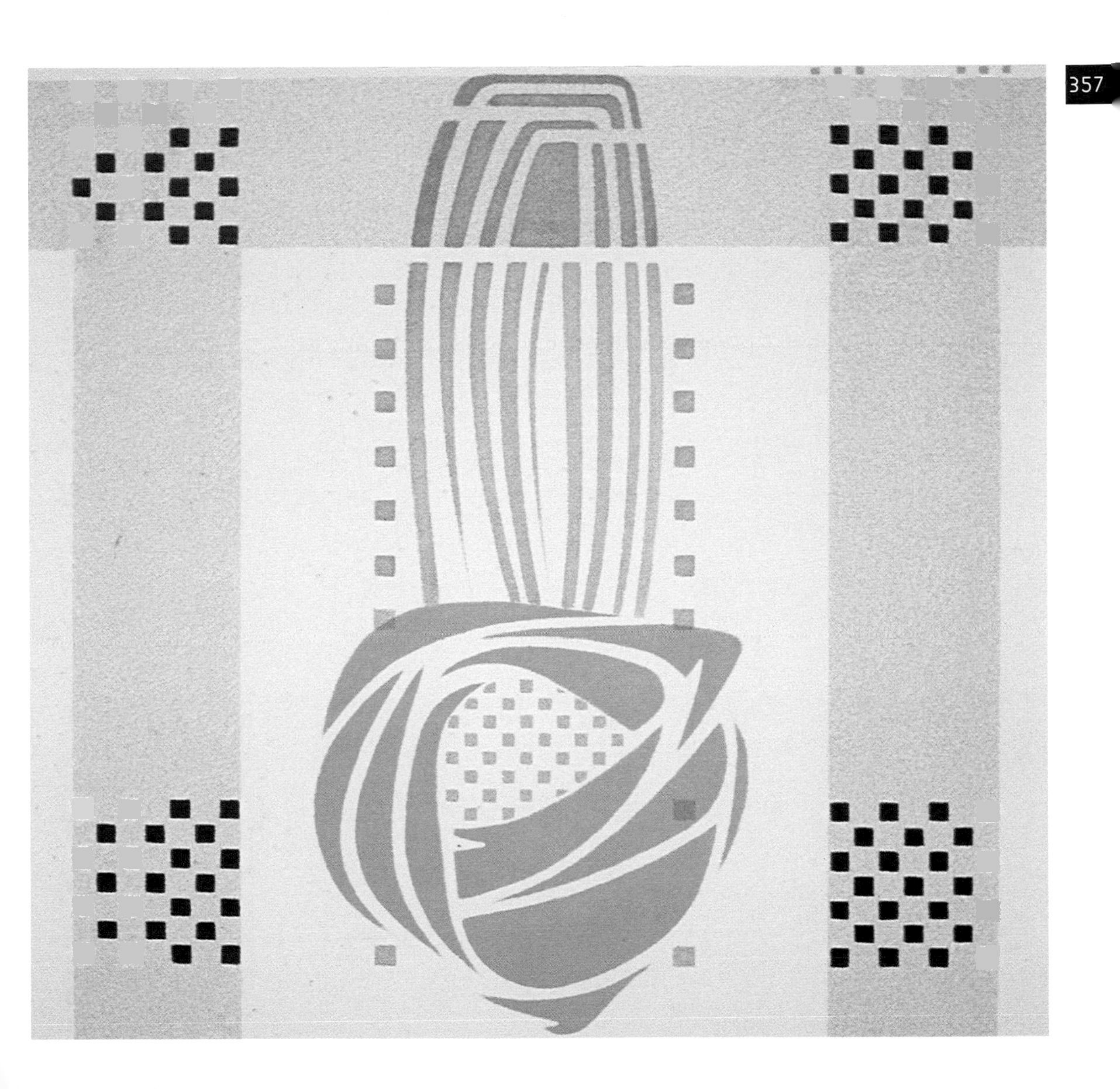

Fabric design, 1916

The surviving sketches for fabric designs that Mackintosh made during his London years offer a fascinating look at the artist's working process. Here, for example, he was experimenting with various colours, building up his pattern in different areas so that he could compare the aesthetic effect. This drawing also demonstrates his technique of using a pencil-drawn grid with which to base his pattern around. This grid technique was seen many times in his drawings, as was his use of varying papers and working materials, although he favoured tracing paper and a combination of watercolour and pencil or ink. His interest in different mediums was further explored through his use of coloured glass, inlaid precious materials and metal panels as decorative details. This sketch is similar to the designs that he created while working at 78 Derngate for W. J. Bassett-Lowke. He produced a series of stunningly modern interior schemes for Bassett-Lowke that centred on bold geometric patterns of triangles and squares. The use of the triangle as a motif was one that the Viennese designer Josef Urban greatly favoured.

CREATED

London

MEDIUM

Pencil and body colour on oiled tracing paper

SERIES/PERIOD/MOVEMENT

London textile designs

SIMILAR WORKS

Ebro fabric sample by Maria Likarz, 1926

Settle, 1916

Shortly after settling in London Mackintosh received a commission to redecorate a small house in Northampton, 78 Derngate, from W. J. Bassett-Lowke. Bassett-Lowke was the affluent owner of a scale-model factory and was a founding member of the Design and Industries Association. He was a strong-minded individual with a keen concept of modern technology and was also a designer in his own right. This meant that the interiors and the furniture that Mackintosh developed for him had to complement Bassett-Lowke's own designs. The commission marked a significant change in Mackintosh's style and techniques. The geometric influence that had been creeping into his work now bloomed with an absorbing intensity. His furniture designs, such as this settle that lived in the hall at Derngate, were predominantly plain and sturdy, their decorative appeal crafted through the use of punched-out squares and simplicity of design. His furniture designed in London was made by highly skilled craftsmen and the quality of their fabrication is evident. Many of Mackintosh's Glasgow designs were assembled by local carpenters more used to working in the shipping yards.

CREATED

London

MEDIUM

Black-lacquered wood with upholstery

SERIES/PERIOD/MOVEMENT

London furniture designs

SIMILAR WORKS

Sofa in entrance hall, Pürkersdorf Sanatorium by Koloman Moser, 1903

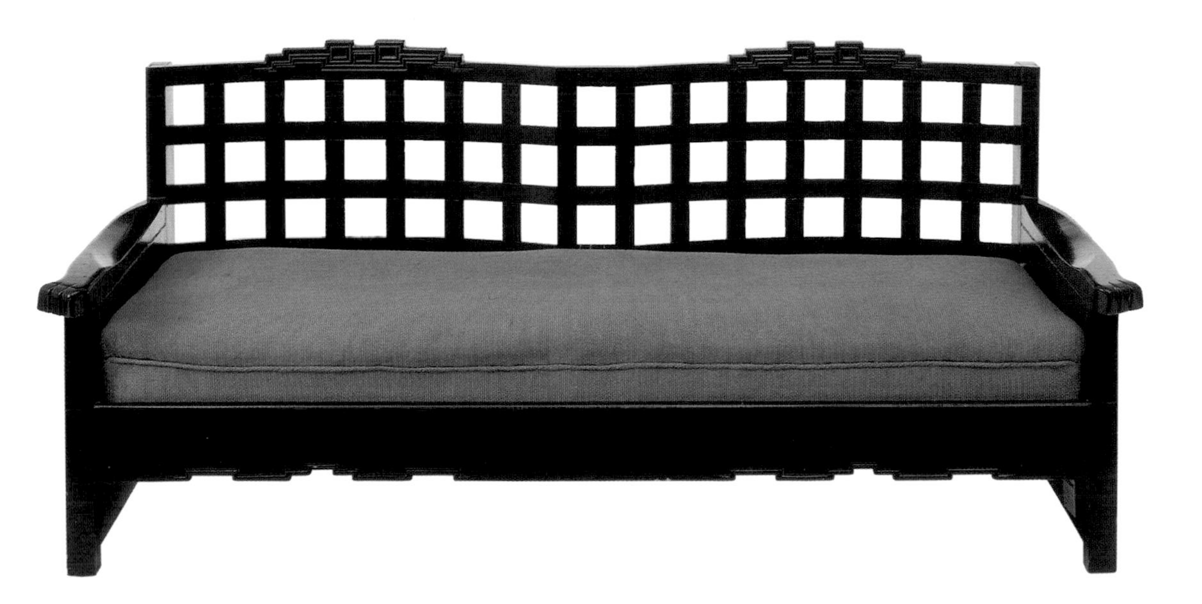

Smoker's cabinet, 1916

Bassett-Lowke was certainly the most knowledgeable of Mackintosh's clients with regard to design and construction, and required functional furniture that was well made and unfussy. One of the most striking aspects of Mackintosh's furniture designed for Derngate is the solidity of it, with every piece demanding attention. The aesthetic effect of the furniture was achieved through the austere and simple form of each piece combined with geometric detailing. Mackintosh developed a dark colour scheme alleviated with vibrant highlights for the hallway at Derngate and designed much of the furniture for this area in a dark lacquered wood. All the furniture in this room was based on a square lattice design for detailing apart from the door screen and the Smoker's Cabinet. Mackintosh's use of bold and simple form can be seen in this smoker's cabinet, which is decorated with diamond and triangle shapes. This is one of the first examples of Mackintosh using erinoid, a synthetic plastic material, as an inlaid design feature in his furniture. Mackintosh's use of synthetic materials in this manner shows his knowledge of the new industries and technologies.

CREATED

London

MEDIUM

Black-lacquered wood with erinoid inlay

SERIES/PERIOD/MOVEMENT

London furniture designs

SIMILAR WORKS

Small cabinet, maple and ebony with ivory knobs designed by the *Wiener Werkstätte*, c. 1905

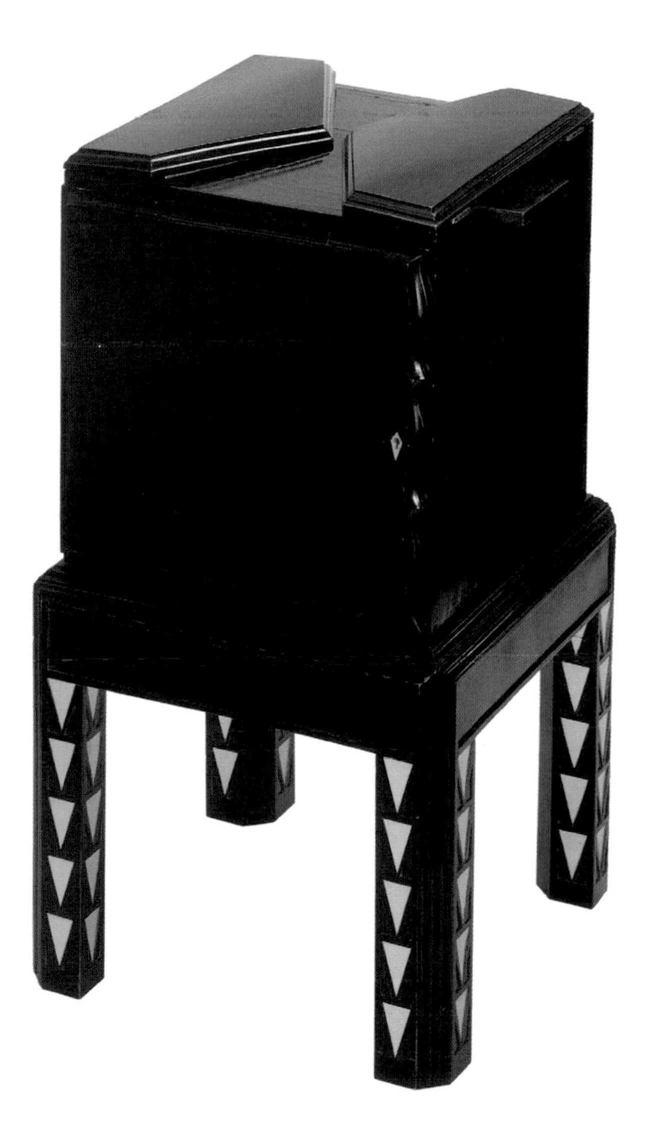

Curtain design for hall windows for W. J. Bassett-Lowke, 1916–17

The Derngate commission required Mackintosh to be truly inventive in order to make the most of the small, cramped existing interior. He made several changes to the house to increase the floor space, one of which was an impressive three-storey extension to the back of the house that is described by Thomas Howarth as 'predating any other Modern Movement work in Britain'. This is a measure of the unique design concept with which Mackintosh approached this project. The first room of the house, the hallway, immediately set the precedent for the rest of the scheme. The front door, which was painted black with inset panels of leaded glass in a triangular pattern, opened into the hall, which served as a hallway and a parlour. The ceiling and walls were painted black with a frieze of vibrant-coloured triangles sitting on a band of black and white chequerboards running around the top. This sketch for curtain fabric draws its design from the theme of the room, with the slight curve in the pattern perhaps representative of the ripple of the curtains as they hang.

CREATED

London

MEDIUM

Pencil and body colour on oiled tracing paper

SERIES/PERIOD/MOVEMENT

London textile designs

SIMILAR WORKS

Furnishing fabric by Madame de Andrada, 1925

Design for a clock face for W. J. Bassett-Lowke, 1917

The design of Mackintosh's clocks is another example of the extraordinary attention to detail that was characteristic of him. It was this attention to detail that made him difficult to work with, but that also ensured his designs were the most impressively cohesive. An amusing indication of the artist's fastidiousness was his insistence that the trees at The Hill House be pruned to the exact shape of the trees in his original architectural drawings and, not content with just that, he apparently rebuked Mrs Blackie for her flower arrangement in the hall at The Hill House because the colours clashed with his interior scheme!

This preliminary drawing for one of the clocks at Derngate expresses the geometry of its intended surroundings and shows Mackintosh developing his colour scheme. The finished clock face was supported by ten columns and the decorative details seen in his drawing were achieved through inlaid ivory and green erinoid. This clock is similar in concept, although more stunning, than one he had designed for The Hill House. Here the black-lacquered surround vividly contrasts with the ivory and erinoid creating a dramatic effect.

CREATED

London

MEDIUM

Pencil and watercolour

SERIES/PERIOD/MOVEMENT

London designs

SIMILAR WORKS

Wall clock by Margaret Gilmour

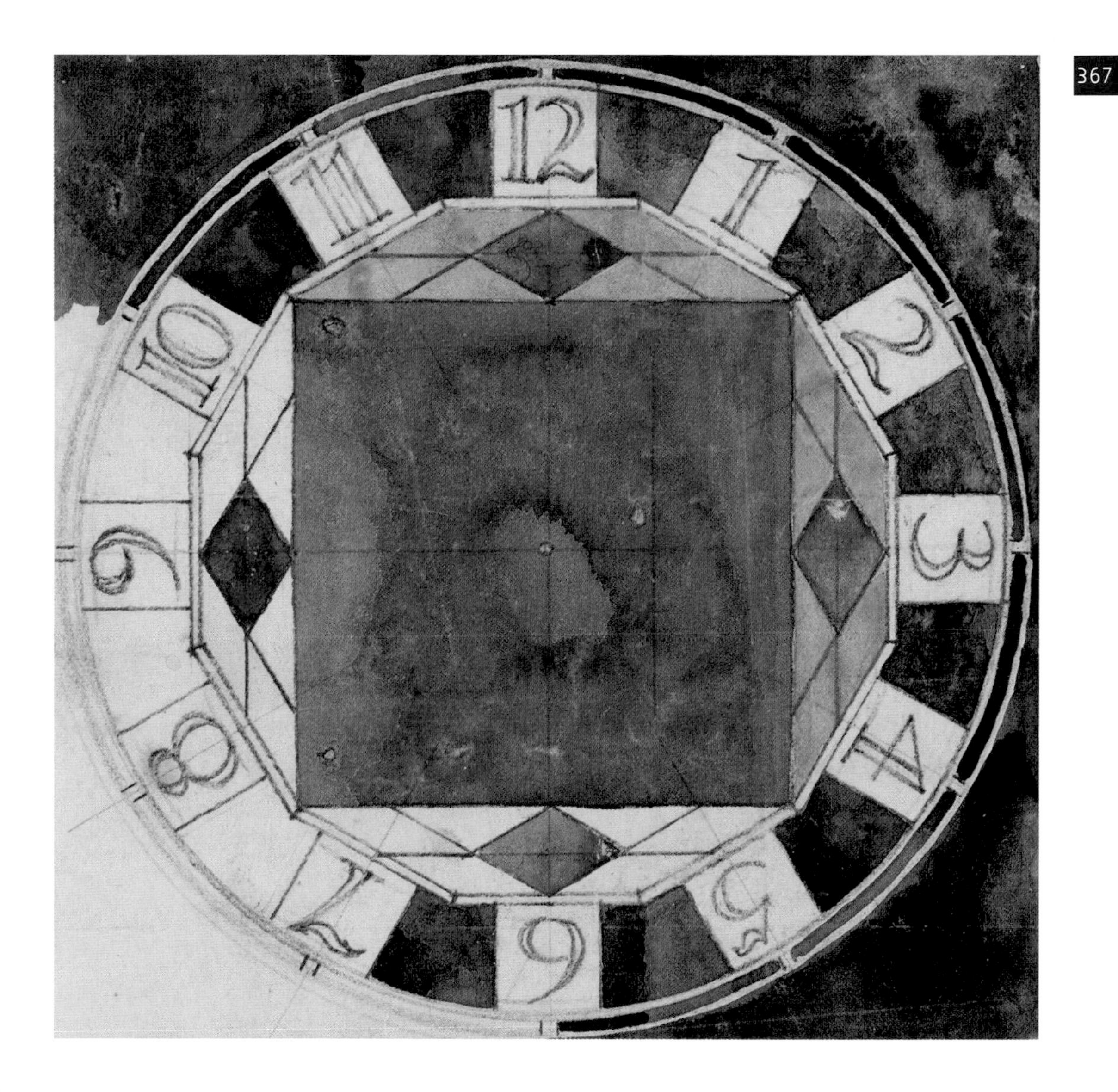
12
1
2
3
4
5
6
7
8
9
10
11

Bedroom at 78 Derngate, Northampton, 1919

The guest bedroom at 78 Derngate was one of the most striking interiors that Mackintosh designed. His style of paring down elements to their most minimal was at its most effective here, where the stunning stripes created an arresting visual effect. The furniture he designed for the room was simple in shape and form, the only decorative details being small punched-out squares on the bed baseboards and a narrow frieze of ultramarine squares highlighting the simple furniture design. This detail was similar to the work of Hans Offner, a member of the Viennese School. The white-painted walls and ceiling were striped with black and white, with ultramarine harness-braid edging the design. Thomas Howarth relates an amusing story told by Mr Bassett-Lowke about a visit from his friend George Bernard Shaw. On showing him the bedroom Bassett-Lowke said, 'I trust the décor will not disturb your sleep', to which Shaw replied, 'No, I always sleep with my eyes closed'.

The techniques and artistic vision that Mackintosh used at Derngate were leading the way towards a new concept of design that was realized through the emergence of Art Deco in the 1920s and 1930s. As with all great artists, Mackintosh was somewhat ahead of his time.

CREATED

London

MEDIUM

Interior design

SERIES/PERIOD/MOVEMENT

London interiors

SIMILAR WORKS

Drawing room by Josef Hoffmann, 1911

Bedroom by Wilhelm Keppler, 1911

Bedroom suite for the guest bedroom at 78 Derngate, 1917

The guest bedroom at Derngate was originally furnished in a similar style to the master bedroom and the mahogany furniture pictured is from this first design scheme. The stunning and unique striped arrangement was the result of a process of redecoration that took place in 1919. Unfortunately no pictures survive of the room as it first appeared. This original mahogany suite retains the simple mass and structure of the furniture from the master bedroom and was a style that Mackintosh repeated for two other private commissions. The pieces are very effective with the clean spare lines of their form being aesthetic and uncluttered. He used his technique of inlaid mother-of-pearl and aluminium to create decorative detail, which he kept to a minimum. He was also keenly aware of the beauty of natural wood and treated the grain in the planes of wood as a decorative feature. As such, he paid great attention to the type and quality of wood that was used in these designs. The furniture in his later scheme was primarily sycamore and was edged with a narrow band of aquamarine squares.

CREATED

London

MEDIUM

Interior design

SERIES/PERIOD/MOVEMENT

London furniture designs

SIMILAR WORKS

Pearwood bedroom furniture by Karl Bertsch, 1907

Washstand

Mackintosh's love of nature was an enduring passion that he frequently referred to in his designs throughout his career. Even in his London years when he was focusing on strong geometric patterns he would still incorporate heavily stylized organic motifs. It was not an unduly surprising change of direction for him to turn to landscape painting at the end of his career.

This washstand that he designed for Walter Blackie to match an existing chest of drawers incorporates a number of characteristic Mackintosh techniques. He has again turned to the stylized tree motif and used a shimmering mosaic of glass and pewter set in plain wood to depict it. Mackintosh often used inlaid coloured glass accents in his furniture favouring the reflective quality of their surface. He was acutely aware of the play of light and how to manipulate it and considered this in relation to the positioning of his furniture. Nothing Mackintosh designed was random and every detail was so placed to create a specific effect. His use of beautiful, warm, dark wood in this washstand contrasts and complements the icy hard finish of the mosaic splashback.

CREATED

Glasgow

MEDIUM

Mahogany

SERIES/PERIOD/MOVEMENT

Glasgow furniture designs

SIMILAR WORKS

Washstand, pine, marble and ceramic tile by E. W. Godwin, *c.* 1870

Screen for the Willow Tea Rooms, 1903

Photos © Hunterian Museum and Art Gallery, University of Glasgow, Mackintosh Collection

Located on the fashionable Sauchiehall Street in Glasgow the Willow Tea Rooms were amongst the most luxurious and innovative tea rooms that Mackintosh designed. The panel pictured here formed part of a screen that separated the Front Saloon from the entrance and corridor leading to the staircase up to the Salon De Luxe. Mackintosh made use of coloured glass and insets throughout the interior scheme at the Willow Tea Rooms and was particularly attentive to the effect created by sunlight filtering coloured rays through the glass panels.

The screen was wooden and painted white, forming a neutral background for the stunningly simple glass panels. Above the screen Mackintosh designed an unusual abstract plaster relief frieze that evoked images of the tree of life theme in a wholly intricate and decorative manner. The white walls and table cloths provided the perfect foil for the dark painted ladder-back chairs, which in turn echoed the strong verticality of the glass-panel design in the screen. Mackintosh's technique of continuing the smallest details through his schemes for a unifying totality was propagated so subtly that one is unaware of the process, but appreciative of the result.

CREATED

Glasgow

MEDIUM

Leaded glass

SERIES/PERIOD/MOVEMENT

Tea Rooms

SIMILAR WORKS

Entrance door to the Petöfi Museum, Budapest by József Vágó

Glass panel from the Willow Tea Rooms, 1903

The Salon De Luxe was one of the most exquisitely jewel-like interiors that Mackintosh designed. The accent for the room was firmly established by the entrance doors, a glittering wealth of sculpted coloured glass whose soft hues and tones were repeated through the room. He used a palette of delicate silver, grey, white and pink, which can be seen in the glass panel pictured and which was reflected in the partially mirrored interior bathing the room in opulent splendour. This glass panel formed part of a frieze that continued around the room, the slender stylized forms echoing the theme of the willow tree and complementing the composition of Margaret's gesso panel, *O Ye, All Ye That Walk in Willow Wood*. The sumptuous extravagance of the room was further emphasized by the elegant high-backed chairs, painted silver with lavish purple velvet seats and a pierced pattern of coloured-glass squares on the backs. His use of coloured-glass accents and mirrors helped to create an exotic atmosphere that appealed to the public, causing people to flock to the stunningly unique restaurant.

CREATED

Glasgow

MEDIUM

Leaded glass

SERIES/PERIOD/MOVEMENT

Tea Rooms

SIMILAR WORKS

Entrance door to a theatre in Budapest by József Vágó, 1913

Author Biographies

Tamsin Pickeral (author)

Tamsin Pickeral has studied Art and History of Art since she was child, and lived for some time in Italy furthering her appreciation of the subject. She has travelled extensively throughout her life, and has recently returned to the UK after nine years spent living an unusual life on a cattle ranch in the US. She now resides in Norfolk with her husband, where she continues to write about art and horses, two of her favourite subjects.

Anne Ellis (foreword)

Anne Elllis is an architectural historian with a classical background, having first lectured on classical civilization then architecture and design at Glasgow University. She still does a few lectures every year for the university's History of Art Department, in between writing articles and reviewing books. For 12 years she was the curator at The Hill House, Helensburgh, designed by Mackintosh, and describes her time there as 'absolute heaven – like living inside a work of art!'. More recently an interest in broadcasting has developed into a regular slot presenting *The Arts Show* for Radio Scotland.

Picture Credits: Prelims and Introductory Matter

Pages 1 & 3: Charles Rennie Mackintosh, *A Southern Town*, Photos © Hunterian Museum and Art Gallery, University of Glasgow, Mackintosh Collection
Page 4: Charles Rennie Mackintosh, *Rome, Arch of Titius* © Christie's Images Ltd
Page 5 (l to r top): Charles Rennie Mackintosh (all): *Wareham, Dorset* © Christie's Images Ltd; Textile design © The Fine Art Society, London, UK/www.bridgeman.co.uk; Sidechair © Christie's Images Ltd
Page 5 (l to r bottom): Charles Rennie Mackintosh (all): Interior of the stair tower of Scotland Street School © Anthony Oliver; Sign for the Willow Tea Rooms © Anthony Oliver; *La Rue du Soleil*, Photos © Hunterian Museum and Art Gallery, University of Glasgow, Mackintosh Collection
Page 6 (l to r top): Charles Rennie Mackintosh (all): Study of a doorway, Naples, S. Trinita Maggiore © Christie's Images Ltd; Glasgow School of Art, exterior from the north-west © Bridgeman Art Library, London/www.bridgeman.co.uk; Glasgow School of Art: the boardroom © Anthony Oliver
Page 6 (l to r bottom): William Richard Lethaby, Design for a room © Victoria & Albert Museum, 2005; Augustus Welby Northmore Pugin, Table with carved and chamfered decoration © Victoria & Albert Museum, 2005; Herbert McNair, *Ysighlu*, from *The Yellow Book* © Estate of Herbert Mac Nair/University of Liverpool Art Gallery & Collections, UK/www.bridgeman.co.uk
Page 7: Charles Rennie Mackintosh (all): Railing from the Willow Tea Rooms © Christie's Images Ltd; Writing desk for The Hill House © The Fine Art Society, London, UK/www.bridgeman.co.uk; Bedroom at 78 Derngate © Anthony Oliver
Page 12: Charles Rennie Mackintosh, Master bedroom at The Hill House © Anthony Oliver
Page 15: Charles Rennie Mackintosh, Detail from an ebonized mahogany writing cabinet © Christie's Images Ltd
Page 16: Charles Rennie Mackintosh, *Collioure* © The Fine Art Society, London, UK/www.bridgeman.co.uk
Page 17: Charles Rennie Mackintosh, Detail of a wall stencil from The Hill House © National Trust for Scotland
Page 18: Charles Rennie Mackintosh: House for an Art Lover: design for a music room with panels by Margaret Macdonald Mackintosh © The Stapleton Collection/www.bridgeman.co.uk

Further Reading

With thanks to the Hunterian Museum, Glasgow, and the Charles Rennie Mackintosh Society

Benton, C., *Art Deco 1910–1939*, V&A Publications, 2003

Billcliffe, R. (ed.), *Mackintosh Textile Designs*, John Murray, 1982

Billcliffe, R., *Mackintosh Furniture*, Cameron and Hollis, 1990

Billcliffe, R., *Mackintosh Watercolours*, John Murray, 1992

Brandstätter, C., *Wonderful Wiener Werkstätte: Design in Vienna 1903–1932*, Thames and Hudson, 2003

Buchanan, W., *Mackintosh's Masterwork: Charles Rennie Mackintosh & the Glasgow School of Art*, Chronicle Books, 1989

Burkhauser, J. (ed.), *Glasgow Girls: Women in Art and Design, 1880–1920*, Canongate Books Ltd, 1990

Crawford, A., *Charles Rennie Mackintosh*, Thames and Hudson Ltd, 1995

Duncan, A., *Art Nouveau Furniture*, Thames and Hudson Ltd, 1982

Duncan, A., *Art Nouveau*, Thames and Hudson Ltd, 1994

Hackney, F. & I., *Charles Rennie Mackintosh*, Apple Press, 1989

Hiesinger, K. B. (ed.), *Art Nouveau in Munich: Masters of the Jugendstil*, Prestel Verlag, 1988

Howarth, T., *Charles Rennie Mackintosh and the Modern Movement*, Routledge, 1977

Jones, A., *Charles Rennie Mackintosh*, Smithmark Publications, 1996

Kaplan, W, (ed.), *Charles Rennie Mackintosh*, Abbeville Press, 1996

Kinchin, P., *Tea and Taste: The Glasgow Tea Rooms 1875–1975*, White Cockade Publishing, 1991

Koizumi, K., *Traditional Japanese Furniture*, Kodansha Europe, 1995

MacLeod, R., *Charles Rennie Mackintosh: Art and Artist*, E. P. Dutton, 1983

Parry, L. (ed.), *William Morris*, Philip Wilson Publishers, 1996

Poulson, C., *William Morris*, Apple Press, 1989

Rennhofer, M., *Koloman Moser: Master of Viennese Modernism*, Thames and Hudson Ltd, 2002

Robertson, P. (ed.), *Charles Rennie Mackintosh: The Architectural Papers*, White Cockdale Publishing, 1990

Robertson, P., *Charles Rennie Mackintosh: Art is a Flower*, Pavilion Books Ltd, 1995

Samuels, C., *Art Deco Textiles*, V&A Publications, 2003

Schweiger, W. J., *Wiener Werkstätte: Design in Vienna, 1903–32*, Thames and Hudson Ltd, 1990

Soros, S. W., *E. W. Godwin: Aesthetic Movement Architect and Designer*, Yale University Press, 1999

Steele, J., *Charles Rennie Mackintosh: Synthesis in Form*, Wiley-Academy, 1994

Toman, R. (ed.), *Vienna: Art and Architecture*, Konemann UK Ltd, 1999

Vergo, P., *Art in Vienna, 1898-1918: Klimt, Schiele and Their Contemporaries*, Phaidon Press, 1993

Wilhide, E., *Mackintosh Style: Design and Décor*, Chronicle Books, 1998

Index by Work

Works are by Charles Rennie Mackintosh unless otherwise specified

Apple 65
Arch of Titus, Rome 161
Argyle Street Tea Rooms
Armchair designed for the billiards and smoking room 325
Armchair, dining chair and occasional table 35
Armchair *c.* 1897 319
Arts League of Service Studios, elevation 139

Blackthorn 249
Blue and pink tobacco flower design 275
Buchanan Street Tea Rooms
Preliminary design for a mural decoration 131
Butterfly Flower 251

Casket, 1909 317
Casket *c.* 1895 31
Certosa di Pavia
Studies of the ceiling decoration 151
Study of a Jesuit Altar 23
Study of an angel statue 153
Collioure 223
Conversazione Programme 27

Daily Record building, Glasgow 107
Decorative panel of beaten metal 289
78 Derngate, Northampton
Bedroom 369
Bedroom suite for the guest bedroom 371
Curtain design for hall windows 365
Design for a clock face 367
Design for the staircase screen in the hall 229
Design based on concentric circles 75
Design for a bookplate (Margaret Macdonald Mackintosh) 287
Design for a Cabinet for H. Bruckmann 41
Design for a decorative frieze (Frances Madonald MacNair) 295
Design for an Exhibition Stand for Francis Smith 49
Design for a printed textile 239
Design for a room (Lethaby) 231
Design for a smoker's cabinet 185
Design for a wall with a table and doors for A. S. Ball 187
Design for W. J. Bassett-Lowke 69
Design with dotted curvilinear element for textile 81
Design with stylized bird motif 263
Detail from an ebonized mahogany writing cabinet 57
Dining room suite 87
Diploma of Honour designed for the Glasgow School of Art Club 285
Domino Clock 71
Dress fabric, 1918 85

Elevation of a wall for the dining room of A. S. Ball 59
Elevation of proposed studio in Glebe Place 89

Fabric design, 1916 359
Fireplace from the Salon De Luxe in the Willow Tea Rooms 113
Floral and checked fabric design 255
The Fort 91
Four Spoons for Miss Cranston's Tea Rooms 109
Fritillaria 253
Furnishing Fabric designed for William Foxton, 1918 211
Furnishing Fabric designed for William Foxton, 1922 209

Glasgow Herald building
Extension to 103
Glasgow School of Art
The Boardroom 183
Design for display and bookcase for the Ladies' Common Room 175
Detail of the ironwork of the north façade 313
Director's Room 39
Glass Detail 181
Library 179
View of a Roof Arch from the West (photograph) 173
View of a Studio (photograph) 177
Views of the Exterior 37, 171
Glass Panel, 1902 51

Here's a Kiss to the Whole World! (Klimt) 301
High-backed chair, *c.* 1898–99 323
The Hill House, Helensburgh
Design for a couch for the drawing room 135
Design for the north wall of the main bedroom 343
Detail of a wall stencil 357
Detail of a wardrobe 345
Drawing room 353
Exterior view 355
Fireplace in the drawing room 347
Garden 247
Master bedroom 351
Rose motif 237
Washstand 371
Writing desk 349
House for an Art Lover competition
Children's nursery room 203
Design for a dining room 195
Design for a Music Room (with Margaret Macdonald Mackintosh) 199
Dining room side table 197
Floor plans 193
Perspective exterior view 53
Sides of the music room and reception room 201
South elevation 191
Title page of folio 189
Hous'hill
Armchair for the blue bedroom 341
Chair in the drawing rooms 339
Desk for the blue bedroom 337
Pen box for the white bedroom 335

Ingram Street Tea Rooms
Chair for the Chinese Room 131
Designs for writing desks 127
Domino table and chairs 129
Hat, coat and umbrella stand for the White Dining Room 125

14 Kingsborough Gardens
Cabinet 55
Detail from a display cabinet 241

Larkspur 67
The Lighthouse 215
The Little Bay 93
Lornes cabinet with printed panels
(Margaret Macdonald Mackintosh) 271

Mackintosh, Charles Rennie
(photograph of) 25
120 Mains Street
Designs for Bedroom Furniture and
Fireplace 45
Fourposter Bed 43
Martyr's Public School, Glasgow
Perspective drawing of 97
The May Queen (Margaret Macdonald
Mackintosh) 291
Metal and leaded-glass hanging shade 243
Miss Cranston's Tea Rooms (photograph) 63,
137, 145
Montacute House, Somerset 33
Mont Louis Flower Study 259
Mosside, Kilmalcolm 205

Naples, S. Trinita Maggiore, study of a
doorway 169

Oh Ye, All Ye That Walk in Willow Wood
(Margaret Macdonald Mackintosh) 299
Opera of the Seas (Margaret Macdonald
Mackintosh) 273
Orvieto Cathedral, a sheet of studies of mosaic
bands 159

Palermo, Campanile Martorana 165
Palermo Cathedral, study of an entrance porch
163
Panel from a lampshade (Margaret Macdonald
Mackintosh) 297
Part Seen, Imagined Part 303
Pine Cones 261
Pompeii, a sheet of studies 167
Poster for an Exhibition
at the Glasgow Institute of Fine Arts 277
Proposed theatre in Chelsea
for Margaret Morris 141

Queen Margaret's Medical College
Proposed Hall of Residence 105
Queen's Cross Church
Detail of a beam above the altar 269
Interior view 267

Reflections 280
Repeating design with stylized flower and scale
motifs 73
The Road Through the Rocks 219
The Rocks 221
Roses on a chequered ground,
textile 207
La Rue du Soleil 147

S. Trinito Maggiore doorway,
Naples 169
Sconce (Margaret Macdonald Mackintosh) 281
Scotland Street School
Interior of the stair tower 101
Perspective drawing 99
Settle, 1916 361
Sidechair, *c.* 1905–10 5, 61
Smoker's cabinet, 1916 363
A Southern Town 217
The Spirit of the Rose (Frances Macdonald
MacNair) (1903) 309
The Spirit of the Rose (Frances MacDonald
McNair) (*c.* 1900) 307
Still Life of Anemones 257
Stork's Bill, Holy Island 47
Studies of decorative ceiling panels, San Miniato
155
Study of the tomb of Carlo Marsuppini, Santa
Croce 157
Stylized Rose 235
Stylized chrysanthemums,
textile design 143
Stylized floral design on trellis
background 265

Table service designed for
E. Bingham and Co. 319
Table with carved and chamfered decoration
(Pugin) 233
Table with mother-of-pearl inlay 83
Textile Design 77
Titania (Margaret Macdonald Mackintosh) 305

Wareham, Dorset 29
Washstand *c.* 1917 79, 373
The Wassail 293
The White Cockade
Illustration for a menu 111
White oval side table 227
Willow Tea Rooms
Design for chairs in the Salon De Luxe 119
Glass panel 377
Ladder-back chairs 327
Railing 315
Rare Ladder-Back Chair 115
Screen 375
Settle from the Dug Out 121
Sign for 117
Windyhill House, Kilmalcolm
Design for a hall chair 331
Exterior 333
Plan of the ground floor 329
Plan of west elevation 133

Yellow Clover 245
Yellow Tulips 211
Ysighlu (MacNair) 279

General Index

Aestheticism 16, 270
Arch of Titus, Rome 158–9
architecture *see under* Mackintosh, Charles Rennie
Argyle Street Tea Rooms 34, 40, 60, 62–3, 126, 322, 324–5
Art Deco 13, 210, 228, 238, 254, 368
Art Nouveau 10–11, 36, 120, 164, 194, 210, 226, 236, 254, 272, 278, 280, 282, 294, 300
Arts and Crafts movement 194, 226, 230, 238, 240, 280, 300, 320
Arts and Crafts Society 80
 1888 Exhibition 230
 1896 Exhibition 36, 184, 238, 240, 288
Arts League of Service 88, 140–2
asymmetry and symmetry 22, 116, 190, 284, 312
Austria *see* Vienna

Baillie Scott, M.H. 52, 188, 190, 194
Baird, John 104
Ball, A. S. 58, 184
Basile, Giovan Battista 164
Bassett-Lowke, W. J. 13, 68, 70, 72, 84, 86, 90, 228, 358, 360, 362, 368
batik craft 208
Bauer, Leopold 188
Beardsley, Aubrey 122, 262, 272, 278, 286
Behrens, Peter 13, 72, 90, 228
Billcliffe, Roger (author) 248
Blackie, Walter 11, 56, 90, 134, 140, 236, 246, 281, 302, 342, 344, 348, 355, 372
Blunt, Arthur Cadogan 88
Braques, Georges 262
British Architect, The 104
Brooks, Miss 90
Bruckmann, H. 40, 58
Buchanan Street Tea Rooms 130–1, 136–7, 302
Burne-Jones, Edward 282
Butterfield, William 233

cabinets 54–7, 184–5
Candida Cottage 84
caskets 30–31, 316–17
Celtic imagery 150, 226, 268, 270, 280, 288, 294, 318
 see also Scottish tradition
chairs 60, 128–9, 338–9
 armchairs 34–5, 320–1, 324–5, 338, 340–1
 high-backed 118–19, 134, 322–4, 326, 330–1, 374
 ladder-back 134, 326–7, 350, 374
Charles Rennie Mackintosh Society 266
Chicago International Exhibition 1923 92
Chiddingston, Kent 248
Classicism 180, 233
clocks 70–1, 366–7
Cochrane, Major John 334
Collins, Mr 202
Collioure 220
colours 28, 84, 90, 154, 158, 202, 210, 222, 228, 238, 248, 250, 258, 260, 270, 282, 298, 344, 350, 352, 356, 358, 362, 366
 black 356–7, 364, 368
 blue 128, 184, 242, 262, 274, 336
 green 210, 220, 260, 262, 274, 342, 344
 red 128, 260, 274
 white 42, 50, 106, 116, 216, 226–7, 254, 274, 290, 326, 336, 346, 356–7, 364, 368, 374, 376
 white rooms 13, 38, 42, 122, 254, 334, 352
 see also glass
Craigie Hall 198
Cranston, Catherine 11, 34, 46, 56, 58, 62, 108, 110, 112, 114, 120, 128, 136, 142, 144, 186, 250, 290, 318, 324, 334
Cranston, Stuart 136
Cubism 262
curvilinear designs 26, 60, 78, 80–1, 350
cutlery 11, 108–9

Daily Record building, Glasgow 48, 106–7
Davidson, Peter Wylie 280, 316
Davidson, William, Jr 56, 132, 204, 316, 328, 332
Davidson, William, Sr 132
Dekorative Kunst magazine 40, 54, 118
78 Derngate, Northampton 11, 68–72, 82, 86, 128, 228–9, 358, 360–71
Design and Industries Association 210, 360
Deutsche Kunst und Dekoration 54

Exposition des Arts Décoratifs, Paris, 1925 254

Fergusson, J. D. 80, 140, 146, 212
fittings *see type of fitting* and under Mackintosh, Charles Rennie
Fleming, Sir James 316
Florence 154–7, 166
form and function, synthesis of 13, 98, 182, 233, 258, 312, 348
Foxton, William 208, 210
France 90, 216, 226, 228, 238, 258
 see also Collioure, Port Vendres
Franklin, Harry 86
Fraser, Claude Lovat 210
Fry, Roger 110
furniture *see under* Mackintosh, Charles Rennie

gardens 162, 174, 234, 246–7
Gaudi, Antonio 10
Geddes, Patrick 226
geometric patterns 13, 34–5, 68–9, 76, 80–3, 120–1, 128, 158–9, 196–7, 210, 214, 216, 218, 220, 238–39, 249, 274–5, 284, 314–15, 324–5, 334–5, 344, 348, 358, 366–7, 372
 chequerboard patterns 70–1, 252, 254, 262, 296, 318, 356–7, 364
 diamond shapes 362
 domino patterns 70–1
 by Frances MacNair 294, 306–7
 squares 82–3, 86, 98–9, 154, 334–5, 342–3, 356–8, 360–1, 368, 370
 trellises 264–5, 296
 triangles 98–9, 154, 228–9, 262, 358–9, 362–5
Germany 11, 40, 54, 58, 66, 194, 226, 278
 influences on C.R. M. 142
gesamkunstwerk 11
gesso panels 274–5
 by Margaret Macdonald Mackintosh 272–4, 290–1, 298–9, 376
Gladsmuir 204
Glasgow 10, 14, 32, 34, 40, 42, 52, 56, 64, 80, 86, 96–107, 132, 134, 150, 154, 170, 180, 184, 186, 200, 208, 212, 252, 258, 280, 292, 308, 312, 314, 324, 336, 360, 374
 Fine Arts Institute 276–8
 International Exhibitions
 1901 48–9, 106
 1911 62, 110
 see also tea room projects *and below*
Glasgow Boys 120, 132, 328
Glasgow Four 42, 134, 174, 184, 234, 236, 238, 240, 254, 258, 276, 278, 282, 284, 286, 292, 302, 306
 influence of 17, 46, 132, 172, 184, 226, 246, 272, 276, 278, 288, 292, 298, 300, 328
 influences on 234, 242, 262, 270, 282, 292, 294
 members 14, 16, 24, 26, 270.
 see also individual members
Glasgow Herald building 32, 102–3, 164
Glasgow School of Art 24, 64, 152, 160, 198, 226, 234, 280, 282, 284
 C. R. M. at 26, 32, 84, 166, 168, 172, 244, 256
 C. R. M.'s designs for 13, 17, 36–40, 60, 62, 170–83, 192, 196, 200, 242, 250, 268, 312–13, 316, 320–1

glass, coloured 50–51, 54–7, 98, 118–19, 122, 154, 180, 194, 242–3, 290, 298, 315, 338, 346, 348, 364, 372, 374, 376–77
Glebe Place, Chelsea 68, 00
Gothic Revival 232, 266
Gregory Brown, F. 210
Grenander, Alfred 186
Guimard, Hector 10
Guthrie, Sir James 160

Henry, George 234, 270
The Hill House, Helensburgh 11, 16, 44, 56, 62, 134, 202, 236–7, 246, 281, 330, 342–57, 366
Hoffman, Josef 10–11, 46, 292, 304
Holy Island 46–7, 244
Honeyman, Joseph 48
Honeyman and Keppie 24, 28, 36, 42, 48, 102, 150, 178, 206, 244, 252
Honeyman, Keppie and Mackintosh 48, 64, 250
Hoppé, E. O. 86
Hornel, E. A. 234, 270
Horstmann, Sidney 84
Horta, Victor 10
House at Bridge of Weir 54
House for an Art Lover
  competition designs 188–203, 342
  built 200
Hous'hill, Glasgow 58, 334–41
Howarth, Thomas (biographer) 78, 102, 284, 364, 368
Hutchinson, John 22

Ideal Home 72
industrial design 210
Ingram Street Tea Rooms 62, 122–7
  Chinese Room 110, 124, 128–29
  Cloister Room 110
  Oak Room 60, 108, 124
  White Dining Room 290–1
interior decoration *see under* Mackintosh, Charles Rennie
Iona, abbey of 150
Italy 22, 102, 150, 152–69, 218, 256, 266

Keppie, Jessie 14, 24, 30
Keppie, John 14, 24, 30, 104, 174, 178, 250
14 Kingsborough Gardens, Glasgow 54–5, 240–1
Klimt, Gustav 10, 46, 242, 270
  Beethoven Frieze 240, 292, 300–1
Koch, Alexander 52, 188

lamps and lampshades 242–3, 296–7, 356
  by Margaret Macdonald Mackintosh 296–7
Lethaby, William Richard 230–1, 238
Leyland, F. R. 262
light 38, 50, 202–3, 264, 290, 298, 315, 350, 352, 372, 374
lithography 26–27, 284–5
Little Ease (house) 90
Liverpool Cathedral 56
Liverpool University 286, 306
Lloyd George, David 110
London 14, 68, 72, 78, 80, 82, 120, 126, 136, 138, 140, 142, 146, 150, 184, 206, 208, 212, 214, 228, 238, 240, 250, 252, 258, 262, 356, 358, 360, 372
Lutyens, Sir Edwin 11

Macdonald, Frances (sister-in-law) *see* MacNair, Frances Macdonald
Macdonald, Margaret *see* Mackintosh, Margaret Macdonald
Mackintosh, Charles Rennie 25
  architecture 11, 13–14, 16–17, 22, 24, 26, 28, 30, 32–3, 36–8, 48, 52–3, 56, 58, 62, 74, 84, 86, 88–90, 96–107, 116, 132–3, 138–41, 152, 158, 160–1, 164, 168, 170–4, 178, 180–1, 188–92, 202–5, 214, 228–9, 236, 246, 250, 254, 258, 264, 266–9, 286, 312–15, 328–35, 342, 354–5
  arrested 40, 66
  attention to detail 44, 154, 318, 354, 366, 372, 374
  see also ornamentation
  character, health and psychology 11, 13–14, 24, 64, 66, 74, 78, 92, 146, 170, 172, 174, 176, 180, 206, 220, 234, 250, 290, 296
  childhood, education and training 22, 24, 26, 28, 30, 32, 150, 158, 166, 172, 174, 176
  fittings 30–1, 122–3, 242–3, 316–17, 318–19, 334–5, 342, 346–7, 366, 374–5, 376–8
  furniture 11, 14, 28, 34–5, 40–5, 54–8, 60, 62, 68, 70–1, 78–9, 82–3, 86–7, 114–15, 118–21, 124–9, 134–5, 184–5, 197–9, 226–7, 240–41, 292, 320–21, 322–5, 334, 33641, 344–5, 344–6, 348, 350–1, 360–2, 368–74
  grid technique 358
  influence of 13, 17, 64, 78, 84, 98, 182, 262, 280, 296, 300, 302, 308, 364, 368
  influences on 10–11, 13, 16, 36, 58, 102, 116, 120, 124, 132, 142, 152, 154, 162, 166, 170, 172, 174, 182, 194, 196, 208, 210, 226–309, 320, 326, 334, 348
  interior decoration 11, 34–5, 38, 42, 44–5, 50, 56, 58–9, 60, 62–3, 68–9, 112, 116, 120, 122–3, 130–1, 136–7, 150–1, 186–7, 190, 192, 194–5, 198, 200–202, 228–9, 236, 268–9, 296, 298, 304, 314–15, 338–43, 346–7, 352–3, 368–71
  marriage 14, 30, 42, 122, 172, 248
  paintings and watercolours 14, 22–3, 28–9, 32, 46–7, 64–7, 80, 84, 90–3, 146–7, 152–64, 168–9, 206, 212–15, 218–21, 234–5, 238, 244–60, 264–5, 274–5, 282–3, 290, 292–3, 302–3, 372
  posters and printwork 26–7, 276–7, 302
  sketches and drawings 22, 32, 166–7, 264, 266, 278
  textiles and fabrics 14, 68, 74–8, 80–1, 84–5, 142–3, 206–11, 213, 222, 238–9, 250, 254–5, 262–3, 355–9, 364–5
  reputation 11, 56, 184, 250, 252, 258, 292, 306
  death of 13, 17, 92
Mackintosh, Jessie (sister) *see* Newbery, Jessie
Mackintosh, Margaret Macdonald (wife) 14, 16, 26, 30, 42, 74, 78, 82, 90, 122, 138, 146, 172, 206, 208, 210, 212, 214, 216, 218, 220, 222, 248, 252, 258, 260, 302
  influence of 16, 50, 62, 280, 300
  influences on 272, 290, 292, 304
  works 28, 62, 72, 76–7, 80, 112, 122, 198–9, 208, 210, 218, 270–74, 280–1, 284, 286–92, 294, 296–9, 301, 304–5, 346, 352, 356–7, 376
  death of 92
MacNair, Frances Macdonald (sister-in-law and wife of Herbert MacNair) 14, 16, 26, 28, 42, 172, 272, 278, 284, 286, 288, 294–5, 299, 308–9
  works 294–5, 306–7
  death of 306
MacNair, Herbert 14, 16, 24, 26, 28, 42, 150, 172, 174, 244, 248, 276–7, 286, 306, 308
  works 278–9
Maeterlinck, Maurice 84, 304
The Magazine 282, 284
120 Mains Street, Glasgow 42–5, 60, 212, 292, 346
Marsuppini tomb 156–7
Martyr's Public School, Glasgow 32, 96, 97–8
McLeish, Minnie 210
Mears, Lady Norah 66
menu cards 62
  by Margaret Macdonald Mackintosh 110–11
metalwork 268–9, 280–1, 290, 312–15, 348, 372
  by Margaret Macdonald Mackintosh 288–9, 302
  by W. A. Davidson 316
Millar, James 48
Minimalism 306, 334
mirrors 376
Modernism 13, 16, 78, 84, 98, 116, 182, 210, 364
Moll, Carl 46
Morris, Margaret 78, 80, 88, 90, 140–1
Morris, Talwin 134, 246, 281, 302
Morris, William 226, 230, 238, 250, 300

mosaics 158, 346, 372
Moscow Exhibition of Modern Architecture and Design 56
Moser, Kalaman 304
Mosside, Kilmalcolm 204–5
mother-of-pearl 56, 78, 82, 86, 334, 340–1, 348, 370
motifs *see* organic motifs, geometric patterns
movement, lack of 222, 308
Munch, Edvard 270
Munich 40
Muthesius, Hermann 11, 58, 186, 188, 200
  The English House 11

Naples 150, 168–9
nature as inspiration 22, 26, 46, 234, 242, 256, 260
  see also organic motifs
New Ways, Northampton 13, 90, 228
Newbery, Francis 14, 26, 28, 36, 54, 170, 172, 176, 206, 216, 234, 236, 280, 282
Newbery, Jessie (sister; wife of Francis Newbery) 54, 206

Offner, Hans 368
Olbrich, M 46
organic motifs 13, 76–7, 264, 266, 286–7, 334, 344, 346, 372
  birds 260–3, 276–7, 322
  flowers and flower motifs 64–7, 72–3, 80–1, 174, 234, 242–3, 248, 250–1, 252–3, 254–5, 256–7, 258–9, 260–1, 264–5, 274–5, 286–7, 312
  roses and rose motifs 42, 54–5, 188–9, 206–7, 234–9, 276–7, 296, 308–9, 356–7
  by Frances McNair 306–7
  trees and tree motifs 26–7, 178, 268, 298, 302–3, 314–15, 315, 322, 326, 346–7, 366, 372–3, 376
  by Frances MacNair 294
Oriental influences 70, 124, 196, 208, 226, 236, 240, 246, 248, 262, 264, 272, 326, 348
ornamentation 13, 16, 38, 98, 322, 334, 336, 338, 350, 352–7, 366
Orvieto 158–9

paintings and watercolours *see under* Mackintosh, Charles Rennie
Palermo 162–5
patterns *see* geometric patterns
Pavia 22–3, 150–53
Perret, Auguste 228
perspective 32, 216, 254, 260, 262, 290
Pettigrew and Stephens 154
Phené, Dr 88
Picasso, Pablo 262
plastics 362, 366
The Plough performing arts group 82, 84, 86
Pompeii 166–7
Port Vendres 90, 146–7, 212, 214, 216–19, 223, 258
Post-Impressionist Exhibition, 1911 110
posters and printwork *see* menus *and under* Mackintosh, Charles Rennie
Pre-Raphaelite movement 122, 152, 242, 270, 276, 282
Pugin, A. W. N. 232–3

Queen Margaret's Medical College, Glasgow 32, 104–5
Queen's Cross Church, Glasgow 40, 266–9

Rabanne, Paco 84
Rome 160–1, 166
Rossetti, Dante Gabriel 122, 242, 270, 276, 282, 298
Rowat, Mrs 54
Royal Institute of British Architects 60
Ruskin, John 122, 230

Salon of the Independents 80, 82
San Miniato 154
Schwabe, Carlos 282, 286
sconces 280–1
Scotland Street School, Glasgow 98–101
Scottish tradition 10, 13, 17, 26, 38, 42, 54, 132, 152, 172, 184, 190, 225, 234, 236, 246, 254, 292, 328, 332, 354
screens 338, 374–5
Secessionism *see under* Vienna
settles 360–1
Shaw, George Bernard 122, 368
Shaw, Norman 122, 230, 266
sketches and drawings *see under* Mackintosh, Charles Rennie
Smith, Francis 48
Soane Medallion Competition 154
Société des Independants, Paris 80, 82
78 Southpark Avenue, Glasgow 44, 60, 212, 308
'Spook School' *see* Glasgow Four
Squire, Harold 88
staircases 202, 330, 332, 354
Street, G. E. 233
The Studio 11, 36, 48, 62, 92, 118, 130, 186, 240, 276, 278, 292, 294
stylization 80–1, 174, 238, 240, 254, 262–5, 296, 342, 372
Surrealism 144
Symbolism 16, 240, 2446, 272, 278, 282, 284, 286, 288, 290, 294, 300, 304

tables 34–5, 82–3, 196–7, 226–7
  Domino tables 126
  by Pugin 232–3
tea room projects 11, 34, 46, 62–3, 108–31, 136–7, 142, 186, 250, 302–3, 318, 322, 324–5
  see also Argyle Street, Buchanan Street, Ingram Street, White Cockade, and Willow Tea Rooms
textiles and fabrics *see under* Mackintosh, Charles Rennie
Thompson, Alexander 104
Toorop, Jan 272, 278
trees *see under* organic motifs
Turin International Exhibition of Modern Decorative Art, 1902 50, 58, 60, 200, 240

Urban, Josef 228

Venice 158
Vicenza, Basilica of 266
Vienna 11, 17, 142, 228, 278, 368
  Academy of Arts 226, 300
  Association of Fine Artists of Austria Exhibition, 1902 300
  Eighth Secessionist Exhibition 46, 50, 122, 184, 186, 188, 240, 292
  Secessionists 40, 66, 226, 240, 292, 300, 304
Voysey, C. F. A. 11, 142

Walberswick 14, 64, 66, 76, 138, 206, 214, 252, 260
Walton, George 34, 62, 130, 142, 302
Wareham 28–9
Wärndorfer, Fritz 50, 198, 274–5, 304
washstands 78, 344, 372–3
Webb, Philip 122
Wells, HG 112
Whistler, James 262
White, Gleeson 11, 36, 130, 240, 276, 292, 294
White Cockade Tea Room 62, 110–11, 250
Wilde, Oscar 122, 272
Willow Tea Rooms, Glasgow 56, 108, 114–15, 124, 134, 252, 314–15, 318, 326–7, 346, 374–7
  Dug Out 70, 120–1, 128
  Salon De Luxe 112–14, 116, 118–19, 120, 298, 326, 374
  sign 116–17
Wilson, Charles 104
Windyhill House, Kilmalcolm 42, 56, 62, 132–4, 202, 204, 246, 328–33, 342, 346
Wood, Francis Derwent 88
World War I 11, 40, 66, 74, 120, 138, 208
Wright, Frank Lloyd 10–11, 252
writing desks 56, 124, 336–7, 348

Zeitschrift für Innendekorationen 52, 188